The Definitive Guide to Strategic Content Marketing

The Definitive Guide to Strategic Content Marketing

Perspectives, issues, challenges and solutions

Lazar Dzamic and Justin Kirby

First published in Great Britain and the United States in 2018 by Kogan Page Limited

2nd Floor, 45 Gee Street
London EC1V 3RS
United Kingdom
www.koganpage.com

c/o Martin P Hill Consulting
122 W 27th St, 10th Floor
New York NY 10001
USA

4737/23 Ansari Road
Daryaganj
New Delhi 110002
India

ISBN   978 0 7494 8222 0
E-ISBN 978 0 7494 8223 7

British Library Cataloguing-in-Publication Data

A CIP record for this book is available from the British Library.

Library of Congress Cataloging-in-Publication Data

Names: Dzamic, Lazar, author. | Kirby, Justin, author.
Title: The definitive guide to strategic content marketing : perspectives,
   issues, challenges and solutions / Lazar Dzamic, Justin Kirby.
Description: 1 Edition. | New York : Kogan Page Ltd, [2018] | Includes
   bibliographical references.
Identifiers: LCCN 2018015408 (print) | LCCN 2018017330 (ebook) | ISBN
   9780749482237 (ebook) | ISBN 9780749482220 (pbk.) | ISBN 9780749482237
   (eISBN)
Subjects: LCSH: Internet marketing. | Marketing–Social aspects.
Classification: LCC HF5415.1265 (ebook) | LCC HF5415.1265 .D93 2018 (print) |
   DDC 658.8–dc23

Typeset by Integra Software Services, Pondicherry
Print production managed by Jellyfish
Printed and bound by CPI Group (UK) Ltd, Croydon, CR0 4YY

Lazar
*To Marc Nohr, Vonnie Alexander, Paul Kitcatt, Jeremy Shaw
and Richard Madden, who taught me how to think, write –
and be a grown-up in the room.
To Patrick Collister, Steve Paler and the Google ZOO team,
for the chance of a lifetime.*

Justin
*My wife and children, who didn't get enough of my attention
while writing this book.
Sophie Berke, who was the catalyst for our more in-depth
conceptualization of this space.
Mathias Bauer (RIP) my former business partner who I still
run my ideas by.
All those academics and industry experts around the globe
who have kindly given me their precious time over the last five
years as part of my ongoing research.*

Both
*Special thanks to Chris McCarthy at Google ZOO for
hooking us up in the first place.*

CONTENTS

Online chapters and downloadable resources are available at
www.koganpage.com/strategic-content-marketing.

FOREWORD

We live in an era of great change. Professionals around the world want to be both fast to adapt and also quick to show the world they are changing. It means that most areas of work feel rather chaotic: people feel vulnerable to sticking to tactics and strategies that have worked before, as there is a need to showcase new thinking and to embrace the new.

Nowhere is this felt more than the entire field of marketing and advertising. There is a collective unstated sense we must thrust ourselves into everything that is new, shiny and technology-based. To do this, we feel we must eschew the rather boring, time-tested, well-proven, deeply effective tactics and strategies of the past.

TV may still work but it's not sexy; radio may reach more people on the planet than anything else, but it's boring. Brand building still creates the very fundamental foundations of our entire industry, but let's have a play with augmented reality.

There are areas of our industry that worked for generations, that have been rebranded and recycled and thrown into the maelstrom of today. What we once called advertorials in the modern age becomes native advertising. Celebrity endorsements have long been part of our history, but now we have a longer tail of people with followers, we now call this influencer marketing.

It's content marketing that covers the real depth of both being one of the oldest advertising techniques and one that is proclaimed to be the newest and most exciting. What we need at times like this is a mature guide through the change in the industry, to hear from experts who span the old and the new, to learn from precocious thinkers who dare to challenge conventional wisdom. This is where this book comes in.

It is a real privilege to know Justin and Lazar and to be given early access to this book. Here you will find real leadership to guide you through the field of content marketing. We will finally see it defined clearly and concisely, we will see the potential of it discussed practically, sensibly and optimistically, but in the context of the past and other media. We will hear from a range of industry experts, offering unique and valuable perspectives from many angles. This book is a great guide to all people on how to respond maturely to the opportunities in content marketing today. Now go get stuck into it.

Tom Goodwin EVP, Head of Innovation at Zenith, and
author of Digital Darwinism: Survival of the fittest
in the age of business disruption *(Kogan Page, 2018)*

PREFACE

Why have we written this book?

A spectre haunts the marketing world. The spectre of 'Content'.

Written in lower case, the word just marks anything people may read, watch or use – allocate their attention to – anywhere and for whatever reason. It's not controversial at all. It's what media and 'cultural production' have been about all along.

Written with a capital 'C', it marks a conscious, dedicated effort by marketers of all kinds to find an alternative for the deficiencies of the traditional advertising model in the digital space. It is an attempt to either 'camouflage' adverts as something else, or to genuinely earn the attention of the consumers. This capitalized version creates a lot of confusion, delusion, derision and ruptures, but also evangelization, experimentation, innovation and change in the global marketing community. It IS controversial.

Digital has stirred all marketing into a state of flux. Certainty is a much sought-after commodity, both by clients and agencies. But the marketing space is all but *certain*. Universal truths are still few and far between. Anything goes. Some traditional, and even old, ways of thinking are still working well; some are not. New approaches are also sometimes working well, merging marketing communications with service, education or entertainment. Content, as the new generic term for the 'not quite the trad-ad' thinking, has arrived; or, more precisely, it has been rediscovered.

Like anything else, there are those in favour of it and those against. Schools of thought are fighting and debating, but many an agency and client seem to be changing the ways they work because of it: their creative practices and skill sets, processes, revenue streams, evaluation models and, also – we hope – the ethics of what they do.

The two of us had started thinking and writing about this space as practitioners transitioning into academia, with more than 45 years of combined experience in marketing communications, digital and Content. We have seen new technologies coming in and dropping out; we have worked in (and with) some of the best-known agencies and platforms in the business and with some of the highest-profile clients in the world.

That experience gave us a unique vantage point between practitioners – platforms, agencies, clients and consultants – who had skin in the game and had to defend it, and academic researchers without calluses and fingernail dirt from the coal face of the daily campaign grind. We became aware of the intellectual gaps in this hot debate, the missing perspectives and the 'filter bubbles'. No one, it seems, is listening to anyone; no one agrees with anyone. The more we observed, the more we had become aware that the marketing industry works on an interesting set of binaries: about its business models, the nature of creative ideas, their application along the customer journey and – the topic of this book – the role of Content. There are walls everywhere, despite the claims that digital is breaking them, and no clear maps or guides on how to get around them.

We decided to map out that territory and to write that guide. Like all the best ones in history – Thomas Cook's or Michelin's, the grandfathers of Content – we hoped it would be part exploration, part inspiration. Thought-provoking and useful. A springboard of a sort, a primer, a reader for getting a quick feel for the dynamics, debates, concepts and challenges that this approach to branding is creating. An unbiased bigger picture. The 'why' of Content, rather than the 'how'. Hence the word 'strategic' in the title. The executional intricacies are being covered every day online by numerous practitioners.

The book will hopefully show how various players across the industry are responding to the digital challenge through the lens of Content. We wanted to look at it as neutrally as possible, with fresh eyes. To reveal, not to judge. To rise above the often partisan pit fights that Content elicits. The way to achieve that, we believe, is to present all sides of the debate, in one place, instead of scattered across hundreds of various digital destinations, blogs, opinion pieces and articles.

As we were charting that map, we looked at all the important and interesting vectors, reflecting the key debates, and how various dots on them join up. It is made of interconnected ideas, approaches, perspectives and points of view. It is laced with premises leading to certain conclusions. We may not have spelt out all of them, but we are sure you will do the maths for yourselves.

It turned out, our attempt to create that map had become a journey for us too: of both professional and academic enlightenment, of learning to listen to all sides without prejudice, and of personal perseverance in stitching together a lot of moving parts into a more cohesive picture. Many of our professional instincts got challenged; some important points of view we held have changed.

One realization was that Content – instead of being the *solution* for the deficiencies of the online advertising, as we initially thought along with many others in the industry – is a *symptom* of the broader, tectonic, changes and shifts in the topography of the media and the marketing world driven by the digital takeover. In its excesses, it is also a *syndrome* that the marketing industry has succumbed to.

We also believe that we have glimpsed the faint outlines of what brand building could become in the near future, when the 'media' could mean something quite different from what we know now: immersive spaces of AR, VR (MR) and intelligent assistants powered by machine learning and, soon, stronger artificial intelligence (AI). In these spaces, it is experience that counts. That made it a more interesting book to write.

What became very apparent were the limitations of the current 'discipline salad'. Working on the book made us realize that the current attempts to define Content are all just different facets of one bigger phenomenon that, at the time of writing, still does not have its universally agreed name – and maybe never will. Hence our using just the capitalized 'Content' as our contribution to the debate, to denote the difference between the *principle* and the *product* of this approach. The realities of the publishing world, and the ways people currently search through this space, however, dictated that we keep the label 'Content Marketing' in the book title. But you'll get our drift as you progress through the book...

There are many aspects of this area that we could have addressed, as the Content spiderweb spreads far and wide, but we decided not to. It is partly due to the constraints of space and partly because they are more tactical aspects. Product placement, Content farms, brand publishing, Content strategy as part of user experience (UX) and information architecture (IA) disciplines, Content platforms and Content analytics are just some. Our primary focus, instead, was the ways in which branding mutates in the digital world and how Content, as one expression of that, may itself only be a transitional phase towards something else.

The book is made to be 'dippable': jump in and out as you like, or as you need a particular thing clarified for your daily work. There is a lot of recommended reading for those who want to dig deeper. We hope that every marketer will have this book on their shelves, as it will save them time. It will also help them make up their own mind about whether, how and where Content thinking could be useful for their brand-building efforts.

We came out of the project convinced that Content is not an isolated thing that should be placed in a department, with its own Chief Content Officer (CCO). It is an ethos and a way of thinking, a signpost to the ways of earning our scarce and volatile attention. It is not a replacement for advertising and not a universal solution. It certainly should not be a set of quick and dirty tactics, as is often the case today. It is a useful lens for keeping the customer in the centre of the picture. That is why we broadened our scope to the discussions of purpose, authenticity, experience, context and ethics. We felt that wider context was the missing ingredient.

And that, in our eyes, is what makes the book unique.

CHAPTER SUMMARIES

We dedicate the *Introduction* to the inability of the industry to define Content in a clear and unified way. We explore five groups of 'vectors' conceptualizing different definition attempts and how they reflect various cohabiting business and intellectual models of the modern marketing industry. We also explore the possibility that Content is not a separate discipline, but a symptom of the wider media evolution, a stepping-stone towards more experience-based brand building.

Part One focuses on big shifts that build the case for the perception of Content as a better promise for marketing in the digital age.

Chapter 1 unpacks in more detail the most-often quoted key challenges that drive the erosion of advertising and marketing communications as we know it.

Chapter 2 outlines the notions behind the Experience Economy and how Content – by focusing on the concept of 'designing for time and place' – may be a tool for fighting product, communications and brand commodification unleashed by the digital space. It also explores interesting new ideas such as Content as profit centre and business model, the enterprise experience businesses and the impact this may have on the evolution of creative and media agencies.

In *Chapter 3* we look at the connection between Content and Purpose – another potential driver for Content's enhanced role in modern brand building – and the dynamics of developing more sustainable brands using Content to better tell their stories and express them in practice.

Part Two covers how Content impacts the ways main industry players change the way they do business, remodel their processes and diversify their revenue streams (see our two online chapters below for additional client and publisher perspectives).

Chapter 4 is dedicated to creative agencies and their challenge of having to move at different speeds in the digital age. It also explores a tectonic rift between the 'deep branding' and 'touchpoint optimization' philosophies that currently divide the agency space, as well as the ways to achieve new integration based not just on bringing together different skills, but – via the new concept of Empathic Utility – on changing the optics of looking at the agency product.

Chapter 5 explores the complexities of the modern media space and the ways media agencies reacted to it faster and more flexibly than many other players. It outlines some new roles and a new kind of reverse integration that media agencies are adopting based on understanding data, technology and their proximity and collaboration with publishers.

Part Three is dedicated to what Content should mean in the world dominated by context, data and the incoming paradigm shift of the new, more immersive media environments.

Chapter 6 looks at the key requirement for Content in the digital age: to be contextually relevant. We explore what context actually means, how it is used by brands to deliver brand value across the customer journey and the importance of understanding the concept of the value exchange to fulfil Content's better experiential promise.

Chapter 7 looks at the role the data-rich world provides for creating empathy-rich Content – and the missing of that opportunity by focusing on just efficient delivery platforms. We reveal how and why data is still more of a promise than reality and how Big Data should be enhanced by additional rich and thick data approaches to drive more empathic moments that matter.

Chapter 8 explores how immersive spaces such as AR, VR (MR) and intelligent virtual assistants could potentially spell one of the greatest challenges for the old interruption communications model – but also one of the biggest opportunities for Content. In the 'world without edges', the new modes of brand building such as 'storydoing' and 'storyliving' disadvantage mere storytelling and potentially redefine what we mean by 'Content creators'.

Part Four investigates the strategic and practical dilemmas with measuring the impact of Content, both from the point of view of measuring the right things – and measuring things right.

Chapter 9 is dedicated to clarifying the controversy and confusion about the possibility and ways to measure the effects of Content on marketing efforts. It investigates various strategic approaches and 'evaluation canvases' for Content, as well as shedding more light on some key (and new) metrics used in this space.

Part Five questions whether Content really is that better promise that it appears to be.

Chapter 10 – The rejecter's manifesto – is a hard-hitting, and often justified, criticism of various approaches to conceptualizing and using Content.

It highlights various manifestations of hype, 'Content myopia' and self-aggrandizing, spectacular waste of budgets and the industry's inability to stop topping-up a vast 'digital landfill' of irrelevant 'stuff' – all fuelled by the tech tunnel vision and inability to understand how attention flows on the net.

Chapter 11 is a rare exploration of the moral and ethical sides of the Content space: opacity and 'dark communications', deliberate baking-in of addictiveness into modern technologies, the unwelcome erosion of separation between editorial and marketing that 'native advertising' and Content in general are forcing upon the mass media, and the surprising shift from an Orwellian future of media repression into the Huxleyan one of cultural trivialization.

In *Conclusions*, we are trying to bring all of that together into a set of key takeaways, as a map of a sort, for navigating the murky, treacherous confluence of Content and brand building in the 21st century.

Online chapters

We have made the important client and publisher perspectives freely available as online chapters, as a flavour of the extensive contributions made by those we interviewed for this book. It helped (re)shape our thinking and conclusions (see *Acknowledgments* for full list). You can read these at the following URL: **www.koganpage.com/strategic-content-marketing**.

Client perspective: in their very own words, clients explain how they see the challenges of the modern marketing space and the role Content can play in them. How do people who hold the marketing purse go about answering the need for building brands at the 'intersection of permission and desire'?

Publisher perspective: in a frank interview, publisher Vince Medeiros reveals how he and his peers try to answer their own formidable challenges of the broken and declining advertising model dominated by the duopoly of Google and Facebook, how they changed the way they recruit necessary skills for the Content age and why modern publishers increasingly launch their own Content creation studios.

ABOUT THE AUTHORS

Photo credit: Jonathan Cole

Lazar Dzamic, former Google ZOO Head of Brand Planning for North and Central Europe, is a creative strategist, writer and academic. Under his guidance, Google ZOO in London introduced the new discipline of 'creative data science', focused on mining the vast universe of Google data to unearth emotional insights for creative storytelling. In his words: to turn Light into Heat. He is an award-winning planning director in several integrated London agencies and is a best-selling author in his native Serbia. He lectures at the Faculty for Media and Communications (FMK) at Singidunum University in Belgrade, where he is now based together with his family, a little notebook and a set of drums.

Justin Kirby is a consultant, educator and thought leader with over twenty years' experience in industry as a digital strategist, producer and entrepreneur. He has been writing about the impact of interactive technologies on business and marketing since the early 1990s, and his books include *Connected Marketing: The viral, buzz and word of mouth revolution* (2005) and the *Best of Branded Content Marketing* (BOBCM) series he conceived and has been curating since 2013. Justin chairs and speaks at conferences around the world, judges awards, consults brands and agencies, and lectures regularly on a wide range of advertising, business, design and marketing degrees.

ACKNOWLEDGEMENTS

We would like to thank our editors Jenny Volich, for commissioning the book, Charlotte Owen, for safeguarding us with energy and optimism through a complicated process and Chris Cudmore, for a reassuring presence.

We are sincerely grateful to all the brilliant people who generously shared their insights for the book:

- Ana Andjelic, Interim Head of Agency, Fashion Tech Lab
- David Berkowitz, Head of Marketing at Storyhunter
- Rob Blackie, Founder at Rob Blackie Digital Strategy
- Adam Boita, Head of Marketing at Pernod Ricard UK
- Paolo Bonsignore, Global Marketing Director at Asko Appliances AB
- Mark Boyd, Founder at Gravity Road
- Mark Bullingham, Group Commercial Director at The Football Association
- Tia Castagno, Global Head of Innovation at Vizeum
- Sylvia Chan-Olmsted, Professor and Director of Media Consumer Research at University of Florida, College of Journalism and Communications
- Patrick Collister, Creative Lead in The ZOO EMEA for Google
- Izabela Derda, former Head of Entertainment at Havas Sports & Entertainment and Head of Content at Havas Media Group
- Gini Dietrich, Chief Executive Officer at Arment Dietrich, Inc
- Scott Donaton, Chief Content Officer at DigitasLBi_US
- Dom Dwight, Marketing Director at Taylors of Harrogate
- Mara Einstein, Professor of Media Studies at Queens College, City University of New York
- Ian Forrester, Global SVP, Insight at Unruly
- Bob Garfield, Journalist, host 'On The Media', WNYC
- James H. Gilmore, Co-founder, Strategic Horizons LLP
- Andy Goldberg, Chief Creative Officer at GE

- Tom Goodwin, EVP, Head of Innovation, Zenith USA
- Simon Gosling, Futurist at Unruly
- Elena Grinta, Adjunct Professor and co-founder of the Osservatorio Branded Entertainment (OBE)
- Chris Hackley, Professor of Marketing at Royal Holloway, University of London
- Jonathan Hardy, Professor of Media and Communications at University of East London
- Mark Higginson, Managing Director at Twenty Thousand Leagues
- Omaid Hiwaizi, Global Head of Experience Strategy at Blippar
- Bob Hoffman, Chief Aggravation Officer at Type A Group
- Thomas Kolster, Founder and Creative Director at Goodvertising Agency
- Martin Lay, former Marketing Director at GO Vauxhall
- Joe Lazauskas, Head of Content Strategy at Contently
- Grace Letley, Strategic Innovation Director at Vizeum
- Rebecca Lieb, Analyst and Founding Partner at Kaleido Insights
- Tim Lindsay, CEO of D&AD
- Marshall Manson, Partner, Brunswick and former CEO, Ogilvy PR UK
- Antony Mayfield, CEO and Founding Partner at Brilliant Noise
- Chris McCarthy, Head of Creative Strategy at The ZOO, Google
- Andrew McStay, Professor of Digital Life at Bangor University
- Vince Medeiros, Co-Founder and Publisher at TCO
- Dejan Nikolic, Co-Founder and CEO at Content Insights
- Dave Norton, Founder and Principal at Stone Mantel
- Neil Perkin, Founder at Only Dead Fish
- Raymond Pettit, Vice President, Analytics at comScore, Inc
- Alex Pickering, Marketing Director, UK and Ireland, for De'Longhi, Kenwood and Braun
- Edward Pilkington, Marketing and Innovation Director, Europe at Diageo
- B. Joseph Pine II, Co-Founder at Strategic Horizons LLP
- Jane Power, Chief Marketing and Customer Officer at Bupa ANZ
- Mark Ritson, Adjunct Professor at Melbourne Business School
- Robert Rose, Chief Strategy Adviser at Content Marketing Institute

- Mark Runacus, Chief Strategy Officer, Data and Insight at Karmarama
- Douglas Rushkoff, Professor of Media Studies and Activism at Queens College, City University of New York
- Sasha Savic, Chief Executive Officer at Mediacom US
- Jan Sebastian Schmalz, Project Manager Games Partnerships at Porsche AG
- Ryan Skinner, Senior Analyst at Forrester Research
- Paul Snoxell, Founding Partner at SNOXISHERE
- Brian Solis, Principal Analyst at Altimeter (a Prophet company)
- Mika Tasich, Creative Technologist
- Simon Thompson, Global Head of Digital Commerce at HSBC
- Ed Warren, Group Chief Creative Officer at Sunshine
- Huw Watkins, Associate Principal Consultant at Q5
- Richard Wilding, Founder and CEO at WMW
- Lee Wilson, Head of SEO at Vertical Leap
- Mark Wnek, Founder and Chief Mentor at The New Breed Talent Army
- Faris Yakob, Founder and Principal at Genius Steals LLC

Introduction
Mapping the Content marketing territory

It is quite telling that the marketing industry has decided not merely to rediscover Content, but to 'create' it again. To invert the original phrase from 1983 by historians Eric Hobsbawm and Terence Ranger about 'inventing tradition' (creating something new, but 'selling' it as if it were old), marketing is now 'reinventing tradition', proclaiming as new, something that was actually the only marketing for the dawn of the electronic media age.

If we look back at examples such as John Deer's 'agricultural journal' *The Furrow* from 1895, or the *Michelin Guide* from 1900, the tradition is even older than radio. We just needed to revert back to already established marketing disciplines, such as contract publishing or direct marketing, to describe it.

This book, and the whole of the Content debate, may have looked differently if that had happened. Instead of hype, we could have had just a level-headed 'back to the roots' approach, borrowing freely from the principles of the great forebears of pre-advertising thinking. A 'retro' movement of a sort, not framed as the future. For all the reasons discussed in this Introduction, that hasn't happened.

Definition dilemma

Despite all the talk, all the fuss, all the evangelizing and even rage, no one actually seems to agree on what 'Content' is. At the moment, there is no universally accepted definition. When we started preparing this book, we collected more than 70! Content seems to us like a massive kaleidoscope: everyone is seeing different combinations of similar shapes. Branded content (marketing), content marketing, branded entertainment and native advertising are only some of the bigger territories with their own labels used in our industry. Although aiming at disciplinary distinctions, they all seem to stem from the same school of thinking; they feel part of a bigger whole – but at the moment we don't have the name for it. This results in quarrels such as whether the umbrella term should be branded content or content marketing; this also resulted in our decision to call it just the capitalized 'Content'.

This definition problem stems from the nature of the modern, digital, media space. Digital is the first meta-medium in our history (Manovich, 2001). It encompasses, in one user space and one set of, admittedly vast, technologies, modes of all previously known personal and mass media. We have image, text, film, sound, voice, conference, broadcast, phone, letter and other two-way messaging modes, as well as other forms of creativity and interactivity. There is a raft of new and hybrid skills required: front-end and backend coding expertise, user experience design, information architecture, creative technology, ad tech, machine learning and artificial intelligence, augmented and virtual reality and many, many more!

Instead of the old certainties, we have what the US Army War College called VUCA to explain the new multi-polar world: volatile, uncertain, complex and ambiguous (Wikipedia, 2017a). It is a perfect description of the digital business and marketing space too.

So, who is going to own this space, creatively? No one and everyone. Most of the previous media modes had their own typical, even *archetypal*, formats: jingle for radio, TVCs for TV, billboards of various set sizes for outdoor (and the same for press), brand films and press releases for PR. They were nails for our hammers in the famous quote by Abraham Maslow: 'If all you have is a hammer, everything looks like a nail' (1966). The category 'nails' – what various players in the industry were built to deliver so it suits their skill 'hammers' – were brand communications, direct, sales promotion, PR, websites, a specific technology… This hardly works any more, as digital is all of that, too. Digital is both brand and direct space, given that *link* – a response device – was baked into its very core and now transformed into a tap or a swipe on mobile. Digital is also the main reputation-building (and -destroying) space, as well as the primary retail space for many categories. Each of these previously separate disciplines, with their archetypal formats, had their own rules and sets of expertise. Business models, organization, remuneration, training and fame were based on these walled gardens.

Digital, because of its meta-media nature, is wreaking havoc with those ingrained models, habits, principles and ways of expressing brands and making money in the process. It forces many players, as evidenced in several chapters in this book, to reappraise how they do business. In some cases, even how to survive. A detailed set of factors driving this transformation is explored in Part One.

Therefore, digital doesn't have its archetypal creative format. We may argue it was the banner. If it ever was, it is now in terminal decline. Branding online is now everyone's game. At the moment, there is not a magical thread that ties it all in. For some, that thread could be Content. For others, not really.

That long list of definitions, and the sentiment of many of the interviews we have conducted for the book, made us realize that current debates about how Content could be defined, or framed, could be clustered into five conceptual groups of 'vectors':

1 Very broad definitions: Content is indistinguishable from the rest of the marketing efforts.

2 Stretching (or renaming) the existing discipline or the area of expertise into Content, powered by various business motives.

3 Frameworks and conceptual approaches based on the ways consumers behave in the digital space, the 'pull' versus 'push' thinking, or digital delivery aspects.

4 Content distinctions based on its authentic feel, credibility borrowed from influencers, narrative duration or non-advertising 'poetics'.

5 A mix of those who completely deny the need for the definition and some more inspired and open-minded ideas pointing to the future evolution of marketing and media – and a potential for the evolution of an equally 'meta'-marketing communications format(s).

Understanding these vectors helps with conceptualizing the whole of the Content space. We do not believe that it is possible, yet, to create a single, all-encompassing Great Unified Theory of Content (GUTC) – a challenge that so far has eluded so many. We think it is too early for that, for all the reasons expressed in this book. But for clarifying the debate, or helping you to take up a position (or not) on the murky Content spectrum, these five groups may help.

Group 1: Content-as-'just marketing' definition approaches

In these definitions, exchanging the word 'content' for 'advertising' or 'marketing' or 'customer relationship management' (CRM) does not change the meaning – not even the veracity – of the statement. Content is indistinguishable from the already established marketing practices. They are also somewhat tautological as they try to define Content using the word 'content', which is in itself not specifically defined. This makes this approach to definitions questionably useful.

Generic definitions of Content

Content Council:

> Content marketing is the discipline of creating content, on behalf of a brand, designed with the specific strategy of influencing consumer behavior in order to drive quantifiable profitable results. (2015)

Branded Content Marketing Association (BCMA):

> Branded content is any content that can be associated with a brand in the eye of the beholder. (2013)

Content Marketing Association (CMA):

> The discipline of creating quality branded content across all media channels and platforms to deliver engaging relationships, consumer value and measurable success for brands. (2013)

iScoop:

> Content marketing is an umbrella term covering a set of strategies, techniques and tactics to fulfil business and customer goals by using content across the customer life cycle and the business functions in a consistent, integrated and continuous way. (2016)

This observation about generic definitions seems to be supported by Professor Sylvia Chan-Olmsted, from the University of Florida, who in our conversation noted that:

> Some marketers see content marketing as an extremely comprehensive, all-encompassing marketing effort, almost like a philosophy or approach to market today.

In many ways it touches upon Professor Mark Ritson's thoughts at the end of this Introduction, albeit in a different sentiment.

Group 2: trade-discipline-based definition approaches

They are the result of the specific existing industry expertise that is now, at least in the eyes of its practitioners, becoming subsumed by Content; alternatively, they are attempts to, more or less credibly, stretch one's expertise into this new, hot and lucrative space, to win new, or new kinds, of clients. It is 'spotting an opportunity' in action.

Following trends and responding to new ways of thinking, which often start as hypes, is critical for the continuous evolution and survival of players in various marketing eco-systems. Nevertheless, it can also give a whiff of 'trendyism': a way to redirect part of the marketing budget pie *this* and not *that* way, an attempt at revenue stretch and differentiation for which Content is conveniently broad enough. It is a growing watering hole in the marketing jungle.

As an act of commercial strategy, it is sensible: if what the organization has done for ages has suddenly become fashionable, why not play on your strengths and benefit from that tide? The only problem is when that particular shade or part of the picture is framed as the *whole* picture. Everyone is parking tanks on the Content lawn.

Here is a quick snapshot of various business stretches into Content based on the Velocity Partners' (2013) report Crap: The Content Marketing Deluge. It echoes the sentiment and the data of the Beckon research in Chapter 10:

- Search engine optimization (SEO) agencies are becoming content marketing shops.
- Social media agencies have discovered content as the new social lubricant.
- Every business to business (B2B) marketing agency is cramming the word 'content' into everything they do.
- Copywriting agencies are now content farms.
- Video production companies are now 'rich content creators'.
- Contract publishers are rebranding themselves as content marketing experts.

Group 3: consumer-centric definition approaches

The other set of perspectives starts with the way people consume content on various platforms. It is different from the previous approaches in the way that it starts with the audience's point of view, rather than what could be sold in terms of products and services.

Probably the most prominent angle here is the one that pits Content versus traditional advertising. In other words, 'pull' versus 'push'. Scott Donaton, former editor of *Advertising Age* whom we interviewed extensively for several chapters, refers to it as 'Invitation versus Interruption'; Professor Andrew McStay, from the School of Creative Studies and Media at Bangor University, has a very nifty name for this elusive quality: the 'opt-in impression'. We may say that it goes all the way back to the early idea of Permission Marketing (Godin, 1999).

It is based on the notion that Content should be something that audiences *want* to get; something they want to spend time on. If earning attention is key, then whatever we call Content must work better than just the paid advertising impression, provided it is executed well. It must have a better 'pull' force. It should make people feel the message is worth their time, versus the mere brute-force interruptive exposure that relies just on paid-for frequency to be noticed and mentally processed. This is reflecting the concept of 'designing for time and space' that we elaborate on in Chapter 2, dedicated to the Experience Economy. It also echoes the considerations about purpose explored in Chapter 3; the context of distributing Content in Chapter 6; and issues with data and ethics in Chapters 7 and 11.

It is handy as it avoids the futile discipline-related debates. Here, it just doesn't matter, as long as people *want* to spend time on it. It is a 'post-discipline' definition thinking, with the user experience and the quality of the output as the focus. The sad truth seems to be, as evidenced in Chapter 10, that a significant portion of Content efforts still falls short of it.

P J Pereira, Chief Creative Officer of Pereira & O'Dell, sums it up in an interview for BOBCM (Kirby, 2014a):

> For me, something that is worth the consumer's time is the best definition of what branded content is. So, if you think more radically and try and stretch that definition, then even a 30-second spot is branded content if it's worth the consumers' time. And I'm fine with that, as I like to play through those lines.

Many definitions of Content stem from this sentiment:

Customer-centric definitions

Branded Content Marketing Association (BCMA):

From a managerial perspective, branded content is any output fully/ partly funded or at least endorsed by the legal owner of the brand that promotes the owner's brand values, and makes audiences choose to engage with the brand based on a pull logic due to its entertainment, information and/or education value. (2016)

IAB:

Content marketing is the marketing technique of creating and distributing relevant and valuable content to attract, acquire and engage a clearly defined and understood target audience... Content marketing differs from advertising, advertising-based storytelling and other promotional vehicles in one specific way: the intent of this mode of communication is to provide useful, educational or entertaining information on its own merit. Content marketing is a pull strategy, unlike advertising, which is push. This marketing technique intends to 'pull' the consumer towards the brand and create a user experience that will ultimately increase brand awareness and preference. (2015)

Forrester:

A marketing strategy where brands create interest, relevance and relationships with customers by producing, curating and sharing content that addresses specific customer needs and delivers visible value... media-led content marketing relies largely on a conscious decision by a consumer to view the content. (2016)

Content Marketing Institute:

Content marketing is a marketing technique of creating and distributing relevant and valuable content to attract, acquire and engage a clearly defined and understood target audience – with the objective of driving profitable customer action. (Pulizzi, 2012)

Cannes Lions:

The Entertainment Lions celebrate creativity that turns content into culture. Entries will need to demonstrate ideas that are unskippable; that is, work that captivates in order to cut-through, communicate a brand message or connect with consumers in a new way. (Matthews, 2016)

[Cannes Lions Brand Experience] In these categories, the jury will consider brand experiences that harness the power of consumer influence to create and develop entertaining and engaging content to further brand's reach and awareness and to drive business. (Cannes Lions, 2017)

Jeremy Bednarski:

Maybe more of a description than an actual definition, but I love how Michael Brenner describes content marketing (paraphrasing): instead of interrupting the things people are interested in, create the things people are interested in. (Cohen, 2016)

Keith Blanchard – Story Worldwide:

Content marketing is the opposite of advertising. It is about engaging consumers with the stuff they really want, in a way that serves your brand's purposes and ideals, rather than just trying to jam your logo into their periphery. It's reaching the exact consumers you want, instead of a vaguely defined demo. It's helpfully providing an experience they want, instead of trying to distract them from the one they came for. In short, it is the very evolution of advertising itself into something more effective, more efficient and much less odious. (Cohen, 2016)

Matt Heinz – Heinz Marketing:

What in sales and marketing isn't content marketing? Sales voicemails, your trade show booth… I like Ann Handley's definition – 'everything the light touches is content!' (Cohen, 2016)

Many case studies mentioned in the book fall into this category. Big ad extravaganzas such as Nike 'The Switch', where Ronaldo swaps his body with a Sheffield kid, but also innovations such as *Melbourne Remote-Controlled Tourist*. From 'just' a great TV ad, to a new breed of thinking: a campaign, a programme, a destination, a user-generated-content proof-of-concept, a manifestation of the trend that travellers like trying it out before they go, and an interactive 'documentary' tourist brochure – all in one!

Several well-known frameworks of 'defining' Content have this way of thinking at their core.

Paid–earned–shared–owned

A particular kind of the 'experience' approach is the often-used paid–earned–shared–owned (PESO) framework, one of the first to articulate what Content could be. It looks at experience from the brand, or media agency-side of it: how they are able to control its dissemination. It is primarily a blueprint for contextual content distribution – framing of the different kind of media spaces that we can deploy for all of our marketing messages, not just Content itself (Figure 0.1).

This model is useful when conceptualizing spaces *where* content should appear, *how* it may be discovered – or, for some of them, what *kind* of content could be deployed. However, as demonstrated in various places in the book, particularly in Chapter 10, one could build the argument that all media are simultaneously just paid and earned. Budget is usually required to create content, as well as to promote it. Still, even with paying for both, content needs to have enough of the pulling power in order to earn the attention of the audience, otherwise it risks being ignored. The only thing we may 'own' is a database, a web page, an app or another digital presence; whether any of those will be effective is another matter. That depends on the skill of creating quality 'pull' content, and then promoting it with a maximum contextual effect.

Google's HHH framework

During our initial book discussions, we both mentioned how we often struggled, along with many other people, to find a satisfactory answer to the question 'What is Content?' Most of the usual interpretations were that Content could be anything: memes, news hijacks, blogs, vlogs, infographics, FAQs, customer service videos, brand magazines, events... even ads. However, that was not very useful when a client brief appeared. Where should one start? How to allocate the budget and the intellectual and creative energy? Just to make better ads? Or to try to better – and more creatively – answer some of the obvious needs and pain points clients' consumers have been searching about across the digital space?

For Lazar, for example, it wasn't until he arrived at Google's creative think-tank ZOO that he got a coherent answer to it. Google being Google, it didn't stop at just discussions and opinions. It had a look at the data. YouTube is the world's biggest video branding platform, as well as the world's second-largest search engine. It is also a place where cultures are created and lived all the time and where people entertain themselves, learn

Figure 0.1 PESO framework, used with kind permission from Gini Dietrich

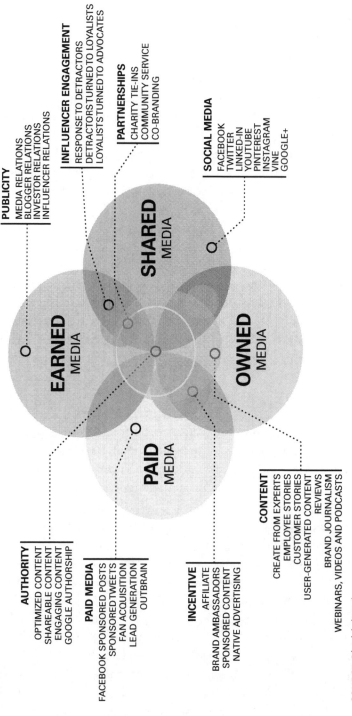

PUBLICITY
MEDIA RELATIONS
BLOGGER RELATIONS
INVESTOR RELATIONS
INFLUENCER RELATIONS

INFLUENCER ENGAGEMENT
RESPONSE TO DETRACTORS
DETRACTORS TURNED TO LOYALISTS
LOYALISTS TURNED TO ADVOCATES

PARTNERSHIPS
CHARITY TIE-INS
COMMUNITY SERVICE
CO-BRANDING

SOCIAL MEDIA
FACEBOOK
TWITTER
LINKED-IN
YOUTUBE
PINTEREST
INSTAGRAM
VINE
GOOGLE+

AUTHORITY
OPTIMIZED CONTENT
SHAREABLE CONTENT
ENGAGING CONTENT
GOOGLE AUTHORSHIP

PAID MEDIA
FACEBOOK SPONSORED POSTS
SPONSORED TWEETS
FAN ACQUISITION
LEAD GENERATION
OUTBRAIN

INCENTIVE
AFFILIATE
BRAND AMBASSADORS
SPONSORED CONTENT
NATIVE ADVERTISING

CONTENT
CREATE FROM EXPERTS
EMPLOYEE STORIES
CUSTOMER STORIES
USER-GENERATED CONTENT
REVIEWS
BRAND JOURNALISM
WEBINARS, VIDEOS AND PODCASTS

SHARED MEDIA
EARNED MEDIA
OWNED MEDIA
PAID MEDIA

SOURCE Dietrich (2014)

Figure 0.2 3H framework

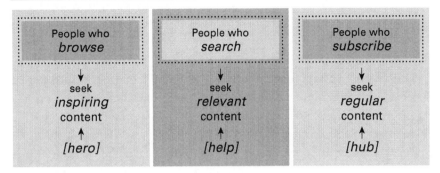

SOURCE adapted from Google 'Build a Content Plan' (2015a)

and look for answers to their needs and problems billions of times across many categories all year round. If there ever was an answer to what Content could be, it was likely to be found there.

YouTube spotted three distinct categories, three 'buckets' that encompass various types of content and user behaviours around them. Three kinds of things people really *want* to watch. Each of them is a permission for a brand to behave in a way that achieves both reach and engagement, as well as for an agency to expand on its creative canvas and the revenue potential. The discovery became known as the HHH, or 3H, Content framework (Figure 0.2).

In many ways – if we are to judge on the number of clients who used it as a way to organize their Content efforts – it is one of the most useful and widely adopted attempts in tying in many current loose ends of the Content definition debate.

Hero is big moments of storytelling we share with friends, full of Emotional Resonance and impact. It is what we talk about at watercoolers, use as examples of great creativity, if and when created by and for brands. The Nike extravaganzas, the Wren 'First Kiss', the Dove 'real beauty sketches' of humanity, the Always '#LikeAGirl' prejudices and the Volvo Trucks Jean-Claude Van Damme 'epic split' humbugs... Hero content – almost always video, but not exclusively – is what 'traditional' creative agencies eat for breakfast. It's a permission for a brand to behave like a broadcaster or an entertainer, amplifying its message through big ideas and adequate supporting spend.

Help content lies at the other end of the spectrum. It is the land of native YouTube 'creators' and a growing number of 'immigrant' brands who are either mimicking or partnering with them. The amount of Help-like content, not just on YouTube, but on the web overall, probably eclipses everything else. The secret is in the name: it is what people look up when they need help with something, when they want to learn. It is tutorials and 'how to' videos, articles, blogs and infographics, white papers and podcasts... on any imaginable topic. It is a permission for a brand to behave like a human being, to listen and answer to the problem, to earn trust.

Hub is more of an approach to packaging and delivering content than a specific kind of it, but one particular trait stands out: the repeated, episodic nature of it. Once consumers come into a brand's gravitational field by discovering it either through Hero or Help, they may like what they saw and may want more; they may have clicked on the 'Subscribe' button on a YouTube channel, or given their e-mail address for a newsletter. They now expect regular doses of magic.

The Hub is where YouTube celebrities are made, the stuff of 'formats'. It is still not very populated by brands. This episodic content, created and launched in regular instalments, is usually based on a specific field of interest and on what a brand (or a creator) has to say about it. The Hub content is a permission for a brand to be a friend or at least a fellow nerd, to explore the sweet spot where people's interests meet a brand's competence and a unique tone of voice, indigenous or borrowed.

One of the most frequently asked questions at this junction is whether brands need all three Hs? They don't. Which of those will be activated depends on several factors.

Factors to consider about which 'H' to use

1 **Which category is a brand in?** It is difficult to see how soft-drink brands may use Help, bar answering an occasional question on the amount of sugar they contain. In reality, most of the brands in this and similar categories may be using just the Hero approach, usually Hub-packaged, as the series of more or less connected micro-Hero entertainment episodes. Pepsi Max UK's 'Unbelievable' channel is an example of that.

2 **What is the brand's expertise?** If a brand has a particular expertise, a specific deep knowledge of topics, needs and trends in a category, it could be a platform for good Hub and Help content. Financial institutions, fashion and beauty, travel, health, food – most of the categories in a market would be of such kind. Volvo Trucks has

cornered their market, Unilever with its AllThingsHair.com is doing similar for hair.

3 **How do consumers behave in the category?** What do they search for? Are there any topics they need help with? Are there any new trends they are latching on to? Are there any perennial, 'evergreen' topics they always need help with, year after year, that are currently not answered well by the competition (deeply, interestingly, creatively, amusingly...)?

Google's 3H framework shows that there are different ways to engage consumers' attention online (2015a). Some of them are more traditional, usually based on Emotional Resonance; some of them are based on what we called the Intent Utility in Chapters 4 and 6, steeped in various – in Google and Facebook parlance – 'Moments that Matter' (2015b). They are where consumers show us, through what they search, what their needs are. 3H is a great way to unify the two sides of the industry's big binary debate – brand inspiration versus touchpoint optimization – into a coherent approach.

There is another way to look at the 3H framework, inspired by our encounters with some of the most respected creative directors in the industry. One of the constant pushbacks was that they do get the Hero bit, as this is what they 'eat for breakfast', a statement usually accompanied by a quick pointing to the awards shelf, creaking with brass and heavy Plexiglas. It was the other two Hs that were the problem. What was their role in them? They considered it the domain of the native 'YouTubers' and, eventually, clients themselves. And it is also boring.

What hides underneath this are the questions of fame and the business model. So far, Hero was the one providing professional recognition and enough production fees to keep the creative agency model going. Hero is the Hollywood, blockbuster kind of fame. Gloss and shine; what makes people *obviously* famous as they become the talk of the town. But there is a way to look at the other two through the lens of fame as well. Help is more like the BBC documentary kind of fame, its life well observed and well told, in its own terms, using the raw materials of it. Agencies and clients may want to consider this question: could you become the BBC of your category? Can you create better 'documentaries' about consumer needs and better answers to them, with more authenticity and grit? Can you be not the James Cameron, but the Asif Kapadia of your category?

It is similar with Hub, where episodic nature of content comes to the fore. Some say that HBO has transformed modern TV with its novel-like approach to creating character and narrative arcs across a number of episodes. So, is there a possibility for creative players to become the HBO of their category, by specializing in episodic, addictive content?

Our deep conviction is that there are no boring products and services, just boring ways to talk about them.

Group 4: definition approaches based on narrative/aesthetic feel

The fourth way Content is conceptualized is through various narrative-based methodological considerations. The feeling of the hybrid nature of Content blurring the lines between marketing intervention and conventional journalism or storytelling is palpable. Content is here anything that feels authentic, genuine and not purely sales-focused, unconstrained by limitations of the traditional commercial media.

TV ad contrivance versus authenticity

Sometimes, in workshops, we play the famous Dove 'Sketches' online film to an audience, immediately followed by the Dove 'Friends' TV advert based on *exactly the same* strategy and message. In both, women are asked to describe themselves, or to try to find something beautiful about them, only to give answers that are falling short of what other people think. It is a phenomenal human insight: a lot of us perceive ourselves as less beautiful than we are. The difference between the films, and the way the audiences see them, is striking. On one hand, with the online film, there is emotion and goosebumps; on another, contrivance and clichés. As of December 2017, the online film has about 70 million YouTube views, the other fewer than 300,000. The narrative and emotional effect – the difference in the 'poetics' – is so obvious that many in the audience are stunned. Not a lot of us, it seems, thought long and hard about the differences between the TV and the YouTube storytelling mechanics.

In a pointed and witty phrase by Hugh MacLeod, if people talked to people the same way advertising talked to people, they would punch you in the face (2006). In the content-saturated digital space, authenticity and tone of voice stemming from a personality of a creator is paramount. That is often reflected in production approaches: less slick, rougher, more spontaneous, more experimental, more cottage industry than big studios, often beyond boundaries of the mainstream TV or even cable spaces due to its often non-standard formats – just somehow more *free*... It seems that advertising gives away a particular 'odour' that many digital users find repellent, given that 11 per cent of the global internet population is blocking it; ad blocking grew by 30 per cent globally in 2016 (PageFair, 2017).

Brands, unchained from the constraints of the strictly regulated TV space and the sensitive fact that in that space they come into our houses uninvited, now have a chance to stretch online and try things they have never tried before. They are still reluctant, as the old muscle memory of advertising is strong, but some are learning. The vast creative cauldron of online video and the new kind of influence is spurring them: the one based on authenticity and purpose. We will talk about this in more detail in Chapter 3.

The restriction of TV seconds versus free time on the web

To be fair to many brands, their hands were largely tied by one convention of the mainstream media: time and space are worth a lot of money, particularly on TV. This is good news for publishers, bad for brands. On the web, there are no seconds, or column inches. It is free, but it is also worthless if one cannot use it well to attract and keep attention. This instantly changes with the way a story is told, as in the Dove 'Sketches' film example, where the story is longer, more intimate, with more cinematic techniques deployed to create mood and atmosphere. There is enough time online to properly develop an *immersive* story. Like in a film. People pay to watch them. Brand films, not counting Lego, are not asking for money to be watched (that comes later), just for consumer attention. That doesn't make it easier to earn it.

The removal of the time restriction puts the emphasis on only one factor: the quality of storytelling. Even on mobiles, a longer story that 'doesn't look like an ad and doesn't feel like an ad' can have a longer watchtime than traditional ads – *particularly* traditional ads! The quote was taken from one such experiment, the *Unskippable Labs: The Mobile Recut*, created jointly between Google's Art, Copy & Code project and agency BBDO New York (YouTube Advertisers, 2015). The longest version of the ad, produced to look and feel like a fun music video, had the longest watch time on mobiles. As the punchline from the video goes: it's maybe not about being shorter, but simply better.

The effect is getting confirmed, year after year, in various online places where video dominates. For example, the most watched branded videos on YouTube every year are several minutes long. It is the same for the most shared global video ads via platforms such as Unruly.

Average video length for top 50 most shared global video ads

– **Top 10**: 4 min 11 sec (does not include 'Kony 2012')

– **11–20**: 2 min 30 sec

– **21–30**: 3 min 5 sec

– **31–40**: 2 min 57 sec

– **41–50**: 1 min 45 sec

– **Top 50 average**: 2 min 54 sec (does not include 'Kony 2012')

SOURCE Unruly Media Data (Jarboe, 2012)

Length in the online spaces, opposite to the common wisdom, may actually be the advertiser's friend. As explored in Chapter 5, where we talk about the impact of Content on media agencies, the problem that advertising is trying to solve may not be simply to increase sales, or even increase saleability, but to reduce 'unsaleability'. It is a word used by Ogilvy and Mather's Rory Sutherland in an interview with BOBCM (Kirby, 2014b). Sutherland defined the reduction in unsaleability as 'to overcome those hurdles to purchase which are preventing people from confidently buying something which ownership would ultimately justify the cost'. As with the shopping channel QVC, he thinks that sometimes this requires more than a six-word headline, or a 30-second spiel.

Infomercials could be seen as an earlier blend of content (info) and advertising (commercials), and a proto-example of content-like narrative thinking. 'Will It Blend?' – content-based brand building that proved one of the early successes of the 'not quite the trad ad' approach in the digital space – was actually an infomercial on steroids (Wikipedia, 2017b): a genius twist on an otherwise, in creative circles, loathed format! The big difference was that word of mouth and building strong memorability were key aims. They were supported by the fact that 'physical availability' online means one click to an e-commerce site. It was a very impactful and surprising 'prank' format that built a strong brand, instead of endless repeating of immediate rewards available if one buys right there and then, while operators are standing by.

Borrowing credibility from influencers

The word *authenticity* comes about a lot when platforms like YouTube – or online video overall – are discussed. It is often quoted as one of the main reasons YouTube 'creators' beat well-known brands hands down in that space, as far as the number of subscribers, views and watch time are concerned. Creators seem to be much better than brands in marshalling attention on those platforms. They even trump, by a wide margin, traditional Hollywood celebrities. In a survey published by *Variety* magazine in July 2015, for a second year running, teens' emotional attachment to YouTube stars is as much as seven times greater than that towards a traditional celebrity; YouTube stars are perceived as 17 times more engaging, and 11 times more extraordinary, than mainstream stars (Ault, 2015).

It seems that a big part of the explanation is that 'native' digital celebrities rarely seem to be 'staged' personas, they are mostly 'them'. A girl next door happening to be good with make-up advice (Zoella), a strange guy in Spandex with an obsession for epic meals (Epic Mealtime), an amiable nerd who can talk about scientific concepts through the eyes of a child (Vsauce), two guys who like exploding things in slow motion (Slo Mo Guys)... There are seemingly no particular talents involved, no super-human beauty or physique, just people like us, talking to us like friends, in a human language, in their bedrooms, gardens, on a street or from makeshift studios. There are no gatekeepers they had to persuade to gain access to the controlled prime-time channels; they earned their fame alone in the most competitive space on earth: the ultra-Darwinian world of the online attention jungle.

To their chagrin, brands are discovering that in the online world they have to borrow credibility much more and in more different ways than in the traditional media sphere, where it could be just bought. Collaboration, not just mere product placement, is often called for, but with a particular challenge for brands: they now need to find a way to align their tone of voice to that of an online star. Or, in other words, they have to accept that their traditional tonality may be amended, stretched or twisted in order to make it compatible and credible. One of the first forays into Content for many brands – and one of the biggest differences from their traditional advertising – would be such collaboration, borrowing that credibility. External content creators could be the beginning of the Content-thinking adoption for brands. However, this particular space has its particular rules that one has to understand to be successful, as the traditional notions of brand control do not always apply.

Group 5: do we need a definition at all?

The Content space seems to be just too wide for all the different practices, and commercial interests in maintaining them, to be herded together into a label that everyone would agree with. When we looked at positions that are not particularly concerned with a specific definition, there were two camps. One maintains that this is an utterly irrelevant question – as is Content itself; the other one is slightly more philosophical about it and points to a transitional and potential role Content could have in the future developments of brand building.

Defining Content is a waste of time

This is a position firmly held by Professor Mark Ritson, Bob Hoffman (of *Ad Contrarian* fame) and various others who think that Content is just a distraction from the real and important work of 'proper' marketing and communications. Their opinions are explored in more detail in Chapter 10, but some are also relevant to this issue of definition. Ritson, for example, is adamant that the question of defining Content is just a huge 'red herring':

Content (marketing) (CM) is an invention that we don't need. It reflects genuine changes in marketing in the last 15 years, but the terms we already have are adequate and we don't need more terms. More terms are not very helpful at all in this world. I think if CM defined itself as a general movement, or a change in the 'ethos' of how marketing is tactically done, I think it would have been fine. But the way that it was parlayed as a revolutionary approach that has distinct strategic implications, with chief content officers (CCOs) and all of that… It's the perfect example of what is one of the flaws of marketing in many cases, which is we just completely fall for our own bullshit and spiral into pirouettes of ever more ridiculous stupidity. It's not to say that there isn't a very interesting thick red line of CM implications for marketing. It's just that it's a theme, I'd say, or a movement, it's not a discipline, it's not a C-suite role, it's not glossary, it's not something that has a 150-year history. Someone was recently saying that it's 'the past, the present and the future of marketing' – it's none of those things.

The other problem is that marketing doesn't need more concepts at the moment, it really needs to get itself really focused quite quickly and we seem to be breeding concepts! It's certainly not CM's fault, but when there was a genuine movement a few years ago to push for a CCO, that didn't do us any favours in the 'proper' parts of the organization. Marketing should have a role there, whether in the form of a chief marketing officer (CMO) or not. But, the discussion on that gets distorted, which I discovered to my horror in one big company when, on my suggestion that they needed a CMO, I was asked 'why not a CCO'? All the terminology and the other ephemera that comes out of this doesn't just hurt CM, it also makes most of marketing look fairly buffoon as well.

(Not) defining content as a temporary stepping stone

If Content is nowadays placed firmly in the context of digital as the first meta-medium in history, it may also bring a meta-question: *what is the problem that Content may help solve – why does it exist at all and what is it for?* This position is therefore not concerned with what content is now and how it is differentiated from any other current marketing activity. It looks to the potential of what it could become.

As elaborated above, one of the key problems that brands are facing in the digital world is how to connect with consumers in the changing media landscape and ways we now consume them. Media fragmentation and clutter are not new problems, but the proliferation of social and 'skippable' media (to borrow Google's word) continues to make traditional advertising approaches online less effective and even inappropriately intrusive.

If we go back to some of the definition conceptualizations above, they are all attempting to answer this bigger meta-question in different ways. This seems to be aligned with a point made in our interview with Professor Chris Hackley, Royal Holloway, University of London, that 'the problem with defining branded content is because it is an evolving hybrid approach that cuts across disciplines'. We would add that the digital space itself is also evolving, hence why the overarching definition of Content is a hard one to pin down. It is like trying to put a signpost in the shifting sands of a desert.

One may argue – albeit against a very strong and credible opposition elaborated above and in Chapter 10 – that advertising is slowly giving way to a new set of optics. Instead of specific communications formats that we are so used to, this new set outlines marketing communications and Content in this new age in much broader terms, still delivering meaning in some specific ways but not in fixed formats. Whatever works, works; naming the items on the costing sheet is not crucial. There is no name for those delivery items and nor is that important; in a potential new marketing communications dictionary of the future they may be called, instead of a 'display ad' or a 'branded film', something as broad as just 'contextual narrative units' (CNUs?) or 'purpose-centric'/'brand-equity-centric utility structures'.

As we said in the Preface and at the beginning of this chapter, Content is in many ways a symptom of the uncertainties of the digital marketing revolution. It is a VUCA-related phenomenon. It reflects the time of transition. Interestingly, anthropology has a concept that is remarkably apt for describing this perspective on defining it. *Liminality* is 'the quality of ambiguity or disorientation that occurs in the middle stage of rituals, when participants no longer hold their pre-ritual status but have not yet begun the transition to the status they will hold when the ritual is complete (Wikipedia, 2017c). During a ritual's liminal stage, participants 'stand at the threshold' between their previous way of structuring their identity, time or community, and a new way, which the ritual establishes. Content may be just one expression of the marketing industry in its liminal phase, 'standing on the threshold'.

In our interview for the book, Professor Andrew McStay thinks that Content at the moment does not have to be more than just some kind of a 'placeholder':

My sense of where advertising is going (and marketing) is that we're seeing a divergence between 'deep branding' and 'touchpoints' that are behaviourally enabled (such as in stores, through Alexa, chatbots and the like). Deep branding has more to do with traditional creative activity, although I suspect that this will increasingly entail higher levels of ad testing for clarity and emotional relevance. My thinking, then, is that content marketing is a placeholder for an understanding of tomorrow's marketing environment. This will become clearer as key technologies (and not just fads) take root: again, I have home internet of things (IoT), agents and bots in mind. (The test for whether it is a fad or here to stay is whether in heart-of-hearts it will genuinely be useful.)

This 'placeholder' frame of mind, unburdened of the definition urge, may just be the needed pressure-relieving valve to carry us through the ever-shifting digital landscape while we are waiting for the fog to clear. Vince Medeiros, an online publisher whom we interviewed for the online Publishers chapter (Online Chapter 2), agrees:

> The true test will be whether it works – or not. Also, crucially: if it doesn't, what will replace it, especially as it becomes increasingly clear that digital display as a main source of revenue for *most* publishers has its days numbered.

It is the point echoed by Catharine Hays, who directs the Future of Advertising programme at the University of Pennsylvania's Wharton School. In the *New York Times* article 'Toasting the Ad Industry and a Book Predicting Its Doom' (Maheshwari, 2017), Hays delivered her answer to the question 'Is advertising dead?' It is the sentence sitting at the heart of this book:

It's the wrong question. The right question is 'What's better than the 30-second ad?'

As we will see in the rest of this book, it is the question that is still surprisingly difficult to answer.

References

Ault, S (2015) [accessed 30 December 2017] Digital Star Popularity Grows Versus Mainstream Celebrities, *Variety*, 23 July [Online] variety.com/2015/digital/news/youtubers-teen-survey-ksi-pewdiepie-1201544882/

BCMA (2013) [accessed 12 December 2017] Defining Branded Content for the Digital Age [Online] thebcma.info/wp-content/uploads/2013/10/BCMA-Oxford-Brookes-Ipsos-Academic-Study.pdf

BCMA (2016) [accessed 12 December 2017] Defining Branded Content for the Digital Age [Online] www.thebcma.info/wp-content/uploads/2016/07/BCMA-Research-Report_FINAL.pdf

Cannes Lions (2017) [accessed 12 December 2017] Spikes Asia Festival of Creativity Entry Kit 2017 [Online] canneslions.com/mediaonline/downloads/SA17_Entry%20Kit

Cohen, H (2016) [accessed 11 June 2017] Content Marketing Definition (Blog) Heidi Cohen, 9 November [Online] heidicohen.com/content-marketing-definition/

CMA (2013) [accessed 12 December 2017] What Is Content Marketing? [Online] the-cma.com/news/what-is-content-marketing/Dietrich, G (2014) *Spin Sucks: Communication and reputation management in the Digital Age*, Que Biz-Tech, Indianapolis

Content Council (2015) [accessed 12 December 2017] About Us [Online] thecontentcouncil.org/About-Us

Forrester (2016) [accessed 11 June 2017] Don't Confuse Media-Led and Customer-Led Content Marketing [Online] forrester.com/report/Dont+Confuse+MediaLed+And+CustomerLed+Content+Marketing/-/E-RES131044

Godin, S (1999) *Permission Marketing: Turning strangers into friends, and friends into customers*, Simon and Schuster, New York

Google (2015a) [accessed 12 December 2017] Build a Content Plan [Online] thinkwithgoogle.com/marketing-resources/youtube/build-a-content-plan/

Google (2015b) [accessed 12 December 2017] Winning the Moments that Matter: Right Person, Right Message, Right Time, Every Time [Online] thinkwithgoogle.com/intl/en-gb/articles/winning-the-moments-that-matter-right-person-right-message-right-time-every-time.html

Hobsbawm, E and Ranger, T (eds) (1983) *The Invention of Tradition*, Cambridge University Press, Cambridge

IAB (2015) [accessed 12 December 2017] Content Marketing Primer [Online] iab.com/wp-content/uploads/2015/07/IABContentMarketingPrimer.pdf

iScoop (2016) [accessed 12 December 2017] Content Marketing Defined: A Customer-Centric Content Marketing Definition [Online] i-scoop.eu/content-marketing/content-marketing-defined-customer-centric-content-marketing-definition/

Jarboe, G (2012) [accessed 11 March 2015] What's the Ideal Length for a YouTube Marketing Video? *Tubular Insights*, 5 November [Online] tubularinsights.com/length-youtube-video/

Kirby, J (2014a) [accessed 11 June 2017] Interview with Pereira O'Dell's PJ Pereira (Blog), *BOBCM*, 29 October [Online] bobcm.net/2014/10/29/interview-with-pereira-odells-pj-pereira

Kirby, J (2014b) [accessed 11 June 2017] Rory Sutherland on Long-Form Branded Content? (Blog), *BOBCM*, 20 August [Online] bobcm.net/2014/08/20/rory-sutherland-on-long-form-branded-content/

MacLeod, H (2006) [accessed 11 June 2017] If You Talked to People (Blog) *Gaping Void*, 9 May [Online] www.gapingvoid.com/blog/2006/05/09/if-you-talked-to-people/

Maheshwari, S (2017) [accessed 11 June 2017] Toasting the Ad Industry and a Book Predicting Its Doom, *New York Times*, 11 June [Online] nytimes.com/2017/06/11/business/media/ads-marketing-end-of-advertising.html

Manovich, L (2001) *The Language of New Media*, MIT Press, Cambridge, MA

Maslow, A H (1966) *The Psychology of Science*, Harper & Row, New York

Matthews, I (2016) [accessed 12 December 2017] What Does Cannes Lions' Shift to an Entertainment Category Mean?, *Campaign Live*, 13 January [Online]

www.campaignlive.co.uk/article/does-cannes-lions-shift-entertainment-category-mean/1379278

PageFair (2017) [accessed 12 December 2017] The State of the Blocked Web 2017 Global Adblock Report [Online] pagefair.com/downloads/2017/01/PageFair-2017-Adblock-Report.pdf

Pulizzi, J (2012) [accessed 12 December 2017] Six Useful Content Marketing Definitions (Blog), *Content Marketing Institute*, 6 June [Online] contentmarketinginstitute.com/2012/06/content-marketing-definition/

Velocity Partners (2013) [accessed 30 December 2017] Crap: The Content Marketing Deluge – The Single Biggest Threat to B2B Content Marketing, *Slideshare*, 10 January [Online] slideshare.net/dougkessler/crap-the-content-marketing-deluge

Wikipedia (2017a) [accessed 30 December 2017] Volatility, Uncertainty, Complexity and Ambiguity [Online] en.wikipedia.org/wiki/Volatility,_uncertainty,_complexity_and_ambiguity

Wikipedia (2017b) [accessed 30 December 2017] Will It Blend [Online] en.wikipedia.org/wiki/Will_It_Blend%3F

Wikipedia (2017c) [accessed 30 December 2017] Liminality [Online] en.wikipedia.org/wiki/Liminality

YouTube Advertisers (2015) [accessed 30 December 2017] Unskippable Labs: The Mobile Recut | YouTube Advertisers [Online] youtu.be/6HHgzEGwil4

PART ONE
Content marketing: a new and better promise?

Why Content is seen as the solution to current marketing challenges

01

Technological change is not additive; it is ecological, which means, it changes everything.

POSTMAN, 1998

In the Introduction we mentioned the idea that Content could be seen as a symptom of marketing's evolution rather than just a solution. We also introduced the VUCA conditions that are enveloping the modern marketing business (and overall). The above quote from 1998, by media theorist and cultural critic Neil Postman, helps explain the desperate need to adapt, to survive and, if possible, to thrive in such an environment. We also showed that instead of trying to define Content on a meta-level, a better approach would be to take advice from visual thinker and author Dan Roam (2009) and start asking better questions about its role:

Whoever best describes the problem is the most likely to solve it.

The beginning of that answer is summed up in expert feedback highlighted in the second phase of the Defining Branded Content for the Digital Age research commissioned by the Branded Content Marketing Association mentioned in the previous chapter (BCMA, 2016):

So, a lot of the reasons for the increase in this [non-interruptive] approach is because there have been fundamental changes in the way that people consume and use media and digital technologies.

We will be looking here at these changing ecological conditions in detail. This chapter explores why Content is seen as a better promise than the (more interruptive) advertising model it challenges. Later, in Chapter 10, we will be hearing from Content's naysayers. Hopefully, presenting the *for* and *against* like this will help you judge where you stand in this heated debate.

Reasons to see Content as a potential solution

Brands losing control: no more faking it?

There is a recurring theme among some marketing academics and practitioners about how companies have lost control of their brands to their consumers thanks to the democratization of media and, specifically, the proliferation of social platforms (McAfee, 2009). It is one that lies behind the attempt to develop a more 'holistic conceptualization' of the term *branded content* in the first phase of the BCMA's research mentioned above (Asmussen *et al*, 2014):

> This loss of control over branded content is an aspect of social media that organizations have to learn to live with. It supports the need for organizations to instil good practices, good customer service and communications across their entire business.

The point being made is that now both its cheerleading customers and critics can create and distribute content connected with a brand. It is one thing to understand this in principle, but a much bolder step to let go and suddenly embrace the kind of *open-source branding* being advocated by Professor Susan Fournier and Dr Jill Avery (2011). They present an upside to consumer empowerment where brands can not only have their customers discuss their content, but also have their fans actually create it for them. Yet, even when sold as a virtue of necessity, any rewards are always going to have to be weighed against the potential risks. These include having your brand hijacked (Wipperfurth, 2005) or reputation wrecked by #brandvandals (Waddington and Earl, 2013), not to mention the own goals.

'Thriving on chaos', along the lines that business guru Tom Peters encourages from the sidelines (1989), is all very well if you are not likely to be caught in the crossfire. This is critical because it is both a real and a perceived risk in a new world where marketing directors now fret about how that new idea they present to their C-suite colleagues could be a career-ending move.

CASE STUDY Coca-Cola #MakeItHappy

Coca-Cola's 'Make it happy!' campaign is a good example of the risk posed by trying to engage consumers and activate them in the co-creation of your branded content. Promoted as part of their 2015 Super Bowl commercial, Twitter users were prompted to reply to negative tweets they found with the hashtag #MakeItHappy. Coca-Cola then transformed the tweets into 'cute ASCII art' along with a message telling the world how they were helping turn the hate that had been found into something happy. According to *The Guardian*, the stunt was subsequently suspended after they were tricked by the Gawker Media team into tweeting Hitler's autobiography *Mein Kampf* line by line from the @MeinCoke Twitter account they had set up (Woolf, 2015).

Of course, the least risky move for organizations is to avoid doing anything that will get their consumers, or society, up in arms. That way, there would be no loss of control. The best that many can currently do is try to engineer their reputation through various image-building projections such as advertising, PR and similar – but by the standards of the web reputation-building norms, this is close to 'faking it'. Plugging the gap between those brand promises and customers' actual experiences is a starting point, given how easily dissatisfaction can get amplified online. These and other effects of digital disruption have been a catalyst for organizations to think more deeply about two key areas:

1 The customer experience 'gestalt' across all touchpoints, so that brand experience as a whole is perceived as more than the sum of its parts.

2 The ontology of the organization (the worthy nature of its existence), so it becomes clearer about who it is, what it does and why it matters – or why anyone should care.

The answers to those questions can be seen to form part of a bigger promise that brands can play in our lives and society as a whole. We will be looking at this more in the following chapters dedicated to the 'Experience Economy' (Chapter 2) and 'purpose' (Chapter 3). The role Content plays here is key to understanding its potential and expectation as marketing's better promise, too.

The social media engagement delusion

Where the consumers go, brands follow, particularly when trying to connect with that elusive 'millennial' generation in social media. Suddenly, everything has become the matter of 'conversation', causing a lot of despair in the brand community because of the massive ineffectiveness issues. The argument here that works in Content's favour is that much of social media activity is irrelevant because it is done just for the sake of it. It is the question of *quality* more than anything else. The notion of failed 'engagement' is palpable. The Pepsi Refresh Project is often mentioned as an example.

CASE STUDY Pepsi Refresh Project

Pepsi have been having their own trials and tribulations when it comes to social media, namely with their Refresh Project exploration of 'how a brand could be integrated into the digital space' (Leslie, 2015). Led by their former Chief Engagement Officer Frank Cooper back in 2010, Pepsi allocated an initial $20 million for this social media marketing campaign as part of a trailblazing shift of one-third of its ad spend to digital and social media (Zmuda, 2010). The cause-orientated campaign offered grants in various categories for worthy projects chosen by online audiences. Many pundits lauded it at the time as being a means to 'deepen the relationship with consumers'. The premise was that they were engaging with 'the crowd' in something more meaningful and positive than simply interrupting them with ads. Despite the social media success that included the gaining of millions of likes and followers, Pepsi made a hasty retreat back to TV after a 5 per cent drop in market share that year, along with suffering the ignominy of getting knocked off the number two spot by Coke Zero.

Ad veteran Bob Hoffman, of *Ad Contrarian* fame, points the finger for Pepsi's 'massive failure' squarely at what he sees as the 'infantile delusion that social media marketing is based on' (2017a):

> The silly idea that consumers want to have conversations with and about brands and share their brand enthusiasms with the world.

Hoffman has much more to say on the topic of Content as well (see Chapter 10). For him, the delusion is wider and deeper than just social media.

Smart Insights founder Dr Dave Chaffey offers a different take on the efficacy of social media marketing, seeing the problem instead as one where more dots need to be joined (Kirby, 2014). For him the problem is not so much that Content and social media marketing have become the de facto ways of conducting engagement in the digital space, but that they are far too often considered separately. The point is that if the approaches become more unified it introduces more 'connected' thinking about the role of Content in customer engagement across their digital journeys. It is about aligning what's in it for both them and the brand, and Content here could play a crucial role.

That unification as an opportunity has not been lost on the PR community, who have moved quickly to assimilate Content and social capability into their practice. So what was once called 'stakeholder engagement' or 'opinion leader programmes' based on the Two Step Flow communication theory of Elihu Katz and Paul Lazarsfeld from the late 1950s (1955), is now being pitched in the Digital Era as 'influencer marketing'. That is yet another example of the 'reinvention of tradition' we discussed in the Introduction, and one where the co-creation of content with those who influence an audience often sits at the heart of the approach.

The ongoing shift to digital and the darkening clouds of the 'adblocalypse'

Live linear TV continues to hold its own in some markets, in part thanks to what is being heralded as the latest new 'Golden Age' of TV. Paradoxically, that has been helped by the rise of internationally acclaimed series commissioned by platforms like Amazon and Netflix – offering premium ad-free content environments!

However, there seems to be a research war going on between the two sides of the TV sustainability debate. On one hand, we have UK's Thinkbox with a raft of distinguished research partners, as explored in Chapter 10, stating that linear TV is still in good health. On the other, there is also growing evidence, including Globalwebindex 'Digital vs. Traditional Media Consumption' report in 2017, showing that traditional media consumption continues to decline overall, with a significant shift to digital in some markets and demographics. This is most notably with those aged 16–34, aka the 'hard-to-reach' millennial generation, who are spending more and more of their time online and increasingly on mobile devices. It is particularly true of fast-growth markets where younger age groups represent a larger percentage of online populations. Even in markets where TV is still strong, online represents 60–64 per cent of the 'millennial' media consumption (Chesters, 2017). That, interestingly, includes how they use the TV set, for example, for playing games and how they use other connected services, including those that are ad free.

The ongoing consumer shift to digital and how brands are responding to it could also be seen in the point made by the D&AD CEO Tim Lindsay, who sees their awards as one of the chroniclers of that shift. If you wind back the clock, he explains in our interview, then half of the awards used to go to ad agencies and the other half to design studios. That started to change, Lindsay thinks, about the time D&AD launched its first digital category in the mid-1990s. Since then, he feels that things have changed out of all recognition:

> We give about 65 to 70 yellow or black pencils each year and only two or three go to what we would now call traditional advertising.

D&AD is still awarding the output of advertising agencies and design studios in the main, but the growing number of new categories being offered and entered helps highlight how the output of agencies is moving way beyond traditional advertising. The changing nature of business models across the marketing industry is something we will be looking at in Part Two. But, as brands adapt on their ongoing digital transformation journey, and try to connect with consumers in an ever-growing number of ways, there are some black clouds mustering.

First, the proliferation of channels, lifestyles and content in the online space is too much for anyone to process. Brands cannot be everywhere – particularly in any meaningful way. It has never been easier to ignore things, particularly brands; one swipe, and it's gone. At the same time, advances in user experience (UX) continue to improve the way that people can manipulate what they see on screens and make choices about whether they like something or not.

This is creating the growing problem of the 'adblocalypse', as highlighted by the following stats from Forrester Research (McQuivey, 2017):

- 38 per cent of online adults in the United States have installed an ad blocker;
- 50 per cent of online adults in the United States actively avoid ads on websites;
- 47 per cent of online adults in the United States actively avoid mobile in-app ads.

PageFair's ongoing reports, mentioned in the Introduction, tell a similar story (PageFair, 2017). If consumer-driven ad blocking wasn't enough of a problem, then Apple's iOS 11 version of their operating system for mobile devices raised the ad industry to a heightened state of alert in 2017.

The inclusion of an 'intelligent tracking prevention' as a default feature in their Safari web browser limits the ability of advertisers to stalk users with ads around the web.

Despite the irony of the annoying nature of ads being one of the factors driving ad blocking, the Coalition of Major Advertising Trade Associations accused Apple in an open letter of sabotaging the economic model for the internet (2017). As highlighted in *The Guardian*, the likely beneficiaries of Apple's latest enabling of ad blocking may be Facebook and Google because, once again, they will profit from the switching of ad budgets to their environments as they are more immune to the falling ad revenues than smaller publishers (Hern, 2017). Their growing duopoly had already accumulated 50 per cent of all US digital advertising revenues by 2017, according to eMarketer, and continues to grow (O'Reilly, 2017). This leaves everyone else fighting over what is left – this is an issue discussed in our online 'Publisher' chapter in more detail.

Unilever's CMO Keith Weed captures the reason we highlight the digital media shift and ad avoidance as part of the better promise of Content during his keynote address at Advertising Week New York (Tan, 2017):

> Today's ad experience is not in line with the empowered consumer's expectation of faster, better, more relevant content.

The point was made as part of presenting Unilever's new '5C' marketing framework (Consumers, Connect, Content, Community and Commerce). It makes the consumer the starting place ('the true north') with Content providing the means to connect and engage them in better and more relevant ways, so brands do not get filtered out (Weed, 2017).

Viewability, ad fraud and other reasons for advertisers not to be cheerful

According to Google's own viewability research (2014), only 54 per cent of online display ads are ever seen, complying with the Interactive Advertising Bureau UK's (IAB UK) minimum criteria for an ad impression of 50 per cent of its pixels to be visible in the browser window for at least one second (2014)! That sets the bar about as low as it can get and so it is hardly surprising that click-through rates of digital display ads are reported by Forrester to be at around 0.35 per cent (McQuivey, 2017).

To add to digital advertisers' ad blocking and viewability challenges, they are also faced with fraud that inflates traffic numbers and click-through rates. The Association of National Advertisers' (ANA) extensive research with digital security company WhiteOps gave some idea of the scale of the problem: advertisers' projected losses to bot traffic in 2016 were around US $7.2 billion (ANA, 2016).

This growing list of issues has not been lost on advertisers. P&G's chief brand officer Marc Pritchard called for the digital media advertising supply chain to clean up its act or face the financial consequences – describing it 'murky at best' and 'fraudulent at worst' (Roderick, 2017). The call for greater transparency and accountability by Pritchard is also linked to the 'crappy advertising' that he sees helping drive our avoidance of it. The hope is that better advertising creative (work) along with greater accountability and efficiency will help advertisers to reap the benefits that digital is supposed to offer when compared to traditional media. How big clients could avoid responsibility for the 'crappy' ads so far is an intriguing question.

It is against this backdrop that Content, if done well, is pitched as a means of escaping the vicious circle described to us by the Content Marketing Institute's Chief Strategy Adviser Robert Rose, who pointed out that any increases in digital ad spend only adjust for the inefficiencies mentioned above. In other words, the attempt is to patch up the hole with more money. Suddenly, Owned media sounds like a good deal...

Brand safety matters

There are other pressing matters for advertisers, not least Amazon being the only contender looking likely to break the growing duopoly of Google and Facebook mentioned above (Hobbs, 2017). But despite ad budgets shifting their way and many advertisers bypassing their agencies to work directly with platforms, the two digital giants have been having their own trials and tribulations.

A spotlight has been shone on the role played by Facebook in the spreading of 'fake news'. This has been followed swiftly by the discovery that brand messages are appearing alongside 'questionable or unsafe content' on Google's platforms, such as videos promoting terror groups. In Google's case, that has resulted not only in a call by advertisers to take the same responsibility as media companies when it comes to brand safety, but also the decision by the media agency Havas Group UK, and reportedly 250 brands, to suspend their ad spending until the problem is addressed (Stein, 2017).

For Faris Yakob, creative consultant and author of *Paid Attention* (2015), the brand safety issue is a problem of advertisers' own making, having outsourced media buying decisions to the algorithms behind programmatic ad delivery platforms. That has come at a cost, because although there are savings to be made from using platforms that automate the digital delivery of messages at scale, by trading in the dark brands become blind to the appropriateness of where their ads appear. It also makes the media buying less about the quality of targeting and what that means about your brand, and simply about the cost efficiencies of reach. So, technically speaking, the 'right' person may be reached and even at the right time, but not necessarily in the right place.

As highlighted in Chapter 11, this could be the result of the 'moral choice' of the algorithmic optimization: racists buy shampoo and washing liquid too and racist signals are not difficult to spot – but should we? Should algorithms have a moral and ethical filter? If so, should it extend beyond just the brand-safe environments? It is an interesting conundrum also raised by Mark Higginson from Twenty Thousand Leagues in his interview with us. He maintains that this is a case of algorithms actually working as intended. So, adjusting for this is a case for making algorithms *less* precise in a way, or in other words, how to take out some signals from the overall picture and deprive some content of ad feeds (and vice versa).

These and the other issues highlighted above represent a perfect storm in digital advertising, as outlined in Hoffman's diatribe about the 'Top 10 Reasons Online Advertising Must Change' (2017b). His argument is that the 'online advertising industry is a preposterous train wreck', which forms part of the longer one he makes in *BadMen: How advertising went from a minor annoyance to a major menace* (2017). Key ethical issues with Content and the directions the marketing industry is heading towards in this regard are discussed in more detail in Chapter 11.

Putting the ethical issues aside, it is not surprising that brand safety is prompting brands to look to other alternatives. One of those is the reported growing investment in owned media. Research by the Spiegel Research Center at Northwestern University, in conjunction with Publicis Media, shows that it may also make financial sense to do so (2017):

> Successful brands have raised their share of sales over five years and have invested more in owned media than they have in paid media. Static or declining brands favoured paid media over owned media traffic demonstrating a negative relationship between ad spend and sales.

It is not a case for not investing in paid media, but that it should not be always prioritized because they serve different purposes. It is about finding the right balance. The challenges of brand safety may spur clients to maximize the experience in spaces they *can* control – but attention still has to be earned.

The new rules of the attention economy

Back in 2008, *Wired* magazine's founding executive editor Kevin Kelly summarized what he described as 'the new rules for the new economy':

> Where ever attention flows, money will follow.

What powers the insight is the fact that our attention is a scarce resource and the 'new currency of business' that Thomas H Davenport and John C Beck wrote about in *Attention Economy* (2001). The principle in the old proverb about the antidote often being found close to the poison has been understood in the ad industry for some time, as JWT's former Chief Creative Officer EMEA Craig Davis illustrates (WPP, 2005):

> Audiences everywhere are tough. They don't have time to be bored or brow beaten by orthodox, old-fashioned advertising. We need to stop interrupting what people are interested in and **be** what people are interested in.

Davis's desire about brands being what people are interested in is where Content becomes the remedy to the lack of customer attention, again according to Keith Weed in an article in *Marketing Week* about the '5C' framework (Weed, 2017):

> We all know that the battle for attention has never been greater. So this is about developing a more sophisticated approach to how we think about our content. In this hyper-segmented world, increasingly that means building one-to-one brand experiences, making content speak to a personalized journey.

Interestingly, Weed includes both interruptive advertising ('interruption') and the content we 'seek out' online as part of the Content 'C' in Unilever's new framework:

- **Interruption**: the more traditional advertising formats used to build brands.
- **Seek-out**: content that either solves problems the people are looking for help with or they are interested in, ie their 'passion points'.

These options are not presented as either/or choices, but framed in terms of the need to get the balance right for their difference purposes: echoing the recommendation from the Spiegel Research Center mentioned earlier. We will explore both sides of this perspective in the book: the Experience Economy considerations in Chapter 2, and the more joined up spectrum of 'push' and 'pull' in Chapters 4 and 6.

Declining ad quality and creative talent diaspora

We touched upon the issue of ad (and Content) quality above. It is one of the main reasons why consumers might be turning away from advertising. There are various forces driving this trend, as explored in several places in the book – with the procurement-led race to the bottom remuneration-wise being mentioned the most often – but the D&AD's CEO Tim Lindsay offers another in our interview:

> There's now demonstrably far less talent across advertising disciplines, but most notably in the creative department, where there's been a diaspora to other sectors including technology companies and start-ups of their own – not necessarily in advertising industry!

The reality for those that remain is illustrated in Lindsay's basic formula of today's agency life: they are now working three times as quickly, for one-third of the money. It is bad for attracting the next generation, as highlighted in the 'Bridging the Talent Disconnect' white paper by the Advertising Educational Foundation in the United States (ANA, 2017). Their findings show that school students are not clear about the career paths available in advertising and marketing, as well as the question of whether it amounts to 'meaningful work'. When it comes to higher education, the report concludes that universities struggle to both keep curricula up to speed (given the rapid changes going on) and manage the conflict between industry demands for job-ready graduates and their academic remit to develop broader critical-thinking skills.

The problem of curricula keeping up to speed is very real and amplified by how Content requires very different and more collaborative ways of working. For example, the traditional 'two-atom' creative team (copy + art) is increasingly becoming outdated, or at least not up to the more complex job of creating Content and solving other bigger communication problems convincingly for dozens of platforms and digital formats. Most of those we spoke to also see that the creative process in Content tends to be less linear and more iterative, requiring teams with much broader skills (eg data and technology), as well as the ability, in many cases, to actually execute ideas rather than just have them. This is not to downplay the need for creative thinking, but without that being framed around more in-depth understanding of the rapidly changing nature of its practical application, the fees become harder to justify.

Pedagogical issues aside, we mention the talent acquisition and retention issues because they create a problem for both agencies and clients trying to understand better the digital mindset. It is also a problem for Pritchard's and Weed's demands for better-quality creative work and the industry having a responsibility to deliver it. One of the most consistent criticisms of Content so far is the poor quality of so much of it. That may be the result of its commodification, reflected in the joke doing the rounds in London that one is not only 2 metres away from a rat at all times – but also only 20 metres away from a content creator! That oversupply of rubbish as the seed of Content's own potential demise is a well-understood issue in Content circles. However, we must not forget that Content is here just following the well-trod advertising route to reduced quality. Actually, most of everything in life is rubbish, usually expressed as 'Sturgeon's Law':

> Sure, 90 per cent of science fiction is crud. That's because 90 per cent of everything is crud. (Science-fiction author Theodore Sturgeon at New York University, c 1951 (Raymond, 1996))

Zenith USA's EVP Product Innovation Tom Goodwin suggests that Content might be better framed to brands in terms of how to do less stuff that has greater impact. In Chapter 4, dedicated to how Content changes the business of creative agencies, we will present an approach that offers less binary choices and may help us avoid getting buried under more of that 90 per cent of Sturgeon's Law.

The emergence of 'non-interruptible' environments

It is against this growing list of issues and challenges faced by brands that Forrester's James McQuivey predicts 'The End of Advertising, The Beginning of Relationships' (2017). He argues that 'display advertising never worked like we pretended'. This is why he suggests that P&G Pritchard's throwing down the gauntlet of 'reform or else' is just a small step towards brands switching to other alternative 'brand relationships' that don't interrupt consumers. Instead, McQuivey recommends the likes of AI-driven personal assistants – Apple's Siri, Amazon Alexa or Google Assistant – as examples of technologies that consumers are adopting to get what they want without interruption.

As we investigate in Chapter 8 about the evolution of Content formats, it is difficult to interrupt people if they are using technologies that they cannot be interrupted on. His prediction, interestingly, coincides with digital advertising still showing the strongest growth and already being twice the size of TV advertising in markets such as the UK (IAB UK, 2017). Digital display ads in the United States look set to overtake even search ads (Peterson, 2016). We will soon know how sustainable that 'spend bubble' is and whether there is an 'ad crunch' just around the corner. The brands' personal assistants that McQuivey suggests are one possible answer to avoid it, and we will be looking at other would-be winners later in the book. Interestingly, he thinks that although tech can make conversations more satisfying to customers, it will require the incorporation of the brand personality the CMO has committed the company to, to make them sparkle. This is also true of Content and arguably a more realistic starting place in these environments. As yet, it is not clear how brands will use agents, chatbots, IoT and other emerging tech to reach audiences at scale to build brand, rather than optimize the (post-) purchase experience.

Feeding 'Moments that Matter'

While the industry tries to understand what's next on the horizon and how they will have to adapt to it, people continue to search for something that is relevant for them in their personal lives. This is what Google (2015) and Facebook (2015) call 'Moments that Matter' (MTMs), which we explore in Chapters 4 and 7. In theory, search should be providing brands with the ability to be there at those moments, particularly those on the consumer's path to purchase. That requires brands to have something there in the first place. It also means feeding the beast, requiring investment in a longer-term game of planning, testing and refining.

As Lee Wilson, author of *Tactical SEO: The theory and practice of search marketing* (2016), explained to us, there are hundreds of signals being processed by Google's algorithms beyond just the quality of the content itself. Freshness, scale, depth of content on a given topic are all important factors, which is why Content hubs that focus on deep information about a subject can really help reinforce the claim to the topic. The theory is that great and well-optimized content can help outperform those trying to bid their way to the top. In reality, gaming Google is more complex than we can do justice here, but creating great Content can be seen as the flipside of winning SEO, because if you have nothing to optimize then you are losing in the ranking game.

If we think about those billions of moments where people are searching for relevant things, including for their entertainment or just something useful, then it helps give a glimpse of the huge space that brands have to play on. This takes us to Content's still unfulfilled better promise, because it allows brands to be there with amusing, inspirational, useful, transformational and, perhaps, beautiful things in moments that matter, in context and on an ongoing basis. Doing so helps brands to focus on the good 10 per cent of Sturgeon's Law – and form part of the bigger promise that brands can play in our lives and at the societal level.

References

ANA (2016) [accessed 12 December 2017] The Bot Baseline: Fraud in Digital Advertising [Online] ana.net/content/show/id/botfraud-2016

ANA (2017) [accessed 12 December 2017] Bridging the Talent Disconnect: Charting the Pathways to Future Growth [Online] ana.net/magazines/show/id/ii-aef-bridging-talent-disconnect

Asmussen, B, Canter, A, Butler, A and Michels, N (2014) Towards the future of branded content, in *Best of Branded Content Marketing 10th Anniversary Edition*, ed A Canter, J Kirby, G MacFarlane and M Welland, Digital Media Communications Limited, London, pp 93–100

BCMA (2016) [accessed 12 December 2017] Defining Branded Content for the Digital Age [Online] thebcma.info/wp-content/uploads/2016/07/BCMA-Research-Report_FINAL.pdf

Chesters, B (2017) [accessed 15 June 2017] A View From Ben Chesters: The Future Is Still Promising for Television, *Campaign*, 16 January [Online] campaignlive.co.uk/article/future-promising-television/1420692

Coalition of Major Advertising Trade Associations (2017) [accessed 12 January 2017] Major Ad Trade Groups Release Joint Letter Outlining Deep Concerns Over Cookie-Handling Functionality of Apple's Safari 11 Browser, *PR Newswire*, 14 September [Online] prnewswire.com/news-releases/major-ad-trade-groups-release-joint-letter-outlining-deep-concerns-over-cookie-handling-functionality-of-apples-safari-11-browser-300519829.html

Davenport, T H and Beck, J C (2001) *Attention Economy: Understanding the new currency of business*, Harvard Business Review Press, Boston, MA

Facebook (2015) [accessed 15 May 2017] Moments that Matter: Finding the Extraordinary in the Ordinary [online] fbinsights.files.wordpress.com/2015/09/facebookiq_moments_whitepaper.pdf

Fournier, S and Avery, J (2011) The uninvited brand, *Business Horizons*, 54 (3), pp 193–207

Globalwebindex (2017) [accessed 15 May 2017] Digital vs. Traditional Media Consumption (Q1 2017) [online] insight.globalwebindex.net/traditional-vs-digital-media-consumption

Google (2014) [accessed 15 May 2017] 5 Factors of Display Viewability [Online] thinkwithgoogle.com/infographics/5-factors-of-viewability.html

Google (2015) [accessed 15 May 2017] Win the Moments that Matter [Online] thinkwithgoogle.com/intl/en-gb/marketing-resources/micro-moments/win-the-moments-that-matter/

Hern, A (2017) [accessed 12 January 2017] Apple Blocking Ads that Follow Users Around Web Is 'Sabotage', Says Industry, *The Guardian*, 18 September [Online] theguardian.com/technology/2017/sep/18/apple-stopping-ads-follow-you-around-internet-sabotage-advertising-industry-ios-11-and-macos-high-sierra-safari-internet

Hobbs, T (2017) [accessed 15 May 2017] Can Amazon Put an End to Google and Facebook's Digital Duopoly?, *Marketing Week*, 12 May [Online] marketingweek.com/2017/05/12/how-amazon-is-taking-on-google-facebook-at-advertising/

Hoffman, B (2017a) [accessed 12 December 2017] Best of 2017: Social Media Agency of The Year For Not Doing Social Media (Blog), *Adcontrarian*, 6 December [Online] adcontrarian.blogspot.co.uk/2017/12/best-of-2017-social-media-agency-of.html

Hoffman, B (2017b) [accessed 12 December 2017] Top 10 Reasons Online Advertising Must Change (Blog), *LinkedIn: Bob Hoffman*, 24 October [Online] linkedin.com/pulse/top-10-reasons-online-advertising-must-change-bob-hoffman/

Hoffman, B (2017c) *BadMen: How advertising went from a minor annoyance to a major menace*, Type A Group, Oakland

IAB UK (2014) [accessed 15 May 2017] Viewable Ad Impression Measurement Guidelines – IAB UK [Online] iabuk.net/sites/default/files/Viewable%20Ad%20Impression%20Guidelines.pdf

IAB UK (2017) [accessed 15 May 2017] Digital Adspend [Online] iabuk.net/research/digital-adspend

Katz, E and Lazarsfeld, P F (1955) *Personal Influence: The part played by people in the flow of mass communications*, Free Press, New York

Kelly, K (2008) [accessed 12 December 2017] Where Attention Flows, Money Follows (Blog) *The Technium*, 25 September [Online] kk.org/thetechnium/where-attention/

Kirby, J (2014) The Future of Branded Content Marketing, in *Best of Branded Content Marketing 10th Anniversary Edition*, ed A Canter, J Kirby, G MacFarlane and M Welland, Digital Media Communications Limited, London, pp 115–46

Leslie, I (2015) [accessed 15 May 2017] How the Mad Men Lost the Plot, *Financial Times*, 6 November [Online] ft.com/content/cd1722ba-8333-11e5-8e80-1574112844fd

McAfee, A (2009) [accessed 12 June 2017] The Illusion of Brand Control, *Harvard Business Review*, 13 November [Online] hbr.org/2009/11/the-illusion-of-brand-control.html

McQuivey, J L (2017) [accessed 15 May 2017] The End of Advertising, The Beginning of Relationships (Blog), *James McQuivey's Blog: Forrester*, 2 May [Online] blogs.forrester.com/james_mcquivey/17-05-02-the_end_of_advertising_the_beginning_of_relationships

O'Reilly, L (2017) [accessed 12 January 2017] The Race Is On to Challenge Google-Facebook 'Duopoly' in Digital Advertising, *The Wall Street Journal*, 19 June [Online] wsj.com/articles/the-race-is-on-to-challenge-google-facebook-duopoly-in-digital-advertising-1497864602

PageFair (2017) [accessed 12 December 2017] 2017 Adblock Report [Online] pagefair.com/blog/2017/adblockreport/

Peters, T (1989) *Thriving on Chaos: Handbook for a management revolution*, Pan, London

Peterson, T (2016) [accessed 15 May 2017] U.S. Display Ad Spending to Overtake Search in 2016, Suggesting TV Budgets in Motion Brands Will Spend More on Banners than Video Ads for Foreseeable Future, *Advertising Age*, 12 January [Online] adage.com/article/digital/u-s-display-ad-spending-overtake-search-2016/302099/

Postman, N (1998) Five things we need to know about technological change, The New Technologies and the Human Person: Communicating the Faith in the New Millennium Conference, Denver

Raymond, E S (1996) *The New Hacker's Dictionary*, MIT Press, Cambridge, MA

Roam, D (2009) *Unfolding the Napkin: The hands-on method for solving complex problems with simple pictures*, Portfolio, New York

Roderick, L (2017) [accessed 15 May 2017] P&G Issues Call to Arms to Ad Industry Over 'Antiquated' Media Buying, *Marketing Week*, 30 January [Online] marketingweek.com/2017/01/30/pg-media-buying/

Spiegel Research Center (2017) [accessed 12 December 2017] The Impact of Owned Media vs. Paid Media on Brand Sales [Online] spiegel.medill.northwestern.edu/paid-vs-owned-media/

Stein, L (2017) [accessed 12 January 2017] Havas Freezes All Google and Youtube Ad Spend In The U.K., *Advertising Age*, 17 March [Online] adage.com/article/agency-news/havas-freezes-google-youtube-ad-spend-uk/308328/

Tan, E (2017) [accessed 15 May 2017] Unilever Marketing Boss Weed Reveals 5C Brand Strategy, *Campaign*, 25 September [Online] campaignlive.co.uk/article/unilever-marketing-boss-weed-reveals-5c-brand-strategy/1445575

Waddington, S and Earl, S (2013) *Brand Vandals: Reputation wreckers and how to build better defences*, Bloomsbury Publishing, London

Weed, K (2017) [accessed 15 May 2017] Keith Weed: Marketers Must Follow the '5Cs' to Connect With Today's Consumers, *Marketing Week*, 5 September [Online] marketingweek.com/2017/09/25/keith-weed-five-cs-connect-todays-consumers/

Wipperfurth, A (2005) *Brand Hijack: Marketing without marketing*, Portfolio, New York

Woolf, N (2015) [accessed 15 May 2017] Coca-Cola Pulls Twitter Campaign After It Was Tricked into Quoting *Mein Kampf*, *The Guardian*, 5 February [Online] theguardian.com/business/2015/feb/05/coca-cola-makeithappy-gakwer-mein-coke-hitler

WPP (2005) [accessed 12 December 2017] JWT Re-Defines Role [Online] wpp.com/wpp/press/2005/jan/27/jwt-redefines-role/

Zmuda, N (2010) [accessed 15 May 2017] Pass or Fail, Pepsi's Refresh Will Be Case for Marketing Textbooks, *Advertising Age*, 8 February [Online] adage.com/article/digital/marketing-pepsi-refresh-case-marketing-textbooks/141973/

Experience Economy

Brand and customer experience as Content enablers

The Content space can sometimes seem like there is a land grab by two competing communication ideologies, which, somewhat cartoonishly, have set up their camps around the dominant terms of 'branded content' and 'content marketing'. Sabres are often rattled, such as Content Marketing Institute's founder and CEO Joe Pulizzi's rallying cry about how 'branded content gives content marketing a bad name' (2015):

> It's a word created by the world of paid media… by advertisers, agencies and media planners… Simply put, branded content looks and feels like advertising. If it looks like a duck and walks like a duck, well…'

A less hyperbolic version of this battle for content budgets is offered by Forrester Research in its 'Don't Confuse Media-Led and Customer-Led Content Marketing' report (2016). They see two types of Content approaches emerging: one that supports brand advertising goals (media-led) and one that supports direct-response goals (customer-led).

Divvying up the Content space like this can seem a bit *to-may-to* versus *to-mah-to* and is symptomatic of a much bigger divide we see forming in adland that we discuss in Chapter 4. The problem of looking at Content this way is that a significant client-driven shift from marketing to customer experience can end up getting overlooked. As highlighted in the IPA's 'Future of Agencies: Systems and Empathy' (2017) report, prepared by Neil Perkin in partnership with Econsultancy, it is an important driver of fundamental change in how agencies now engage with clients and conduct work.

Not only does this shift create challenges and opportunities that we will be looking at later, it also represents another direction where Content may help reshape marketing. Content's role in this shift becomes not just something that is seen as a *better promise* compared to traditional advertising, but part of the progression towards the *bigger promise* offered by the evolution of markets towards the Experience Economy.

What has Content got to do with the Experience Economy?

Every quarter in the UK there is a flurry of articles about consumer spending shifting into the 'Experience Economy'. For example, 'Just do it: the Experience Economy and how we turned our backs on "stuff"', by James Usborne in *The Guardian* (2017). They are usually linked to the release of government economic statistics and often supported by recent market research with data from banks and other sources. But what is the Experience Economy and how are the dots joined to Content?

As flagged up by many of the experts we interviewed for the book, one usual way of showing the role of Content in modern marketing is via its link to customer experience (CX), as a stepping-stone to the full experience-based economy:

Content > Customer Experience > Experience Economy

Customer experience (CX)

Defined by Forrester as:

How customers perceive their interactions with your company, customer experience focuses on the ability to optimize customer touchpoints and journeys for the fulfilment of customer and company objectives. (Manning, 2010)

Or, in a very neat definition by Professor Mark Ritson in Chapter 6, 'It's not what the company thinks or does, it's what the consumer goes through!'

Experiential marketing is another way of joining the dots, as are the other paths between the two, usually obvious because they include the word 'experience': user experience (UX) design, service experience design, and similar.

Helpful content and customer journey

If we take the CX route, then a simple way of connecting the Experience Economy to Content is through Google's Help category, from their HHH framework mentioned in the Introduction. Helpful content covers all parts of the customer journey, as explored in Chapter 6. Using 'helpful content' loops us back to the millions of 'Moments that Matter' (MTMs) mentioned in Chapter 1, which includes all those problems that customers need solving. As SEO expert and author of *Tactical SEO* (2016) Lee Wilson explained to us, when done well, addressing MTMs like this helps provide the kind of 'evergreen' content that has a longer shelf-life because it continues to remain useful. Not only does Content like this support existing customers, but its discovery through organic search and pay-per-click (PPC) advertising can also help drive demand by introducing the brand to new customers and reminding the former that their offerings are worth considering or buying again.

CASE STUDY   Cash from Content – Unilever's 'All Things Hair' YouTube channel

In theory, 'being there' and 'being useful' can both improve people's lives, but also bottom lines. Unilever's 'All Things Hair' YouTube channel was built on the insight gained from analysing Google's data that showed how influential video bloggers providing beauty and style tips on YouTube were generating large audiences. Unilever decided to hire those 'vloggers' to co-create relevant content with them before promoting it via display and search adverting. Within 10 weeks of launch, All Things Hair became the number one hair channel on YouTube: clocking up over 50 million views (Neff, 2015). Unilever has subsequently relaunched the platform as an owned and operated (O&O) channel with an integrated e-commerce platform, which also includes links from content to retail partners.

Content as utility – Customer Experience Management

Helping improve people's lives is the tip of the iceberg in terms of how CX and content marketing are and can be connected. Once the initial dots are joined, it is possible to go beyond help and into the Customer Experience Management paradigm:

> **Customer Experience Management (CEM or CXM)**
>
> Defined by Gartner (2017) as:
>
> > The practice of designing and reacting to *customer* interactions to meet or exceed *customer* expectations and, thus, increase *customer* satisfaction, loyalty and advocacy. It is a strategy that requires process change and many technologies to accomplish.

The crossover between Content and CEM/CEX is being manifested in many ways, but one is particularly interesting: customer service apps and other technologies. This would fit into the 'utility content' type of content marketing that Rebecca Lieb identifies in *Content – The Atomic Particle of Marketing* (2017); a mortgage calculator would be an example. Here, Content becomes an enabling technology for delivering more interactive services and experiences that we *use* to *do* something – rather than content-like stuff we read, look at, watch or listen to. This could be seen as a tech *expression* of Google's Help category, rather than a content *type*.

It is an area that shows how digital provides massive scope for brands to connect with their customers in ways that are useful, rather than just bombard them with messages. Once the door from Content to CX is opened through providing 'utility', then you also enter the worlds of (experience) design and wider innovation spaces such as around product, platform, business, service and similar.

Content and customer experience as one?

The idea of digital as a meta-medium, mentioned in the Introduction, helps explain why Content is so difficult to define and separate out from all the other marketing communications disciplines that also use content. It is also why the lines between marketing and other business areas start to blur, as well as between the real and virtual worlds with new spaces such as augmented reality (AR) and mixed reality (MR), which we will be looking at later in this book (in particular, Chapter 8).

As the Content Marketing Institute's (CMI) Chief Strategy Officer Robert Rose explained to us as part of our research, we encounter a similar problem when we start trying to unpick Content from the customer experience space:

If you look at Lego, they offer the experience of their LEGOLAND®
amusement parks. Well, these encompass digital, physical and all kinds of
different means of delivering a customer experience. You could say that
this is because they are an events company now. But are they? Are they
an events company that just so happens to manufacture plastic bricks, or
are they a manufacturer of plastic bricks who now uses the experience of
an amusement park to actually facilitate the sale of more bricks? I don't
think it matters ultimately.

Rose is the co-author of *Experiences: The 7th era of marketing* (2015) and
also co-wrote *Killing Marketing* (2017) with his colleague and CMI founder
Joe Pulizzi about 'how innovative businesses are turning marketing costs
into profit'. They are looking at the business strategy of becoming more integrated with media and offline customer experiences more broadly. In short,
the point is that it doesn't matter any more if you are in the widget business,
you also need to be in the widget experience business!

CASE STUDY   Trek Bikes – Rays MTB Park

Rays MTB Park in Cleveland, Ohio, is an indoor venue where mountain, cross-
country and BMX bikes can be rode and rented. Trail rides, ramps, jumps and
foam pits allow riders to learn new skills and keep fit all year round, whatever the
weather outside. Trek Bikes purchased the business in 2010, and are now rolling
out the concept in other cities. It is a good example of a brand expanding from
making bicycles and related products into being an *experience business* in the
same category, ie where the *experience is the product* sold (Trek Bikes, 2017).

Towards more integrated business platforms

The premise of Pulizzi and Rose's *Killing Marketing* (2017) is that perva-
siveness of technology enables companies to incorporate those experiences
as part of becoming a more integrated platform. Enter the new 'black' of
the strategy world, where businesses have to become multi-dimensional
and offer all manner of products and services to be able to create multiple
revenue streams.

It is the thinking behind the 'Day One' company philosophy espoused by Jeff Bezos in his '2016 letter to shareholders' (2017). Becoming an integrated platform allows forward-thinking businesses to be more agile, responsive and ultimately resilient. The idea is to keep 'stasis' at bay and embrace future trends so they can 'pivot' to wherever they need to be next. Ford could morph from a car manufacturer to a transportation company as they start to move into driverless vehicles; Facebook becoming a product company with Oculus Rift Virtual Reality; and Amazon's acquisition of the Whole Foods Market organic grocery.

The downside of becoming a multi-dimensional platform is that it can create confusion about what a company is and does. It is also reflective of a radical statement by Saatchi and Saatchi's former CEO Kevin Roberts, who describes the 'super-crazy VUCA world' we now live in and why strategy, the big idea, management and even marketing as we know it are all dead (Draycott, 2012):

> We don't just live in a VUCA world – a volatile, uncertain, ambiguous and complex world – we live in a super VUCA world… The more time and money you spend devising strategies the more time you are giving your rivals to start eating your lunch.

If having your lunch eaten wasn't enough, Silicon Valley looks set to eat the world (Mahdawi, 2017), thus the point that Zenith's Tom Goodwin makes about the battle now being all about the interface to the consumer:

> Uber, the world's largest taxi company, owns no vehicles. Facebook, the world's most popular media owner, creates no content. Alibaba, the most valuable retailer, has no inventory. And Airbnb, the world's largest accommodation provider, owns no real estate… In this age, the customer interface is everything. (2015)

The reinvention of marketing?

Becoming a more integrated platform that offers a greater array of experiences is clearly a broader business effort than just marketing communications. But as Rose explained, CMOs have the opportunity to drive that diversification by having the remit to build the customer's experiences into their brand-building ones:

> The remit of marketing these days is to have a very large part of the top of funnel experience/pre-customer phase; increasingly they have some level of remit over customer experiences post-transaction, but rarely do they have the remit over creating those types of experiences that add revenue lines or business value.

This, of course, poses various new challenges to CMOs, as well as spectacular opportunities. It requires thinking more broadly about what they do rather than just looking at their suite of products and services to work out how they describe value in different ways.

As usual, Red Bull will pop up here. It is the standard bearer that Rose highlights as an innovative company revolutionizing their marketing efforts by making the shift from being 'revenue-takers to revenue-drivers':

> It's published by Red Bull Media House who are a separate division rather than part of the marketing arm responsible for the promotion of the soft drink. That is not to say they don't face the same challenges as other media owners when it comes to making money, including the selling of their content, advertising and sponsorship. But from an accountancy point of view they are a separate business unit that doesn't sit on the expense line.

It is the creation of this kind of media product that people actually buy, which Pulizzi and Rose are looking at in their new book. It is one they think is a great example because it also happens to be part of Red Bull's main marketing effort. However, challenges for this are also formidable and explain why we don't have a lot of Red Bulls around...

'Disneyfication' and the enterprise experience eco-system

The above point, if it could be pulled off, is potentially massive. Take Disney, for example. It is a company cross-connected in hundreds of ways between different expressions of their business eco-system. Everything is content, marketing, experience and business – at the same time! Films, parks, merchandise, apps, products, toys...

Lego is another example of a brand with an integrated portfolio of products that includes TV and film (branded entertainment), as well as customer experiences that could be mapped like this. These types of brand eco-systems help develop a deeper customer experience, which in Lego's case helps sell more playsets, hence the following quip made by Jess Coulter, Chief Creative Officer at Samsung, in his blog:

> The Lego Movie is entertainment produced by a brand. And it's great entertainment that is loved by critics and audiences alike. Lots of people went to the theatre to see it. Now they rent it or buy it at home. Or watch it on a plane. And now they're more emotionally connected to the brand. Now the Legos are a bit more magical. So they buy more Legos. And go to Legoland. Wait, isn't this Disney's model? Maybe Frozen is the gold standard. (2014)

The Disney example loops us back to the 'reinvention of tradition' idea we discussed in our Introduction, because the concept of what the author Andrew Davis and others call 'Content Brands' is not new (Pulizzi, 2015). However, Rose sees a progression that he jokingly calls his 'owned media curve' that looks a lot like the Nike swoosh. His Content maturity model starts with the value of owned media brand publishing in the pre-Digital Era and projects out to 2025. It shows how the value of Content has gradually increased again since a dip in the early days of the web, as it evolves from a marketing approach to business strategy on its way to becoming a business model, as shown, in Figure 2.1.

Figure 2.1 Owned media value curve, used with kind permission of Robert Rose

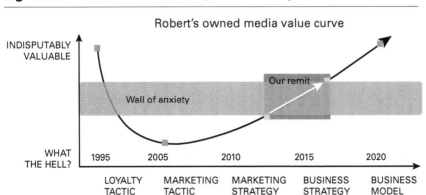

SOURCE Boye (2016); The Content Advisory (2017)

This potential transformation of Content from communications to potential business model was also echoed by several experts in Chapter 5. In the pre-Digital Era, Rose explains in our interview, Content was epitomized by the loyalty magazine. Brands used this type of brand publishing because print was a cost-effective format for delivering a post-sale experience to an audience they knew how to reach and had permission to do so:

> They bought something from you, so you had their address and could send them a copy, or you could simply put that experience in front of them directly because they were a captive audience like on an aeroplane.

The difference now is that digital connects brands to customers across their journeys and so brands can now reach, engage and subscribe audiences pre-purchase too. On the opportunity side, the key realization for brands that Rose sees is that the fusing of the real and the virtual worlds means the *product experience* does not have to be the centre of the universe any more:

> Customers can come in to us and subscribe in numerous ways, one of which may be this experience we create that gets them subscribed at this or that point of their journey; or maybe it's because of the product experience itself having been convinced by an ad that leads to the discovery of our blog, digital magazine or customer event, etc.

This change that digital has brought about is something that Rose also sees happening even in the B2B space:

> If you look at Salesforce now, they offer consulting and agency-like services at the top of the sales funnel, and at the other end they have events like their Dreamforce conference and World Tour. Their suite of software products may still be at the centre of their universe, but they now have an eco-system of experiences.

What is described here may need a different name to distinguish it from both Content and customer experience (CX) disciplines. It is an expression of the Experience Economy – an 'enterprise experience strategy', so to say – but whatever we call it, Red Bull, Lego, Salesforce and many others mentioned are just some examples of where it may be working. Developing those strategies will, however, also require a very different set of skills and thinking than the 'big idea' of the more linear traditional advertising campaigns – something we will explore more in the following chapters.

The Experience Economy: a bigger promise

The idea that consumers will increasingly shift a larger percentage of their disposable income and attention from goods and services to experiences is not a new idea. Alvin Toffler coined the term the 'Experiential Industry' to describe the phenomena in his far-sighted book *Future Shock* (1970). This precedent was acknowledged with considerable depth by B Joseph Pine II and James H Gilmore in *The Experience Economy* (1999a). It comes from a different direction that is potentially more relevant for what we are looking at in this book.

From mass customization to the Experience Economy

We asked Joe Pine about the origins of the Experience Economy model. The story he shared was that the light-bulb moment occurred during a workshop based on his earlier book, *Mass Customization* (1993). While explaining that mass customizations automatically turn goods into services, he was asked what they turn services into. He shot back that they turn a service into an experience, which led to the conclusion that experiences are a distinct economic offering with a transformational potential:

If you go all the way along the through-line of the 'progression of economic value' from commodities you end up at transformation, which is what happens when you customize an experience. These create life-transforming experiences that change us in some way.

Think of Pine and Gilmore's Experience Economy progression as a stairway to a better, brighter and ultimately more profitable place. Climbing the stairway from parity commodities (or worse) to transformative experiences requires customization of offerings so that they become more relevant to customer needs. It is that link between customization and greater relevance that helps create differentiation and premium offerings. Not doing so introduces the risk of commodification and falling down into a more competitive place.

An antidote to commodification

Despite *The Experience Economy* being published during the height of the dotcom boom, Pine and Gilmore really only addressed the impact of the rise of digital technologies shortly after its publication in their 'Are You Experienced' article for *The Industry Standard* magazine (1999b).

The article pulled no punches with its opening line about how the 'internet is the greatest force of commodification known to man', and went on to warn that unless businesses figured out how to provide a compelling online experience and how to charge for it, they would be gone. Ironically, Pine related that only two years later *The Industry Standard* had folded.

Pine and Gilmore's writing on the wall recognized both how the internet can simultaneously commoditize things (as we are now seeing with what some are calling the offline retail apocalypse), and how it also provides the means for exceptional experiences (for example, as the backbone for smartphones, virtual reality, 360 Retail and similar).

In the creative agency world, it is the 'commodification of capability' driven by technology, squeezed margins and working timescales that was the catalyst for the IPA's report mentioned earlier. The report uses the Experience Economy model as a lens for not only showing how the 'progression of economic value' can be understood, but also how a maturity model of agency value can be pegged against it. It presents this 'progression of agency value' as three steps for adapting and surviving the growing threat of commodification:

1 **Delivering services**: deliver traditional marketing and advertising services.

2 **Staging experiences**: originating and crafting platforms for customer experience for and with clients.

3 **Guiding transformation**: guiding real transformation in the relationship that the client has with its customers, and also within the organization itself.

The progression is supported by findings from Econsultancy's 2017 'Digital Trends' report, which includes the three most important digital opportunities picked by an international panel of client-side respondents:

- customer experience (22 per cent);
- creating compelling content for digital experiences (16 per cent);
- data-driven marketing (12 per cent).

Despite these opportunities, Gartner's 'Hype Cycle for Digital Marketing' showed the content marketing category beginning to decline in 2015 having reached the peak of 'inflated expectations' (Sorofman, 2015). Part of the problem is the way that Content 'strategies' are far too often, particularly in B2B, reduced to 'listicles' of undifferentiated tactics, of the type '7 content formats every marketer needs' (Cohen, 2013). Not only does this run the risk of limiting the range of possibilities for clients to engage their customers, it also commoditizes the solutions being offered. The problem is compounded by the term 'content marketing' increasingly becoming understood to mean any marketing that uses content. That makes putting the word 'content' in front of 'marketing' redundant, which diminishes Content's potential to be a better promise.

A bigger promise

The way the IPA's report pegs the 'progression of agency value' to the Experience Economy can also be seen as antidote to Content's commodification, and similar to how Rose, earlier, sees the lines blurring between Content and customer experience. In spite of coming from different places, often presented as opposites, they are both plotting similar paths towards a better place for brands and those who help them. But as Pine and Gilmore (2016) point out, the bigger promise of the Experience Economy can also get diluted as a result of the different ways the term 'experience' is now used so ubiquitously, including:

1 **In name only**: when one takes what they currently do and calls it an experience in name only: the 'Deli Sandwich Bar' that renames itself the 'Deli Sandwich Experience' without adding anything else to what is offered.

2 **Customer Experience Management**: the perfectly valid application where some thinking about the time people spend with the organization is applied to operations, for example to help provide a better service.

3 **Experiential marketing**: not just providing flat advertising, but something more event-based where we are not charging for the experience but stage one to drive more sales of products and services.

4 **User experience (UX):** where we are thinking about new and improved ways of navigating and using the digital realm, including virtual and gaming experiences.

5 **Experience offering:** where a price is attached to the experience, treated as the output of the enterprise, not just for the marketing of it; the experience is the product that people actually purchase.

The blurring of lines between CEM/CXM and CRM could be seen as yet another. But examples 2, 3 and 4 do show how brands are at least thinking about aspects of how we experience a brand at different points along the customer journey in the real and digital realms. From an Experience Economy point of view, though, Pine and Gilmore think these approaches mostly only provide incremental improvements to existing offerings that keep commodification at bay.

Standing out by creating memorable experiences

There are two further problems here: one is the increasing equating of the term 'customer experience' with service design, as a very in-demand emerging discipline with broader (or, sometimes, narrower) application to new product development or service (re)engineering; the other one is the commodification of the term itself: where 'customer experience' is just the incessant delivery of performance marketing outputs via CRM technologies.

Pine and Gilmore think this gets in the way of embracing the true Experience Economy because, once implemented, there is a danger of believing these programmes offer distinctive experiences when they don't. That is not to say that the likes of CX or CEM cannot legitimately be used to help improve a customer's experience, not least being part of customer service. But it's not the same as creating new-to-world offerings that are valued more by customers, so that it can be sold at a premium. Pine and Gilmore encapsulated this distinction with the following slogan:

> If you do not create a memory, then you have not offered a distinctive experience.

As they explained, what is offered has to be something that reaches inside of people and engages them. This is not something they think is achieved by making things just 'nice, easy and convenient', or making things more frictionless – because these are not experiences that actually get noticed.

Designing for 'time and place'

Pine and Gilmore's book (1999a), which is as relevant today, especially for Content, as it was when it was published nearly 20 years ago, includes a set of design principles to help create more memorable and meaningful experiences. The Content space currently lacks something similar, but the starting place we see is the customer-centric way of **designing experiences around time and place**, as Pine explains:

> Our experiences happen in a particular place, and the primary measurement of experience is time. Time is all wrapped up in experience, and so experience design is fundamentally designing the time customers spend with you.

This was reflected in several places in the book. It is also similar to the way Norton and Pine frame the creation of more innovative/unique customer experiences around the notion of 'time well spent' in their article for *Strategy & Leadership* (Norton and Pine, 2009):

> Most company leaders fail to understand the critical importance of innovating experiences that increase the value of the time their customers choose to spend with them.

Thinking about the 'value' of someone's time like this is very different from figuring out what a brand has to say about itself or products and aligning those messages with an audience or customer segment. It is perhaps this more human-centred experience design 'mindset' based around time that helps distinguish Content as an approach from more interruptive marketing communications such as advertising.

We see the idea of designing for time and place as a key piece of a much bigger jigsaw that helps connect up many of the others we discuss in this book. First, it is a useful way of showing the connection between Content and the experience and attention economies. It could also be seen as an inevitable consequence of marketing's evolution as it adapts to the changing media landscape, and why Content can be seen as a symptom or a 'placeholder' phase.

More specifically in the Content space, designing for time and place is becoming more evident by the way the *audience-first* thinking from entertainment and publishing worlds is meeting the more human-centred 'design thinking' problem-solving approach. This crossover is linked to the 'systems and empathy' dynamics identified in the IPA report as being the key to shaping the future of agencies. Those two dynamics are derived from the way Charles Leadbeater combines systems and design thinking as a lens for creating more 'highly convivial, charged, shared experience' as part of better urban planning (2014). It is the two key 'tenets' of the design thinking that we think are particularly important here:

- **Iteration**: the build-to-learn agile development *process*.
- **Empathy**: the framing *mode* for understanding the way people do things and why – for example, by putting yourself in someone else's shoes.

The more *iterative* (design) process is very different from the more linear advertising campaign one that progresses from brief through 'big idea' to production, distribution and measurement in a more linear way. Also, empathy, or an empathic mindset that puts you in someone else's shoes, provides an opportunity to think about customer experiences so that solutions do not have to be so narrowly marketing-focused.

That takes us into innovation territory, which brings different ideation and problem-solving thinking to the table, like the way Norton combines Clayton Christensen's theory of 'Jobs To Be Done' with how time can be designed around his four archetypes of customer happiness: functional, emotional, social, aspirational (Norton, 2015). The emotional and functional archetypes represent the two ends of the spectrum of the Empathic Utility concept we discuss in Chapter 4. It is a way of framing the ways that brands can connect and engage consumers at MTMs along their journeys that are based around designing for their time at those 'places'.

Being more empathic also introduces a practical ethical dimension and one where design can become more respectful of users' time and more supportive of our needs, intentions and deeper human goals. That shift from being manipulated by design to where it is on 'our side' is the space that former Googler-turned-academic James Williams explores, as the antithesis of the attitude that the 'user is the product', challenging the assumption that 'the large-scale capture and exploitation of human attention' is either 'ethical and/or inevitable in the first place' (2015).

We look at ethical considerations later in the book, but this more moral perspective is baked into the Experience Economy by the way its evolutionary progression leads to the guiding of our (personal) transformation. The 'transformation economy' is not something Pine and Gilmore think we have reached yet, or are even close to, but as authenticity is relevant to experiences, Pine thinks 'meaning' is something that is relevant to take into account when guiding transformations.

Gilmore adds to this by introducing the notion of 'purpose':

> The Experience Economy is about engaging people, but you do have to ask engaging in what way and to what end. This is where you get the purpose. As we say in the book, all commerce is moral choice. It is a moral choice to decide what you will produce and sell in the marketplace, and it is a moral choice about what you decide to consume.
>
> People talk about purpose and visions of companies. Do companies, when defining their purpose, spend enough time thinking about how they want to encourage people to spend their time? Because of all economic output – commodities, goods, services, etc – it is experiences that most influences how people spend time. Experiences are time consuming, so how do you want people to consume their time?
>
> If you have purpose, a point of view or philosophy as a business it allows you to speak to the public about how you exist in a certain way. This provides more explicit articulation of the purpose by the enterprises and more explicit understanding and thinking about it by the consumers.

We will be looking at purpose in Chapter 3 as part of building more sustainable brands and the role Content has to play in this. Transformational experience paradigms aside, the immediate effect may be in helping alleviate the most common downside of Content overproduction that we mentioned in Chapter 1: the Sturgeon's 90 per cent crud.

References

Bezos, J P (2017) [accessed 11 June 2017] 2016 Letter to Shareholders [Online] amazon.com/p/feature/z6o9g6sysxur57t/

Boye, J (2016) [accessed 11 June 2017] Robert Rose: Keynote: Content – It's Not the Players – It's The Game, *Slideshare*, 10 May [Online] slideshare.net/j_boye/robert-rose-keynote-content-its-not-the-players-its-the-game

Cohen, H (2013) [accessed 11 June 2017] 7 Content Formats Every Marketer Needs in 2013 (Blog), *Heidi Cohen*, 8 January, heidicohen.com/7-content-formats-every-marketer-needs-in-2013/

Coulter, J (2014) [accessed 11 June 2017] Lego: The LEGO® Movie (Blog), *Best of Branded Content Marketing (BOBCM)*, 14 January [Online] bobcm.net/2015/01/14/the-lego-movie

Draycott, R (2012) [accessed 11 June 2017] Marketing Is Dead Says Saatchi & Saatchi CEO, *The Drum*, 25 April [Online] thedrum.com/news/2012/04/25/marketing-dead-says-saatchi-saatchi-ceo

Econsultancy (2017) [accessed 12 December 2017] Digital Intelligence Briefing: 2017 Digital Trends [Online] econsultancy.com/reports/digital-intelligence-briefing-2017-digital-trends

Forrester (2016) [accessed 11 June 2017] Don't Confuse Media-Led and Customer-Led Content Marketing [Online] forrester.com/report/Dont+Confuse+MediaLed+And+CustomerLed+Content+Marketing/-/E-RES131044

Gartner (2017) [accessed 11 June 2017] Customer Experience Management (CEM) [Online] gartner.com/it-glossary/customer-experience-management-cem

Goodwin, T (2015) [accessed 11 June 2017] Battle Is for the Customer Interface, *Tech Crunch*, 3 March [Online] techcrunch.com/2015/03/03/in-the-age-of-disintermediation-the-battle-is-all-for-the-customer-interface/>

IPA (2017) [accessed 11 June 2017] IPA Future of Agencies: Systems and Empathy [Online] ipa.co.uk/Framework/ContentDisplay.aspx?id=12292

Leadbeater, C (2014) [accessed 11 June 2017] The London Recipe: How Systems and Empathy Make the City Centre for London [Online] charlesleadbeater.net/wp-content/uploads/2014/05/CFL_THE-LONDON-RECIPE.pdf

Lieb, R (2017) *Content – The Atomic Particle of Marketing*, Kogan Page, London

Mahdawi, A (2017) [accessed 11 June 2017] It's Not Just Amazon Coming for Whole Foods – Silicon Valley Is Eating the World, *The Guardian*, 13 May [Online] theguardian.com/commentisfree/2017/jun/20/amazon-whole-foods-silicon-valley-global-domination

Manning, H (2010) [accessed 11 March 2015] Customer Experience Defined (Blog), *Forrester / Blogs*, 23 November [Online] go.forrester.com/blogs/10-11-23-customer_experience_defined/

Neff, J (2015) [accessed 11 June 2017] How Unilever Tapped 'I Want That Hair' Moments by Aggregating Blogger Videos, *Advertising Age*, 15 October [Online] adage.com/article/special-report-ana-annual-meeting-2015/unilever-tapped-i-hair-moments/300939/

Norton, D (2015) *Digital Context 2.0: Seven lessons in business strategy, consumer behavior, and the internet of things*, Gifted Press, Colorado Springs

Norton, D W and Pine II, B J (2009) Unique experiences: disruptive innovations offer customers more 'time well spent', *Strategy & Leadership*, **37** (6) (November), pp 4–9

Pine II, B J (1993) *Mass Customization: The new frontier in business competition*, Harvard Business School Press, Boston, MA

Pine II, B J and Gilmore, J H (1999a) *The Experience Economy: Work is theatre and every business a stage*, Harvard Business School Press, Boston, MA

Pine II, B J and Gilmore, J H (1999b) [accessed 11 June 2017] 'Are You Experienced?', *The Industry Standard*, 9 April [Online] strategichorizons.com/wp-content/uploads/IndustryStandard-9904-AreYouExperienced.pdf

Pine II, B J and Gilmore, J H (2016), Integrating experiences into your business model: five approaches, *Strategy & Leadership*, **44** (1), pp 3–10

Pulizzi, J (2015) [accessed 11 June 2017] Can We Please Stop Using Branded Content? (Blog), *Content Marketing Institute*, 6 October [Online] contentmarketinginstitute.com/2015/10/stop-using-branded-content

Pulizzi, J and Rose, R (2017) *Killing Marketing: How innovative businesses are turning marketing cost into profit*, McGraw-Hill Education, New York

Rose, R and Johnson, C (2015) *Experiences: The 7th era of marketing*, Content Marketing Institute, Cleveland

Sorofman, J (2015) [accessed 11 June 2017] Content Marketing World 2015: Caution Flags for Content Marketers (Blog), *Gartner for Marketers*, 14 September [Online] blogs.gartner.com/jake-sorofman/content-marketing-world-2015-caution-flags-for-content-marketers/

The Content Advisory (2017) [accessed 5 February 2018] Marketing at a Profit: Transforming Strategic B2B Content Creation in a Post Digital World, *Slideshare*, 6 April [Online] www.slideshare.net/BigBlueMoose/marketing-at-a-profit-transforming-strategic-b2b-content-creation-in-a-post-digital-world

Toffler, A (1970) *Future Shock*, Random House, New York

Trek Bikes (2017) [accessed 11 June 2017] Rays MTB Park [Online] trekbikes.com/us/en_US/company/our_brands/rays_indoor_mtb_park/

Usborne, S (2017) [accessed 11 June 2017] Just Do It: The Experience Economy and How We Turned Our Backs On 'Stuff', *The Guardian*, 13 May [Online] theguardian.com/business/2017/may/13/just-do-it-the-experience-economy-and-how-we-turned-our-backs-on-stuff

Williams, J (2015) [accessed 11 June 2017] Why It's OK to Block Ads (Blog), *Practical Ethics*, 16 October [Online] blog.practicalethics.ox.ac.uk/2015/10/why-its-ok-to-block-ads/

How Content can help build sustainable brands with better purposes

If you don't know where you're going, then any road will take you there.

This simplified version of the exchange between Alice and the Cheshire Cat in Lewis Carroll's *Alice's Adventures in Wonderland* (1865) links the previous chapter to this one. In short, *direction* and *purpose* are two sides of the business strategy coin; understanding *where* we want to go and *why*, so that we can figure out *how* to get there.

Chapter 2 may have pointed to where things may be heading more broadly, as the lines between Content and experience continue to blur. In this, we aim to explain how Content, perceived as a better promise versus traditional communications, relates to building organizations with an enhanced sense of purpose.

The backdrop for it could be summed up by Simon Sinek's mantra from his best-selling book *Start With Why* (2011):

> People don't buy what you do; they buy why you do it. And what you do simply proves what you believe.

Content, more than traditional advertising, can help formulate and express that purpose. But, first, we need to know what it is.

Purpose starts with *why*

In 1960, Hewlett Packard's co-founder David Packard gave a speech to employees about *why* a company exists in the first place:

I think many people assume, wrongly, that a company exists simply to make money. While this is an important result of a company's existence, we have to go deeper and find the real reasons for our being. As we investigate this, we inevitably come to the conclusion that a group of people get together and exist as an institution that we call a company so they are able to accomplish something collectively that they could not accomplish separately – they make a contribution to society, a phrase which sounds trite but is fundamental. (Collins and Porras, 1996)

This snippet from Packard's speech helps answer *why we do what we do/ why we are here*, emphasizing that this is by no means a new idea. However, the following tongue-in-cheek, but accurate, observation from our interview with Thomas Kolster, author of *Goodvertising: Creative advertising that cares* (2012), shows there is still a lot of confusion around *purpose*:

> Purpose has become a bit like Pokémon where everyone is searching for it, but they don't know why.

We will be looking at the consequence of this confusion later, although it is not surprising with broad ontological questions like this.

We have identified four principle vectors to show that when it comes to purpose, it is not only becoming increasingly essential to *start with why*, but that there are other perspectives to think through and understand. The vectors are just a thin slice. We hope they provide a starting place for explaining the rise of purpose-driven/values-led organizations, before bringing it back to Content's role in that.

Four vectors driving purpose/Content connection

1 branding in the Digital Age (no more faking it);
2 sustainability for growth and good;
3 the mega trend of *individualization;*
4 the cultural connection.

Without drifting too far into business-strategy territory or getting bogged down in defining all the interrelated terminology, we thought it would be helpful to offer both our explanation of purpose and look at the business advantage of having one, before exploring these vectors below.

Purpose explained

In short, *purpose* is not the same as *mission, vision* or *goals* – they are the more dynamic aspects that shape the business strategies about not only what companies do, but also what they plan to become and the impact this will have/what is achieved. Purpose is not the same as organizational *ethos* either, although they are connected through *internal culture* and the more permanent underlying shared values and principles that help shape attitudes, aspirations and motivations required to achieve goals.

In short, **purpose is the organizational *raison d'être* and more permanent nature of its existence, which the other components and strategy get built around**. As Packard's above quote highlights, the reason for *being* does not have to be about making money. Often, money is the consequence of purpose.

Let's take Disney as an example again: its purpose was and still is 'making people happy'. Their core values or principles remain the same or similar, such as 'creativity, dreams and imagination', 'no cynicism', etc. One of the benefits of the stability of the clearly defined purpose and values is the constant evolution of the hiring practices, channels and products they deploy to achieve it (Collins and Porras, 1996). It allows their strategy to be more dynamic, which means they can continue to evolve and make profits in new and different ways (Jones, 2015). Whatever keeps making people happy is 'them'.

The purpose advantage

There is no shortage of supporting research and quotable stats about the business benefits of organizations that have purpose (*Harvard Business Review*, 2015; EY, 2016), including:

- significantly outperforming their peers;
- having more engaged and satisfied employees;
- being more innovative and likely to achieve transformation goals;
- creating better-quality products and services;
- fostering loyalty and more likely to be recommended by customers.

However, trying to evaluate these findings more systematically is problematic. First, there is an assortment of methodologies being used. Comparing apples with apples is also complicated by all the different terms used, among them 'purpose-driven', 'values-led' as well as 'purposeful', 'meaningful', 'sustainability' and 'sustainable brands'.

Two research projects stood out for us. The first was the The Business Case for Purpose conducted by EY's Beacon Institute, which defines organizational purpose as follows (*Harvard Business Review*, 2015):

> An aspirational reason for being which inspires and provides a call to action for an organization and its partners and stakeholders and provides benefit to local and global society.

The most notable finding was that despite the long list of advantages of having a purpose, as identified by executives surveyed, and that 90 per cent believed that their companies understand these, less than half thought it actually informs their business strategy and day-to-day decision making.

Those organizations seem to be missing a trick according to findings in Corporate Purpose and Financial Performance research by Professor George Serafeim and colleagues (Serafeim and Gartenberg, 2016). What they show is that having a purpose may not be enough alone. For example, having purpose-driven comradery where people feel part of a team is no guarantee of financial performance. But what their analysis does show is that having a purpose matters and can be linked to growth – if it is both clearly articulated and middle management has bought into it.

Below are the four key vectors behind the rise of purpose as a business and marketing perspective – and Content opportunity.

1 Branding in the digital age: no more faking it

As we touched upon this in Chapter 1, brands feel that they are losing control. The old ways of branding are creaking under stress. A useful reminder of what a brand stands for is the way that Robert Jones, at branding consultants Wolff Olins, defines it in his book *The Big Idea* (2001):

> A brand is a promise (of an experience), and one that must be kept.

It is the keeping of promises that lies behind James H Gilmore's and B Joseph Pine II's book *Authenticity: What consumers really want* (2007). At the time of writing it, they saw marketing in general, and advertising in particular, 'becoming giant phoniness-generating machines making fake promises'. We will come back to this at the societal level in Chapter 11, but the issue we raise here is linked to the impact on reputations and bottom lines.

It is a significant problem now that the digitally 'empowered consumer' has more ways than ever to express their dissatisfaction when brands fail to deliver on expectations. As Robert Bean, advertising veteran turned branding consultant and author of *Winning in Your Own Way: The nine and a half golden rules of branding* (2009), explained in a previous interview of ours (Kirby, 2013):

> What were walls that the companies could control in the old days have now become windows. Anyone can see into any organization from any number of different vantage points.

Bean's point is that digital is very good at helping to expose what he calls '**disorganizations**' – brands that try to engineer a reputation, or fake it, now run a much greater risk of being found and called out. This is why he thinks it is more important than ever for companies to become clearer about who they are and what they are about, as well as be true to themselves. The building of strong brands is something that needs to start from the *inside out*, what he calls the three pillars of culture, product (or service) and reputation:

> I mean that the people inside the business are completely aligned around what it is they're trying to do, so you have a culture that is producing a commensurate product that when managed properly creates a commensurate reputation.

Bean thinks that the answer should be articulated in what he calls a 'single organizing principle'. It culminates in condensing purpose and other variables into an aphorism or organizational mantra that is reminiscent of the 'single-minded proposition' familiar in advertising, although here it applies to the organization as a whole rather than just communications. Who might be best suited to telling these stories and distilling big and complex ideas into more simple propositions that can be grasped by people and inspire them is something we discuss more in Chapter 4.

2 *The rise of sustainability for growth and good*

The Disney example above shows how a purpose doesn't have to be social per se, but it is useful to understand why sustainability has risen up corporate agendas and social purposes are being worn more visibly on their sleeves now.

Being a 'sustainable' brand could simply mean business growth and commercial success over the longer term. To avoid any ambiguity, we are specifically using the term 'sustainability' here to refer to corporate purposes that are based on their *social and environmental impact*. One simple reason why these issues have become a corporate concern is that their customers now expect them to be: approximately one-third of them according to international research conducted by Unilever in 2017. It is a growing trend across the globe that Trendwatching.com half-jokingly explains as follows (2015):

Consumers don't want to make the world a better place. They want brands to do that for them.

Their analysts admit the issue is more complex, though. Yet, their point is that consumers are setting higher standards for brands than they adhere to themselves – not least because they blame them for creating the problems in the first place, including the consumption behaviours they find so difficult to quit. Given consumers' scepticism of the 'endless brand sustainability initiatives and CSR-speak', Trendwatching.com makes the following recommendation:

> The only meaningful path left for brands is to stop talking and *act*.

Peter Fisk makes a similar point in his book *People Planet Profit: How to embrace sustainability for innovation and business growth* (2010):

> Sustainability is no longer an adjunct to business. It is no longer a separate department, or even a team within the corporate affairs department concerned only about compliance and reputation. It is no longer enough to have some worthy goals, a sustainability strategy as an appendix to the business plan, or a sustainability report as an afterthought.
>
> CSR (corporate social responsibility) strategies were typically peripheral compensation for the damages already done, relieving the guilt of companies that couldn't see the light. They were the clean caring icing on the big dirty cake. They sought to protect superficial and increasingly fragile reputations.

That is not to say that CSR initiatives cannot provide inspiration for brand storytelling, as Elena Grinta highlights in her book *Branded Entertainment* (2017). But the point Fisk also makes is how the *bigger promise* here is much more than that:

> It is about moving the issues of sustainability from the fringes to the heart of business. It demands that business leaders rethink fundamental strategic questions – why we exist, where we should focus, how we are different, and why people will choose it, want to work for us, and invest in our business.

From a marketing perspective, there are still those like Mark Ritson who remain unconvinced and think brands should remember it is about profit, not purpose (Ritson, 2017). For Fisk, there is no paradox or conflict between 'growth and being good' because saving the planet is a business opportunity. He quotes Kraft Food UK's former vice-president and area director Ben Clarke to reinforce the point:

> Sustainability is now about profit... it is the opportunity of the twenty-first century.

3 The mega trend of individualization

The value derived by aligning the 3Ps advocated by Fisk, as part of ensuring sustainable commercial success over the longer term, is one way to explain the rise of sustainability and social purpose from a business perspective. There is another one, from the consumer side, also useful for brands.

In Chapter 2 we mentioned both *Mass Customization* (1993) by B Joseph Pine II and *The Experience Economy* (1999) that he co-wrote with James H Gilmore. Behind both is the mega-trend of 'individualization', which according to Pine is all about getting closer and closer to the individual. That is the basis of the 'worldview segmentation' idea that Pine and Gilmore introduced in *The Experience Economy*, which Pine explained in our interview is built on the following insight, which helps explain why authentic purposes matter in the new age of individualization:

> People increasingly buy only from those companies whose purposes are aligned with who they are as individuals, and that's when they are viewed as authentic.

The idea of brand being a reflection of a consumer's self lies behind Pine and Gilmore's imperative for organizations to have a purpose based on the particular worldview:

> In the world of 'paid for' experiences, people increasingly question what is real and what is not, and it's not just that they don't want the fake from phony, but they want the real from the genuine. That's why 'authenticity' becomes the consumer sensibility in the Experience Economy, ie the primary buying criteria that people use to choose what and what not to buy.

In *Authenticity*, which can be seen as the sequel to *The Experience Economy*, Gilmore and Pine (2007) use the term *Authentic* as an attribute (*adjective*) of *Experience* (*noun*): authenticity is the important quality of the experience being offered, and reason to buy.

The critical connection to brand building here is also the way they link authenticity to individualization by wrapping up our purchasing decisions in identity formation. Gilmore offered the following explanation, based on the way Virginia Postrel sums this up in her book *The Substance of Style* (2003), where she writes that when people buy something they look at the offering and say: *I like that, I'M like that*:

> Consumers look at any offering and say I am the kind of person who drives a car like that; I am the kind of person who eats in a restaurant like that; I am the kind of person... It's not just the affordability or the quality; it's also about whether a purchase reflects who you are, ie is it true to me?

Pine and Gilmore's introduction of identity formation above reframes *relevance*. *I like that* is not just about what interests us, but something more deeply personal based on our values/beliefs (I'M like that). It is the 'being true to self' part of this identity formation that they use as the basis for their two key standards of authenticity:

- being true to yourself (based on your identity, who you are at your core);
- being what you say you are (to others).

It is these two standards that make purpose an essential aspect of our identity and why we exist in the world and why we must be *true* to be perceived as authentic.

4 *The cultural connection*

What individualization, authenticity and similar terms denote is nothing more than a set of *cultural* constructs. This is where the purpose story becomes both complicated and potentially powerful as, in its essence, it reflects all aspects of culture: in this case *societal* and *business*. Consumers, brands, organizations – they are all manifestations of both, and the role of Content as a better promise could be analysed with that in mind too.

Chris McCarthy, Head of Creative Strategy EMEA at Google ZOO, shared a powerful observation in 2015, in one of our earlier interviews (Kirby, 2015):

> Brands need to understand that connecting with people is a social exercise that is conducted through the messy, murky construct called culture: the stuff we consume, talk about, watch and interact with.

McCarthy's point is two-sided: culture works both internally and externally, it impacts both employees of an organization and its customers; both of these mindframes have cultural origins and modes of expression; both are connected to meaning and purpose. That is why they are also crucial for Content considerations.

On the internal side, it is about how the *why* behind purpose, along with core values/principles, helps get employee *buy-in* so brand promises can be delivered. Richard Wilding, CEO and founder of internal communications specialists WME, suggests one way of thinking about this would be to paraphrase Postrel's mantra above, so that internally it becomes '*I value that, I'M like* that'. How a creative agency may play a role in that space is explored in Chapter 4.

Externally, for consumers, the wider cultural brand picture requires brand narratives to go beyond just adding a superficial 'authentic' twist, as implied in the title of Annette Simmons's *Whoever Tells the Best Story Wins* (2007). Authenticity is not just about the tonality or aesthetics of brand communications, it is about making sure brand values are 'lived'. Sinek would approve.

This leads to a potentially massive conclusion: **there is no good Content strategy without aligning the brand and organizational ones, driven by the bigger purpose.** Furthermore, Content and Culture could not exist side by side, but are nested within each other: **Content is the expression of Purpose and Culture!** (See Figure 3.1.)

Obviously, the picture is markedly different from how Content is being defined and used currently, with glaring examples in Chapters 10 and 11. But, looked at through this lens, it does start giving off the shimmer of a potentially better promise for brands that care about defining and manifesting their purpose. This is highlighted in the raft of academic and consultancy approaches tapping into a vast reservoir of multi-disciplinary research methodologies to generate insights in this space.

Figure 3.1   'Nesting' of Content strategy within purpose and culture

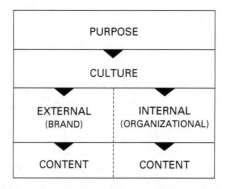

SOURCE authors

One is the very in-demand domain of 'brand culture' ruled by the well-known names such as Douglas B Holt or Grant McCracken, *among* others. They write about how brands can better be understood by examining the role they occupy in the cultural landscape and how their strategies can be shaped by doing so. It is one that looks at, among other things, how neither brands nor consumers are completely in control of the branding process, exploring cultural trends and also codes such as storytelling conventions.

This cultural framing takes us not only into the territory of the arts and humanities, but also into the realms of human and social sciences that offer a range of methods for getting richer insights into what is relevant and meaningful to people.

As Christian Madsbjerg and Mikkel B Rasmussen mention in *The Moment of Clarity* (2014), brands occasionally hire ethnographers and anthropologists to conduct research around new products (normally around their launch), but these rarely go deep into corporate culture. Their management consultancy ReD Associates uses more qualitative and ethnography-based methods to look outwards at the cultural worlds full of consumers to help organizations better understand their ontology/why they exist, or at least when it needs fixing if purposes are not clear. Compared with the *inside out* branding approach advocated by Bean, earlier, it is not the opposite of it, just further upstream. It helps organizations check their assumptions and presuppositions about the market to start making things people want, and also talk to them in ways that are meaningful and helpful. This avoids both misunderstanding consumers and being misunderstood.

The interesting thing is that their method is slow, big and long, which is the opposite of the '*Fail Fast, Fail Often*' mantra of Silicon Valley. That is to do with the kinds of problems they are trying to help solve, which is often when management intuition reaches its corporate and geographic cultural limits.

There is a data angle too, because their argument is that both traditional research and specifically Big Data are limited when it comes to explaining the important *why* we do what we do. Understanding the world needs the capturing of 'both its *big* quantities and its *thick* qualities'. It is about insights gained from what they call 'thick data', or the *thick description* from anthropology and sociology. It is the means by which the cultural context of people's behaviour is unpacked by looking at how we place meaning on what we do and say, as well as on things, to help get what is going on *between* us, not just *in* us. We will talk about it more in Chapter 7.

Finally, the cultural connection helps us to frame Professor Andrew McStay's idea in the Introduction about how Content may just be a 'placeholder' approach – the 'liminal phase' – in the evolution of marketing as it responds to what is next on the horizon.

All of the above, the way purpose, culture and Content are connected, could be summarized in Figure 3.2. It is the framework that explains *why* Content could be perceived as a better promise from both how it is being executed today and how it may evolve in the years to come if the current, seemingly inevitable, demise of online advertising continues.

In the next section we look at *how* Content may tap into purpose and culture to fulfil that promise.

Figure 3.2 Content purpose jigsaw: the 'why' of Content

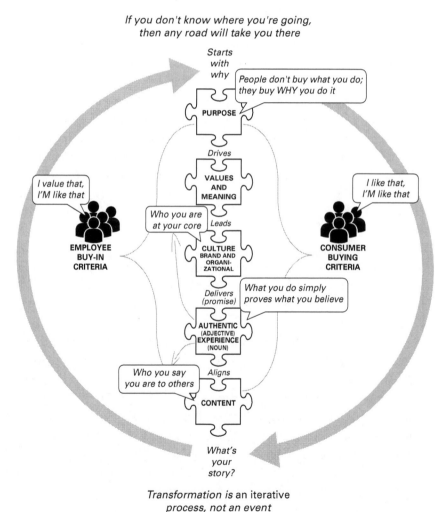

Content starts with purpose?

As research above shows, clarifying and articulating purpose can have practical business implications. For Content specifically, this could mean both *storytelling* and *storydoing*. The latter is important here because not all content is storytelling, as Rebecca Lieb rightly points out in *Content – The Atomic Particle of Marketing* (2017). Stories seem to be the default level of modern branding and a proven way to connect with consumers on an emotional level, with big long-term business implications as, again, shown in the IPA's 'The Long and the Short of It' report (2013):

> The longer the time frame, the more emotions drive profit.

But they are not the only way. The first to point to that difference to us was Scott Donaton from DigitasLBi. He referred to a useful distinction between 'Storytelling' and 'StoryDoing©' made by the co:collective agency in the United States as part of brand performance analysis they conducted in 2013:

> There are two kinds of companies in the world today: **Storytelling companies** that convey the story of their brand, business or product by telling that story, usually through PR or paid advertising; and **storydoing companies** that consciously convey their story through direct action.

StoryDoing is another name for Sinek's 'what you do simply proves what you believe' or Pine and Gilmore's two standards of authenticity cited above. Donaton also helps link this 'values-in-action' storytelling distinction to our progression from 'purpose starts with *why*' to 'Content starts with purpose:'

> Purpose can be a social purpose, or other purpose, but every brand has to have a *why* whatever that is. The *why* of a brand is the Story of a brand, and so once a brand knows its *why*, it knows its story. Storytelling is the best way to express this purpose and the related values. The important thing is the storytelling has to be credible and real, and supported by the actions of the organization. It has to be lived.

Google's Hero content has so far been the mainstay of culturally relevant storytelling for brands, but it is not quite clear yet how purpose is leveraged as the backdrop for other Content categories and more experiential offerings. Donaton thinks that the direct connection between a brand's *why* and its story is one that can change not just Content creation strategies, but media and planning ones too:

> If you begin with the purpose and have everything flow from that, then I think you are beginning with the story and to some degree they become inseparable. If you start the marketing there, rather than with a product or a campaign or a time frame, and really build everything out from that, then not only will the story flow be impacted, but ultimately so will where you place your media.
>
> Your choice of how to spend media dollars might then become less focused on the demographics of an audience, and more about whether the Content you are trying to be associated with is connected to what you actually do and why, like how you improve people's lives in some way. That's such a fundamental change to media planning and buying, so it will take time to work out how we get there, but I think that starts by going back and building everything out from the *why*.

Attributing growth to social currency is not always clear, as demonstrated by the Pepsi Refresh Project case study. If, as the co:collective research suggests, demonstrating purpose in practice powers business performance, that is a significant finding. It has measurement implications too, and is a prompt for further research in this field. We will explore 'storydoing' and what it could mean in the world of 'mixed reality' in Chapter 8.

There is another term introduced by the co:collective consultancy relevant to us here: the 'core story'. It is similar to Bean's *single organizing principle*, mentioned above, although it evolved from being an ad-like slogan to something more narrative-based.

Like Bean, the co:collective's founder and CEO Ty Montague has a long history in advertising that includes being Chief Creative Officer and Co-President of JWT North America. He is also the author of *True Story: How to combine story and action to transform your business* (2013). Again, the title of the book describes the **blurring of lines between business transformation, branding and brand communication** that both he and Bean are keen on. There is not really a name as yet for what sits in the middle of those three circles, but it potentially represents where the evolution of the creative agency might be heading. Whatever it is called, the role purpose plays in the development of more 'narrative brands' is becoming apparent.

Saying that, it is easier for some brands to fulfil that role than the others – especially in the consumer packaged goods (CPG)/fast-moving consumer goods (FMCG) categories. Not everyone wants to have a relationship with a bag of crisps, and it is more difficult to create a strong and believable purpose story around that. Maybe some brands will never be purpose-led, as long as they fulfil some basic need that relies on impulse and habit buying, without a lot of consideration. In that regard, to use Byron Sharp's phrase, just having good 'physical availability' may suffice.

Or, as we have seen elsewhere in the book, there is no such thing as a trivial or boring company, product or service, just boring ways to talk about it. All it takes is a new lens to look at things through.

Whenever we have spoken to experts, the same companies tend to get cited as examples of good narrative brands, the likes of Chipotle, Patagonia, Tesla and Toms, whose values and social purpose help storytelling become an empathy machine. However, as the following Chipotle case study powerfully reminds us, story is not enough if the experience fails:

CASE STUDY Chipotle Mexican Grill

Until the E. coli crisis in 2015 wiped billions off shareholder value and saw customers desert their much-loved brand in droves (Carr, 2016), Chipotle had used a range of creative marketing that, among other executions, included a series of short animated films promoting their ethical food agenda, a comedy series premiered on Hulu and their Cultivate festival of 'food, music and ideas'. These activities had gained them huge earned and shared media success, as well as a slew of advertising awards, including a Cannes Lions Grand Prix. They had also been expanding rapidly at a time when their former major investor McDonald's and others in the sector were contracting. Since they went public in 2006 until its peak in 2015 before the outbreaks their share price had grown by a whopping 3,340 per cent and the number of restaurants opened had grown by 300 per cent. This was achieved by spending less of their revenues on marketing and their marketing budget being a fraction of the major players (less than 10 per cent of McDonald's in 2015). Their fall from consumer and market grace as result of their food-safety crisis only goes to show that a good story, even a purposeful one, is not enough. The brand still has to deliver on the promise of its experience. Failing to do so in Chipotle's case has resulted in having to invest heavily in rebuilding its brand story. That has involved increasing the percentage of revenue it spends on marketing from 1.5 per cent before the crisis to up to 4.8 per cent in the highest quarter since, as well as adopting many of the promotional and loyalty 'gimmicks' used by bigger fast-food competitors that it had previously shunned (Wohl, 2017). These were ones that its CMO had previously described in FastCompany in 2012 as being like the crack of marketing because 'once you're on it, it's really, really hard to get off' (Sacks, 2012).

Not every business has a founder whose desire to help further the advancement of humankind or save the planet is hard-wired into the organizational ethos. That doesn't have to be always founder-driven. P&G and Unilever are examples of multi-national companies who would be close to this territory. They could also be seen as part of the fundamental shift in marketing that Donaton alludes to above – or just an example of 'purposewash' that we explore in the section below.

Building an empathetic communications strategy is something that *Goodvertising*'s Thomas Kolster thinks larger brands have to adopt because the ad industry is in existential crisis, so sustainability is seen as the fix or a bridge that could make brands relevant again and where the good guys win. The other force here is how the democratization of media has lent a helping hand to smaller start-up businesses who have an authentic purpose built into their DNA:

> The democratization of media is putting a lot of pressure on bigger brands that are suddenly faced with the little guy who seems to make their authenticity much easier for people to understand from the get-go. Anyone can set up a business now, so why go to one of the big guys rather than a smaller company, which could have even been set up by one of your friends or peers? Authenticity almost comes by default for the little guys and that is why you've got bigger companies trying to emulate this with mixed results, because it is harder to build that in retrospectively. But they need to, so that they also have a story to tell, and those about sustainability and improving people's lives bring it all back to very human subject matters that resonate with people.

Vizeum's Global Head of Innovation Tia Castagno also agrees that purpose drives Content strategies and that having a social purpose certainly helps when it comes to authenticity:

> It is usually possible to work with a brand to discover its purpose based on what it does and why, and then build a Content strategy around that. At one end of the scale, there are some brands that are authentic just by virtue of what they do. Tesla is an example. They use Content to simply tell their story because it is a great one as a result of their purpose.
>
> In the middle is a brand like IKEA. They started off as an everyday furniture brand, but they have developed a purpose that is very aligned

with what they do, which is creating the right environment for the future, whatever that is. For example, in China people are often constrained by very small spaces and so the purpose of IKEA there becomes helping them build the home of the future, which is perfect for that space. Similarly, in Sweden where the market is very environment-orientated their focus is more about sustainable solutions, and so on.

The real problem Castagno sees occurring far too often is not whether brands have a social purpose or not, but when Content strategies get built around some manufactured quasi higher purpose, or exist only to disguise more profit-orientated agendas:

At the other end of the scale, there are brands creating very convoluted stories driven by Content that seem to mask, or at least hide, their real purpose. That doesn't work any more because consumers are much more switched on to brand identities that are manufactured or overlaid in a way that don't make sense or ring true other than to sell more products.

Put another way: where purpose is confused with 'purposewash'.

The rise of purposewash

In an op-ed piece for the UK's advertising magazine *Campaign* in April 2017, the CEO of the D&AD creative awards Tim Lindsay argued why it is time for the industry to take a long look at itself (Lindsay, 2017). The opening sentence highlighted the irony of life imitating art after *Saturday Night Live*'s 'Pitch Meeting' satire on purposeful communications featuring Alec Baldwin was subsequently outdone by what he described as the crassness of a real commercial by Pepsi (Saturday Night Live, 2017).

CASE STUDY   Pepsi – 'Live for Now'

In 2017, PepsiCo released their 'Live For Now' 'short film' for Pepsi featuring the reality-show star Kendall Jenner – the idea being 'to project a global message of unity, peace and understanding'. Instead, the ad caused widescale ire and ridicule for the way it used protest imagery to help sell a fizzy drink; by doing so, it appeared to trivialize the likes of Black Lives Matter, Occupy and the Civil Rights Movement along with the issues they address – prompting Martin Luther King Jr's daughter Bernice to tweet, 'If only Daddy would have known about the power of #Pepsi.' A day later, Pepsi pulled the ad, acknowledging they had clearly missed the mark and apologizing for any offence caused (Monllos, 2017).

It is the poster child for confusion surrounding purpose we talked about earlier, causing much schadenfreude in ad agencies for having been created by Pepsi's in-house team Creative League Studio. The latest blot on the cultural landscape generated significant coverage in the trade press with accusations of 'echo chambers and big-footing clients', but some of the most cutting criticism was to be found on a dedicated Reddit thread (Schultz and Graham, 2017):

> In-house just doesn't cut it, as there are too few people in the chain saying 'no'. Advertisers clearly don't have the self-discipline.

> In-house creative directors are jaded, tired old-timers who simply want to get paid and go home.

Throwing stones in glass houses is never a good idea because there is no shortage of similar crassness by agencies where 'emotive' messages have crossed lines and resulted in a backlash. This includes the 'Favourites' TV ad by Leo Burnett London for McDonald's UK in 2017, featuring a boy being told about his dead dad's shared fondness for Filet-O-Fish. McDonald's subsequently withdrew the ad after a catalogue of complaints about 'inappropriately and insensitively using bereavement and grief to sell fast food' (Roderick, 2017).

The stream of such examples is now called 'purposewash', a rapidly adopted collective term that now comes in a few choices of prefix colours such as 'green' or 'pink'. Even iconic purpose-driven brands can slip: Dove has managed to undo much of their previous 'empowering' success of their Real Beauty Campaign with two reputation-damaging examples:

CASE STUDY   Dove 'Bottlegate' – May 2017

Dove re-presented the six ordinary women in their underwear from the original 'Real Women' campaign in 1997 as different-shaped bottles of shower gel. According to *The Guardian*, Dove's idea was to 'evoke the shapes, sizes, curves and edges that combine to make every woman their very own limited edition'. The result was only to help heighten female insecurities, the very opposite of what the campaign aims to address, and at the point of purchase on store shelves (Craik, 2017).

CASE STUDY   Dove 'Whitewash' – October 2017

As if accusations for patronizing women were not enough, Dove subsequently faced calls for boycott after accusations of racism. This was prompted by an ad for a new campaign going viral that appeared to show a sequence of a black women being turned white after using their shower gel. The ad was promptly pulled with an apology – and a promise to tighten up internal content-approval processes (Daneshkhu, 2017).

It is difficult to know how much lasting damage these mistakes have on big brands, despite any embarrassment they cause. For Mark Ritson the problem he describes in *Marketing Week* is less about reputational damage, but how the industry has become full of 'softies' who no longer see what they do as the means to commercial ends, such as growing awareness and driving preference as part of the ultimate aim of increasing sales. He thinks branding has, instead, become all about 'beliefs, missions and lofty ideals' (2017):

> Every brand and every newly arrived CMO is not looking for a surge in sales; instead they want to link their brand to a cultural issue faster than you can say 'purpose'.

Given that around 20 per cent of ads featured during the 2017 Super Bowl could be described as 'purposeful' or 'politically themed', he may have a point. Hence the cringing immigration-to-transgender ideas for Cheetos ads being pitched to clients in the SNL spoof mentioned above. It seems that cultural trends discussed above have truly arrived.

However, there is a strong opposition to it, not just from Ritson. In a recent round-up of the tide of 'purposewash' ideas in 'Is this the end for brand purpose?', *Creative Review* (2017), Nick Asbury of Asbury & Asbury pointedly reminds us how the industry sees the purpose of *purpose* being profit, or at least some calculation of the earned and shared media 'conversation'.

Unlike Ritson, he objects not just that the ads are not focused on the product and getting people to buy them; it is the very 'monetizing of social causes' and the glib answers offered as part of engineering an illusion that consumers are doing good by what products they choose. Asbury tears down the whole notion of purpose as a success factor, unless that purpose actually sits at the core of the brand. Without it, he doesn't think brands are any good at doing social issues. Without this authenticity, says Asbury, they just come across as being overzealous 'me-toos':

> Not only do they now believe in this issue, but they're also going to be the one who 'leads the conversation' and tells you about it. There's never a sense of humility or genuine engagement, because brands always have to cast themselves as the hero.

Grinta asks the same: 'with what authority?' do brands play the hero here.

Perhaps more damning is Asbury's belief that the idea of 'doing good is good business' is disingenuous because of the way it engenders smugness about having a higher purpose beyond profit – when there usually isn't one. He quips that the famous quote by DDB's founder Bill Bernbach about 'a principle isn't a principle until it costs you something' has become inverted so a principle isn't one 'until it makes you money'.

Interestingly, Asbury sees a silver lining in this cloud of 'purposewash'. He thinks it will encourage the 'logic' of purposeful communications to be challenged and more critically evaluated not only by consumers, but also the media and ad industry who have been too quick to laud and award campaigns without sufficient scrutiny. It goes to the heart of the role of the mass media in a commercial society, as captured in another quote by Bill Bernbach, echoing our topics in Chapter 11 (Wikipedia, 2017a):

> All of us who professionally use the mass media are the shapers of society.
> We can vulgarize that society. We can brutalize it. Or we can help lift it onto a higher level.

Restoration of trust

In a clickbait-ridden world of fake news and 'alternative facts' there is growing acknowledgement in media and ad industries about not only their role in the erosion of trust in society at large, but also responsibility to put that right. The 'colossal job' the media industry has on its hands to rebuild trust was the theme of the keynote by British film producer Lord Puttnam at the IPA Festival of British Advertising that marked their 100th anniversary in 2017 (Oakes, 2017):

> For me the most alarming 'change' to have occurred is the seeming collapse of 'Trust' – trust in institutions of all kinds, including government, trust in the media, and pretty well all other sources of information – most alarmingly 'trust' in what is referred to as 'the system'.

Lord Puttnam doesn't think that the problem will be solved by the use of analytics and algorithms alone, nor by simply trying to fix a system that is so thoroughly discredited. He thinks the answer is actual human intervention, which will require deep soul searching to understand why things have gone so horribly wrong and for the industry to get behind finding a solution for what he describes as a far more *sustainable* 'social settlement'.

The D&AD's CEO Tim Lindsay thinks the ad industry can play a part in helping bring about that wider sustainability by doing their bit to get clients to do the right thing and prosper as a consequence:

> We need to start working with clients to stop being complicit in selling shit people don't need, to pay for with money they don't have, to impress those who don't care.

A good starting place to restore trust in general would be to foster more of it between brands and agencies. At the same time, business relationships based on a procurement-led race to the bottom are not really a solid basis for performing the kind of 'speaking truth to power' that Lindsay advocates. It is also hard to see how the in-built asymmetry in power makes things any better when bottom lines are under threat. That is not only true for agencies, but for the media too, which is a bigger cause for concern that we discuss in Chapter 11.

A popular quote attributed to Unilever's former Global SVP of Marketing Marc Mathieu, gets closer to what that mindset shift might entail:

Marketing used to be about making a myth and telling it. Now it's about telling a truth and sharing it.

It sounds very much like the old 'truth, well told' line by the McCann advertising network. It could be a start, but it doesn't address the *doing* part of the problem. We have already touched on the need for walking the talk, and some way of monitoring and measuring both promise (Simms, 2005) and values gaps is likely to be helpful (Freeman and Auster, 2015).

As mentioned above, it may have practical consequences:

CASE STUDY Stop Funding Hate (SFH)

Launched in 2016, Stop Funding Hate is a crowdfunding campaign that aims to encourage companies to stop advertising in those UK newspapers that it accuses of spreading 'fear and division to sell more papers'. This includes targeting specific brands whose *values* they claim are at odds with the papers they advertise in. The campaign, along with related criticism on social media, has prompted brands to pull ads, review their ad placement to bring it in line with their values and, in some cases, such as LEGO and The Body Shop, end their advertising in the newspapers being targeted (Wikipedia, 2017b).

Something similar has been happening in the United States, with a number of companies pulling their advertising from the right-wing news site *Breitbart*. This includes The Kellogg Company who were specific that their decision was made on the grounds that it was not aligned with their values as a company (Woolf, 2016).

For many companies, though, especially global, there is an underlying fundamental tension between profit and any kind of social purpose. This is illustrated by the Co-op Group's chief executive Richard Pennycook's response to calls by Stop Funding Hate to stop advertising in what they describe as 'Hate Media' (Bond, Milne and Fedo, 2016):

We do need to be cognizant of commercial realities too, in terms of which advertising channels yield the best results.

The questions highlighted above pose another: what kind of social corporate activism is the market ready to tolerate? The problem that activist companies face is that by default they may end up switching off part of the category. Hence Pennycock's response only echoing what Byron Sharp strongly advocates in *How Brands Grow*, about the need to always talk to the whole market (2010).

The 'devil you do, devil you don't' nature of the issues we have covered here doesn't come with easy answers. Building towards solutions using the design thinking-type iterative method and empathy mindset is a possible start, as is the more 'thick description' method for understanding as advocated and used by Madsbjerg and Rasmussen (2014). But as the Cheshire Cat said to Alice, it 'depends a good deal on where you want to get to'.

References

Asbury, N (2017) [accessed 12 December 2017] Is This the End for Brand Purpose?, *Creative Review*, 19 June [Online] creativereview.co.uk/end-brand-purpose/

Bond, D, Milne, R and Fedo, L (2016) [accessed 12 December 2017] Lego Split with Daily Mail Puts Pressure on Other Groups, *Financial Times*, 13 November [Online] ft.com/content/08995af6-a8fe-11e6-809d-c9f98a0cf216

Carr, A (2016) [accessed 12 December 2017] Chipotle Eats Itself, *Fast Company*, 16 October [Online] fastcompany.com/3064068/chipotle-eats-itself

Carroll, L (1865) *Alice's Adventures in Wonderland*, Macmillan & Co, London

co:collective (2013) [accessed 12 December 2017] Story Doing [Online] storydoing.com

Collins, J C and Porras, J I (1996) Building your company's vision, *Harvard Business Review*, (September–October), pp 65–77

Craik, L (2017) [accessed 12 December 2017] How Beauty Giant Dove Went from Empowering to Patronizing, *The Guardian*, 15 May [Online] theguardian.com/fashion/2017/may/15/beauty-giant-dove-body-shaped-bottles-repair-damage

Daneshkhu, S (*2017*) [accessed 12 December 2017] Unilever Pulls Dove Ad after Complaints of Racism, *Financial Times*, 9 October [Online] ft.com/content/32e16984-acf4-11e7-beba-5521c713abf4

EY (2016) [accessed 12 December 2017] Winning with Purpose [Online] ey.com/Publication/vwLUAssets/EY-purpose-led-organizations/$FILE/EY-purpose-led-organizations.pdf

Fisk, P (2010) *People Planet Profit: How to embrace sustainability for innovation and business growth*, Kogan Page, London

Freeman, R and Auster, E (2015) *Bridging the Values Gap: How authentic organizations bring values to life*, Berrett-Koehler, San Francisco

Gilmore, J H and Pine II, B J (2007) *Authenticity: What consumers really want*, Harvard Business School Press, Boston, MA

Grinta, E (2017) *Branded Entertainment: La rivoluzione del settore marcom inizia da qu,* Franco Angeli, Milan

Harvard Business Review (2015) [accessed 12 December 2017] The Business Case for Purpose [Online] hbr.org/resources/pdfs/comm/ey/19392HBRReportEY.pdf

IPA (2013) [accessed 12 December 2017] The Long and the Short of It [Online] ipa.co.uk/document/the-long-and-the-short-of-it-presentation#.WjqmniOcZE4

Jones, B (2015) [accessed 12 December 2017] Mission Versus Purpose: What's the Difference? (Blog) *Disney Institute,* 23 April [Online] disneyinstitute.com/blog/2015/04/mission-versus-purpose-whats-the-difference/

Jones, R (2001) *The Big Idea,* Profile Books, London

Kirby, J (2013) [accessed 12 December 2017] What Makes a Brand? Branding Expert Robert Bean on the Single Organising Principle (Blog), *MyNewsDesk: Like Minds,* 10 December[Online] mynewsdesk.com/uk/likeminds/blog_posts/what-makes-a-brand-branding-expert-robert-bean-gives-us-his-views-22586

Kirby, J (2015) [accessed 12 December 2017] Google's Chris McCarthy: A View from the Zoo (Blog), *BOBCM,* 30 March [Online] bobcm.net/2015/03/30/googles-chris-mccarthy-a-view-from-the-zoo/

Lieb, R (2017) *Content – The Atomic Particle of Marketing,* Kogan Page, London

Lindsay, T (2017) [accessed 12 December 2017] Why the Advertising World Should Take a Long Look at Itself, *Campaign,* 19 April [Online] campaignlive.co.uk/article/why-advertising-world-long-look-itself/1430822

Madsbjerg, C and Rasmussen, M B (2014) *The Moment of Clarity: Using the human sciences to solve your toughest business problem,* Harvard Business Review Press, Boston, MA

Monllos, K (2017) [accessed 12 December 2017] Pepsi Pulls Its Much-Hated Kendall Jenner Ad, Saying It 'Missed the Mark': Brand Apologizes to Viewers and to its Endorser, *Adweek,* 5 April [Online] adweek.com/brand-marketing/pepsi-pulls-its-much-hated-kendall-jenner-ad-saying-it-missed-the-mark/

Montague, T (2013) *True Story: How to combine story and action to transform your business,* Harvard Business Review Press, Boston, MA

Oakes, O (2017) [accessed 12 December 2017] Lord Puttnam Warns Ad Industry: Trust Is The Most Urgent Task Ahead, *Campaign,* 9 March [Online] campaignlive.co.uk/article/lord-puttnam-warns-ad-industry-trust-urgent-task-ahead/1426792

Postrel, V (2003) *The Substance of Style: How the rise of aesthetic value is remaking commerce, culture, and consciousness,* HarperCollins, New York

Ritson, S (2017) [accessed 12 December 2017] Mark Ritson: Heineken Should Remember Marketing Is About Profit, Not Purpose, *Marketing Week,* 10 May [Online] marketingweek.com/2017/05/10/heineken-marketing-purpose-profit/

Roderick, L (*2017)* [accessed 12 December 2017] McDonald's Pulls 'Dead Dad' Ad after String of Complaints, *Marketing Week,* 16 May [Online] marketingweek.com/2017/05/16/mcdonalds-dead-dad-ad/

Sacks, D (2012) [accessed 12 December 2017] 34_Chipotle: For Exploding All the Rules of Fast Food, *Fast Company*, 7 February [Online] www.fastcompany.com/3017469/34chipotle

Saturday Night Live (2017) [accessed 10 March 2018] Pitch Meeting – SNL [Online] youtu.be/imUigBNF-TE

Schultz, E J and Graham, M (2017) [accessed 12 December 2017] Fair or Not, In-House Agencies Take Heat for Pepsi Gaffe, *AdAge*, 7 April [Online] adage.com/article/agency-news/pepsi-gaffe-puts-target-house-agencies-fair/308604/

Serafeim, G and Gartenberg, C (2016) [accessed 12 December 2017] The Type of Purpose That Makes Companies More Profitable, *Harvard Business Review*, 21 October [Online] hbr.org/2016/10/the-type-of-purpose-that-makes-companies-more-profitable

Sharp, B (2010) *How Brands Grow: What marketers don't know*, Oxford University Press, Melbourne

Simmons, A (2007) *Whoever Tells the Best Story Wins: How to use your own stories to communicate with power and impact*, AMACOM, New York

Simms, J (2005) [accessed 12 December 2017] Customer Expectations: Promises, Promises, *Campaign*, 13 July [Online] campaignlive.co.uk/article/customer-expectations-promises-promises/484849

Sinek, S (2011) *Start With Why: How great leaders inspire everyone to take action*, Penguin, London

TrendWatching (2015) [accessed 12 December 2017] Brand Sacrifice [Online] trendwatching.com/trends/brand-sacrifice/

Unilever (2017) [accessed 12 December 2017] Report Shows a Third of Consumers Prefer Sustainable Brands [Online] unilever.com/news/Press-releases/2017/report-shows-a-third-of-consumers-prefer-sustainable-brands.html

Wikipedia (2017a) [accessed 30 December 2017] William Bernbach [Online] en.wikipedia.org/wiki/William_Bernbach

Wikipedia (2017b) [accessed 12 December 2017] Stop Funding Hate [Online] en.wikipedia.org/wiki/Stop_Funding_Hate

Wohl, J (2017) [accessed 12 December 2017] Chipotle's Marketing Menu for 2017: Biggest Campaign Ever, Fewer Promos, *AdAge*, 10 January [Online] adage.com/article/cmo-strategy/chipotle-s-marketing-menu-2017-biggest-campaign-fewer-promos/307461/

Woolf, N (2016) [accessed 12 December 2017] Breitbart Declares War on Kellogg's after Cereal Brand Pulls Advertising from Site, *The Guardian*, 30 November [Online] theguardian.com/media/2016/nov/30/breitbart-news-kelloggs-advertising-boycott-alt-right

PART TWO
How Content changes the way we all do business

Creative agency 04
perspective

How Content impacts creativity, process and revenue

We are effectively entering an era that I affectionately call the death of the advertising industrial complex. Advertising has become a tax that the poor and digitally illiterate have to pay. If you are wealthy you get to opt out, but brands are still dependent on it.

PROFESSOR SCOTT GALLOWAY, AUTHOR OF *THE FOUR: THE HIDDEN DNA OF AMAZON, APPLE, FACEBOOK AND GOOGLE* (*FINANCIAL TIMES,* 2017)

The idea that 'Don Draper has been drawn and quartered' is a narrative that some we have spoken to think is hugely overstated and needs challenging. The backdrop for this chapter is perhaps best summed up by Unilever CMO Keith Weed's pithy phrase in a speech at Advertising Week New York 2017 (Tan, 2017):

While advertising isn't dying, it has to evolve.

The Darwinian metaphor is on the money given the ad industry's structural issues and competitive pressures.

Porter's Five Forces applied to advertising agencies

Industry rivalry: the slashing of marketing budgets and shrinking of agency rosters announced by big advertisers like P&G and Unilever in 2017 will not only increase interagency competition, but lead to half of them going out of business, according to Forrester (2017).

Threat of new entrants: advertisers can and are now buying creative and production services directly from both media owners and platforms like Google and Facebook who have both access to audiences and better understanding of them (Oakes, 2017).

Threat of substitutions: there is a growing list of those taking a slice from the same pie, but most notably through the rise of data-driven marketing, consultancies moving downstream to offer marketing services, and reintegration of creative services into media agencies.

Buyer power: trust and other issues including digital capability and opportunities to connect directly with customers have led clients to build in-house expertise and/or use more specialist agencies.

Supplier power: those formerly in the supply chain can now sell creative and production services directly or through media agency partners, including production companies, talent agencies, creative crowdsourcing platforms and pretty much anyone with influence over a sizeable audience.

The commoditizing effects of these forces along with the industry's very real talent acquisition and retention problems shine a light on the serious health challenges. As agencies adapt to survive, we have identified a big divide in the agency world that could shape the future of agency practice for years to come. Also, we believe there is an opportunity for reconciliation, as explored below.

One way into this is through the macro trends detected in the IPA's Future of Agencies report, in partnership with Econsultancy (IPA, 2017). These include the increasing importance of content and data, and what they describe as the client-driven shifts from products to services, campaigning to always-on and marketing to customer experience. The report looks at how agencies should be reshaping their propositions and consolidating capabilities.

Operating speeds

One interesting challenge in the IPA's Future of Agencies report relates to different speeds of action required today:

Whilst it is not incumbent for every agency to create an offering that spans a wide spectrum of proficiency, it will become ever more important for agencies to understand exactly where they sit along a spectrum that might be characterized as the difference between 'fast' and 'slow'.

Table 4.1 The 'speed spectrum'

Fast	Slow
Performance	Brand
Tactical	Strategic
Campaign	Consulting

SOURCE adapted from IPA Future of Agencies:
Systems and Empathy report (IPA, 2017)

The IPA 'speed spectrum' (Table 4.1) is reminiscent of the old 'above/below the line' divide.

It also presents a big challenge to anyone with the ambition of offering a one-stop shop. As Karmarama's Chief Strategy Officer Mark Runacus points out in our interview, it is difficult to see how one agency can sustain operating at those different speeds for marketing's broadening scope over longer time frames:

> Let's assume that you are genuinely developing that content eco-system, everything from traditional TV to hourly social media; all done by the same team in order to ensure consistency. I believe the traditional agency model cannot operate at those different speeds.

'Gear selection' is something he sees being wedded to the agency's business model. The default one for ad agencies, for example, is something our various interviewed experts see as being slow. In our chats, they highlight fee-based remuneration incentivizing this because the longer ad agencies draw out the process, the more time they capture and the more they can bill.

Operating models

There is another way of looking at the link between speed and operating models offered by the 'Value Discipline Model' outlined by Michael Treacy and Fred Wiersema in *The Discipline of Market Leaders* (1997). Their premise is that market leadership requires one of three disciplines to be picked as the main, and also some proficiency in the other two:

1 operational excellence;

2 customer intimacy;

3 product leadership.

Strategy and innovation consultant Huw Watkins thinks it as valid today as when it was first proposed and applicable across multiple sectors. If you take the Performance (Fast) and Brand (Slow) vectors in Table 4.1, he points out that they have very different destinations and therefore their operating models are going to be, and should be, equally different because no single organization can excel at both:

> If you place these different models within the Value Discipline framework, both obviously require substantial levels of customer intimacy to function and prosper. However, the 'Performance' model is clearly aligned to the 'Operational Excellence' axis whereas the 'Brand' one is aligned to Product Leadership'. To succeed, organizations need to choose their discipline, and align their strategy and operating model accordingly because they have fundamentally different shapes and culture. This decision drives everything within an organization: the people you hire, their skills, the business measures and reporting, your tools, levels of automation, processes and so on.

The scenarios of how 'gears' and disciplines could be mixed are too varied to cover here. However, we have picked three bigger areas of consolidation as they help provide additional context to the big divide we discuss below.

PR: the content business of the future?

When it comes to selecting the fast gear, Runacus thinks that PR agencies were among the quickest off the mark:

> PR agencies understand brand, how to create earned currency, and the need to do it quickly. However, most PR agencies struggle to deliver anything at scale because it is always about 'today'. They may struggle with those bigger narrative arcs that creative agencies are used to. But if they can learn that and if they put in some kind of a programmatic expertise, I'd say they may be the Content businesses of the future.

Former Ogilvy PR's CEO Marshall Manson, in our conversation, believes there is a philosophical reason for this, which drives a practical one:

Philosophically, when you start to talk about content marketing the real imperative is making things that people want to consume and share, and that is really analogous to traditional PR skills and with those that are being successful in social and digital. Practically, those people who instinctively understand how to work in a more nimble way – to solve practical problems, get stuff produced affordably and out in the real world quickly – are most commonly found in PR.

Salesforce: the ad agency of the future?

The possibility to connect to customers across their journeys is coinciding with increasing pressure on CMOs to drive growth. That has resulted in the shifting of client budgets to more data-driven marketing, which marketing adviser Lindsey Slaby thinks has helped marketing automators to widen their window of opportunity (2017):

Salesforce becoming the ad agency of the future is a REAL THING.

We discuss the platformization of marketing more in Chapter 9. Proliferation of 'martech' (marketing technology) also creates an opportunity for those who aim at aligning purpose and profit, the longer and short-term business strategies. That blurring of lines between strategy transformation and the role of marketing and customer experience in its delivery has allowed consultancies to move downstream to eat agencies' lunch. Not only did Accenture acquire creative agency Karmarama and its CRM sister company Crayon in 2016 (Accenture, 2016a), their Interactive division is now the 'world's biggest and fastest-growing digital agency' (AdAge, 2016) – and they are rolling out Content studios around the globe (Accenture, 2016b).

Runacus helps with joining some additional dots here by showing how data gets put in the middle of the advertising (slow) and performance (fast) sides:

With CRM we can be credible players, particularly because we understand measurement and results. However, we can sometimes be too measurement focused and 'systems first', to the detriment of a good story. That is probably the only thing good integrated agencies need to overcome: to be able to tell bigger, more consistent stories. By putting data in the middle, we found new ways for advertising's muscle memory to use data. What Karmarama brought to the party is a passionate belief in 'brand purpose' and the CRM team adopted that as well, which meant that we became more confident in our discussions with clients about CRM, which quickly led to discussions about 'experience'. CRM really is the engine that delivers the experience. Nowadays, experience IS the brand.

The link Runacus makes between brand purpose and experience is one we look at more below, but Faris Yakob highlights how 'experience' is far too often a misnomer for badly done CRM:

What is being called experience design is really just a massive performance marketing system. The challenge with the customer experience versus the brand-growth marketing piece is that although they are not antithetical, they are not perfectly aligned. A good experience does not mean having a brand annoy you by constantly trying to get you to buy their product. But in performance marketing terms there is limited cost to doing that and so they can A/B test it to death.

Not only does Yakob think that it creates more noise, but more targeted communications via CRM are generally less likely to generate the kind of earned and shared media success, such as putting the Fearless Girl bronze statue commissioned by State Street Global Advisers in front of the Wall Street bull (Schultz, 2017). Clients are still looking for ideas that resonate beyond their working media spend, which is the way he sees the difference that advertising brings. It is close to the intersection of advertising, PR and publisher's thinking explored above and further in the book. This also touches upon another often-mentioned intersection: advertising and entertainment.

Next-generation entertainment companies

As ad veteran Mark Wnek stresses in Chapter 10, one should never forget that most agency creatives are would-be long-form creators: writers of movies, TV shows and novels... As we discuss in Chapter 5, long-form content creation forms part of the ad industry's heritage that goes back to the early soap operas. There's a new breed of 'next generation entertainment' companies emerging from the ad industry who are 'reinventing that tradition'. They have embraced the argument that 'entertainment and advertising industries must converge to survive' made by former AdAge editor Scott Donaton in *Madison & Vine* (2005).

Google's Hero 'bucket' comes to mind here. The Cannes Lions Entertainment subfestival launched in 2016, building on the exponential growth of their former 'Branded Content and Entertainment' award category. The approach could be seen as the antithesis of the data-driven marketing automation mentioned above: one where relevance can too often get narrowly framed around customers' digital journeys and how they get nudged along their paths to purchase. Not only that, but as Sunshine's Chief Creative Officer Ed Warren explains, the approach is fundamentally different from the message focus of advertising:

> As culture has become a lot more adept at avoiding advertising, the changing nature of the entertainment landscape has opened up more opportunities for brands to become producers of entertainment. This is leading to different conversations, often outside of the marketing department, about something that is being viewed more as a product rather than as advertising. That allows us to create cultural products that people want to consume and in a way that those who still think in terms of messages rather than audiences are finding it hard to crack because that way of thinking is ingrained in their muscle memory. Entertainment is not a message-led form. No one left *Jaws* saying 'I really enjoyed that movie because it was really clear'.

The 'product' versus 'message' distinction is interesting because it is an example of the kind or more empathic 'designing for time' idea we discussed in Chapter 2. Gravity Road's co-founder Mark Boyd explained how that thinking was embedded in their agency from the onset, but like Warren above, he also sees it as distinguishing what they do from advertising:

> When we set up Gravity Road we had a working hypothesis that has served us well. We wanted to create the types of things that people wanted to spend time with rather than do advertising that is about what people want to tell you.

However, this is far from plain sailing. Faris Yakob sees the other side of the coin too, that the ability to have an impact on culture is often overstated:

> Hollywood is really good at making movies. But only 1 in 10 makes them money. Half break even and half lose money. That's just the way culture works. It is inherently unpredictable, which makes it a risky business.

It is echoed by ad contrarian Bob Hoffman in Chapter 10 too.

Nonetheless, brands seem to be becoming more comfortable with the approach and are being pitched with both new branded experiential ideas and entertainment formats by creative and media agencies, talent agencies, as well as specialist producers, including those who create content that people actually pay to watch. We highlight this space because it is one of the ways that capability is being repackaged to help brands answer the problem of engaging audiences and their increasingly fragmented attention. Like the other two above, it can also be placed on one of two sides of the active fault line that is becoming apparent in adland.

The binary equation of agencies and its two tribes

In Chapter 2, we mentioned that the battle for Content budgets could often seem like a contest of two camps: branded content and content marketing. Also, as above, it became obvious that there are different speeds at which agencies now have to operate. It can all be seen as part of a bigger divide that shaped the industry for years, and may even intensify in the future.

Zenith USA's Tom Goodwin had a neat thought experiment in our interview, as to what would happen if marketing was reinvented today:

So, if you put every existing form of tactic, skill set and approach into an amorphous bucket, and you then had to segment it in a new way, then what you would probably do is create two buckets: brand advertising – and that would be like a whole world of how to create materials to promote the brands where the brand metrics have no expectation of any immediate results – and then you have another bucket that is more like performance marketing, where it is about cashing in some of the equity by getting people to act as a result of the content.

Goodwin thinks segmenting advertising and marketing like this inevitably leads to thinking less in terms of channels and tactics, or creative versus media, and more in terms of brand versus performance goals. This is something he thinks is more helpful because it leads to conversations about platforms, and what is the role of the brands in them and what role performance plays there.

Goodwin's two buckets may be reminiscent of the old ATL/BTL divide, but this time reimagined for the inherently hybrid brand/direct journeys powered by digital. Everyone is now poised to eat everyone else's lunch. It breeds complexity, as recognized by both big agencies and big clients such as P&G's chief brand officer Marc Pritchard, who admitted at the 4A's Transformation 2017 conference (Sherwood, 2017):

P&G fed the complexity beast by hiring thousands of agencies globally... With a specialist for everything, it was difficult to determine who was in charge of anything.

Pritchard also acknowledged big brands' own role in the very audience fragmentation and clutter problems they are trying to solve:

We bombard consumers with thousands of ads a day, subject them to endless ad load times, interrupt their screens with pop-ups and overpopulate their screens and feeds... but all of this activity is not breaking through the clutter. It's just creating more noise.

His suggested solution is to stop chasing tails and have the courage to do less, with the creative focus being on developing 'fewer and better ideas that last longer' (B&T Magazine, 2017). What we hope to do next is provide a way of thinking about how that may be achieved. This, in turn, may help provide more clarity about who should lead on what, where, when and how, as well as the talent required to deliver it. A good place to start is to try to unpack the big divide mentioned above. Not just Tom Goodwin, but many other well-known names in the industry have highlighted this binary nature of today's marketing industry.

Deep branding versus touchpoint optimization

Professor Andrew McStay sees the brand and performance buckets mentioned above as two pathways that are diverging along the following lines:

- **Deep branding:** linked to traditional brand-building activities of creative agencies, which is increasingly entailing higher levels of ad testing for clarity and emotional relevance to improve impact and distribution efficiency.

- **Touchpoint optimization:** can be linked to performance goals and marketing optimization as the accessing of customers along their journeys becomes increasingly tech and behaviourally enabled, including in-store, via virtual assistants and traditional programmatic and CRM.

Forrester: media-led versus customer-led content marketing (2016)

- **Media-led:** evolution of advertising that supports brand advertising goals.
- **Customer-led:** evolution of direct marketing that supports response goals.

Google: HHH framework (2015a)

The Hero and Help content categories from Google's 3H framework could be mapped on to these trajectories, and also helps explain the different frequencies involved and scale of the different experiences (cultural-level versus more individualized):

- **Hero:** lower-frequency large-scale tent-pole events or 'go-big' moments designed to raise broad awareness through a shared cultural-level experience.
- **Help:** higher-frequency always-on 'pull' content optimized to user intent that is often more personally relevant for that micro-moment.

Adam&Eve: culture versus collateral

David Golding (2017) at Adam&Eve has his way of talking about it:

- **Culture:** more creatively driven big-culture-moment ideas with higher production cost that create shared experiences and build mass awareness, generate fame and 'talkability' through earned and shared media.

- **Collateral:** more iterative, data-driven and programmatically delivered marketing with lower production costs where multiple variations are tested and optimized to nudge customers along their purchase path.

The above are simply illustrative of even more similar conclusions. The IPA's 'speed' table above (Table 4.1), for example, could have a more detailed interpretation (Table 4.2) based on the chasm.

Table 4.2 is by no means an exhaustive list of the attributes of the two trajectories, but it helped frame our discussions with a broad spectrum of agency experts about how Content changes the way they do business.

Table 4.2   The 'binary table' of the marketing industry

Brand	Performance
Creative advertising	Marketing optimization
Deep branding	Touchpoint optimized
Brand-building goals	Response goals
Creativity/Ideas-led	Data-driven/Technology-led
Hero content	Help content
Emotional relevance	Informative/Educational/Useful
Higher production costs	Lower production costs
Large-scale tent-pole events	Optimized to user intent
Big culture moments	Micro moments
Raise broad awareness	Nudge along path to purchase
Lower frequency	Higher frequency
Evolution of advertising	Evolution of direct marketing

SOURCE authors

A new set of optics to resolve the binary equation

This big divide can eventually result either in total divorce, where agencies will specialize along either side of the fault line, or in partial marriages of the kind we mentioned in the 'Operating models' section above. R/GA agency's operating principle of *Stories + Systems* (Law, 2014) and *Systems and Empathy* dynamics put forward in the IPA's Future of Agency Report (2017) attempt to do something similar by suggesting a mind-meld of these binary modes of thinking.

The *empathy* dynamic that the IPA raises may provide the bridge when framed around Google's Moments that Matter (MTMs) concept mentioned in Chapter 1 (Google, 2015b). Each of the moments may be viewed as a micro-contextual delivery unit that could – and we think, should – work in terms of how we engage customers at those access points across their journeys. It focuses the mind on what gets delivered there – and why. There is, we believe, a new set of optics the industry should think about as an opportunity above and beyond current business models. We touched upon the basis of this thinking when exploring Experience Economy in Chapter 2.

This set of optics has two primary lenses that, combined, create a new third one. In our experience, there are just two ways an organization of any kind may try to earn people's attention. They do reflect the industry's current binary divide, but are also different as they are agnostic of any specific discipline, platform, business model or customer journey considerations. They work, and can work, anywhere, anytime, anyhow.

Emotional Resonance (ER)

'Just move me, dude', was the phrase attributed to Dan Weiden, of Weiden & Kennedy fame, in one article about how advertising works (Weigel, 2013). It is very apt, as it neatly encapsulates a vast space of relevant research demonstrating how emotion is important for branding. Think IPA's report again. It could be taken as the proxy for brand marketing.

Advertisers had known that for a long time, but the digital space, unencumbered with the restrictions of time and space, seconds and inches, had found that the length of their messages matters less now. It's the story that counts. That is the reason that we have witnessed, in the last couple of years, a new wave of strong storytelling brand examples that resonated with tens of million of viewers globally. P&G Always '#LikeAGirl', Dove 'Real Beauty Sketches', Wren 'First Kiss', Saddlebag 'How to Knock Off a Bag', Knorr 'Flavour of Home' and John Lewis and Sainsbury's Christmas ads are just some of them. Another expression of the Hero approach, this time on YouTube, is Pepsi Max UK's 'Unbelievable' channel that works as a kind of a 'Hero/Hub' approach, packaging a few bigger moments of spectacle during the year with a raft of more numerous smaller entertaining and inspiring pieces.

'Make them cry, with tears or with laughter', another often-quoted industry adage, is getting a new lease of life in the Content space, to the sigh of relief of many a creative team. In this space, well-executed things that people willingly seek, share and consume, whether powered by a deep insight, or of the 'humbug' variety (Feldwick, 2015), IS also Content. In the salient phrase by the consultant Jay Baer (2014), that particularly applies to the Hero angle if done right, 'Content is fire, social media is gasoline'.

Intent Utility (IU)

The emotional kind of magic we discuss above is difficult to control, however, and even the best don't manage to do it often, particularly for the same brand. After all, John Lewis and Sainsbury's Christmas ads happen only once a year. At the same time, there is a universe of intent revealed every moment on Google, YouTube and many other digital touchpoints. There are about 1 billion queries per month on Google relating just to hair. Brands simply *have* to be there, delivering 'utility' to that revealed intent, in ways that are much richer than just the old terse keyword-stuffed line on a search-engine results page (SERP) – the smart ones are, as shown with Unilever's 'All Things Hair' case study in Chapter 2. This could be taken as the proxy for performance marketing.

Here is how we think it may work. If we plot the IU (performance marketing) on one axis and the ER (brand marketing) on the other, we would get a familiar planning tool of the 2x2 grid that contains four possible scenarios of how Content could work (and largely does) today (Figure 4.1).

The space that is high on IU and low on ER would be the 'left-brain' side of the debate (to use that outdated analogy, still favoured by many in the industry); the one that is high on ER and low on IU would be 'right brain'. The one with neither is why most of Content (and most of modern advertising) has built an awful reputation. However, the top-right corner is the new concept: a very rare animal today (and it shouldn't be). It integrates aspects of both sides of the debate, by changing the way we conceptualize them, as described below. This is the space to consider and conquer. This is the

Figure 4.1 Empathic Utility grid

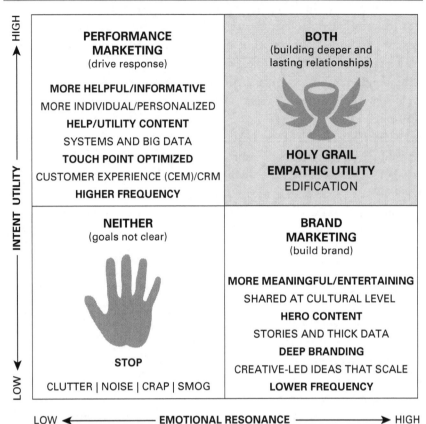

SOURCE authors

bridge. It makes the archetypal unit of delivery in this space not a specific format, but a way of thinking. We call it Empathic Utility (EU).

However, to push the thinking even further, we actually don't believe that EU is just a quadrant, regardless of how tempting its simplicity, as it still indicates something separate from the other two, something that sits in its own corner. Instead, we think of EU as a spectrum. Every time a brand 'touches' the consumer, it should have the MTMs 'charged' with contextually relevant units of EU. At the top of the funnel that is likely to be mostly ER; as you progress along, more IU gets mixed in until certain situations in the journey become almost-all IU (but we don't advocate that, as there are no boring products or services, just boring ways to frame them or talk about them). EU is like a Pantone scale of endless shades between pure emotions and pure utility, with intensity of both to be chosen depending on

Figure 4.2   Empathic Utility spectrum

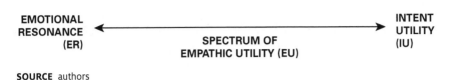

EMOTIONAL
RESONANCE
(ER)

SPECTRUM OF
EMPATHIC UTILITY (EU)

INTENT
UTILITY
(IU)

SOURCE authors

the contextual situation. It's a slider tool for creating meaning (Figure 4.2); a thermostat for an air-conditioning unit in charge of creating customer-friendly ambience... We are sure you will have your own metaphor too.

EU has several perspectives that make it different and potentially groundbreaking.

Empathic Utility perspectives and benefits

- Every MTM is an opportunity to deliver not either brand or optimization, but both! That does not depend so much on the operational or organizational capabilities, but on changing the optics of the problem. It is not new: it has been known for a long time as brand response.

- What is emotional or interesting does not always have to be slow or expensive; it is our business models that make it thus.

- What is useful does not have to be boring; again, it is a question of optics.

- But, to reconcile the two things above we need a different mix of skills, processes and incentives, above and beyond the two-atom creative team mentioned in Chapter 1.

- It is a predominantly digital approach, because TV is mostly time-limited and more broadly targeted, which limits its IU aspect.

- EU could be seen as the convergence of thinking from different insight-generating disciplines, specifically those from product and platform design such as human-centred design (HCD), design thinking, user experience design (UX), information architecture (IA) and good old account planning.

- The EU spectrum is discipline-agnostic and context-pious: as long as one is trying to 'design for time and space', to use the idea from Chapter 2, it is working; it doesn't matter whether it is offline or online, business to business (B2B), business to consumer (B2C), consumer to consumer

(C2C) or human to human (H2H), on which platform or which part of the customer journey, whether it is for communications or apps.

- EU is also media paradigm-agnostic: it works across all media spaces, traditional or new, including the internet of things (IoT), AR, VR/MR, artificial intelligence (AI) and whatever else may come round; again, as long as we are designing for time and space.

- EU also works as an experience-generating lens *inside* an organization, as it is a universal composite: it has the two most important ingredients of ANY experience.

- We see EU as a purpose-building approach that can help bridge the promise and values gaps discussed in Chapter 3. The role brands play at MTMs actually proves what they say they are about.

- Finally, it gives a more ethical expression of whatever brands, agencies, platforms and other industry players do: if the focus is on maximizing EU – and data privacy, transparency, non-addictiveness and non-predatory thinking should be part of it – the likely outcome is going to be more constructive for brands long-term.

Empathic Utility sits at the centre of the triumvirate of forces driving modern marketing. It is a linchpin (Figure 4.3) between them and provides the set of optics enabling a robust answer to probably one of the best questions ever asked in the history of marketing, posited by Tony Stead, one of the first planners in the business and the creator of the name 'Account Planning':

Why the f***k should they?' (Griffiths, 2014)

Why people should think or do – give their time and attention – what organizations would like them to think or do (see Figure 4.3).

How to develop the Empathic Utility optics – a chance for agencies

Like everyone else, as we have seen above, the ad industry is having to ask existential questions about their *why*, and the opportunity for agencies is not just how they figure this out for themselves, but also how they help clients do the same. That takes them from simply responding to marketing

Figure 4.3   Empathic Utility as the linchpin

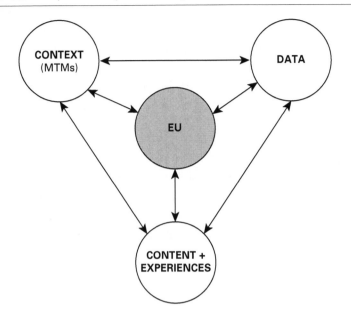

SOURCE authors

communications briefs, to helping solve much broader and deeper business challenges. In turn, this takes them into the business strategy and transformation arena. That is becoming an increasing virtue of necessity because of the velocity of consultancies like Accenture heading their way. The impact zone is where they collide at the 'virtuous circle' of 'Purpose starts with why and content starts with purpose' presented in Chapter 3 (see Figure 4.4).

Figure 4.4   Agencies versus consultancies – Content impact zone

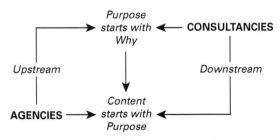

SOURCE authors

What this means in practice is that those formerly responsible for the external communications could now move upstream to help clarify and articulate purposes. The opposite is true as well because of the way transformation is often a response to the way technology is driving marketing mission-creep further along the customer journey and particularly into post-purchase areas like customer service. Richard Wilding, founder of internal comms specialists WMW, helps explain how the dots are joining up here:

> Companies need to sell their products and employ brand agencies to help them. Brand agencies have cottoned on – at least, the smart ones – to the notion that the product a company sells should be some form of manifestation of their purpose, and building purpose into brands is becoming a necessary (but not sufficient) criterion for their success.

Articulating why

In terms of opportunities for agencies, the first is this defining and articulation of purpose and, as discussed in Chapter 3, it is being done in a variety of ways; an example is Robert Bean's 'Single Organization Principle' where purpose and other variables get condensed into an ad-like slogan, or where the organizing principle or ethos is developed into more of what the co:collective calls a 'core story'. When it comes to mapping value to client 'jobs to be done' it's one that ad agencies seem to be ideally suited for. They are still the masters of taking something and distilling it to the core essence of that thought.

Aligning people with purpose

Whether agencies want to define and articulate purpose is another matter, but that's the opportunity that brands competing in the digital world of declining interruption seem to be offering. It is also the stepping-stone into a bigger opportunity to offer the new value that is identified in the IPA's report:

> Employee experience is often the poor relation in transformation initiatives but is a critical element in achieving organizational objectives and an opportunity for agencies to deliver new value. Whether through transformation initiatives, visioning work, internal campaigning and comms, this is a relatively untapped but essential opportunity.

The idea for this stems from the progression explored in Chapter 2: the empowering, motivation and engaging of employees, so that organizational goals get realized, becomes part of agency practice as they evolve along the Experience Economy progression from delivering services, through staging experiences, to *guiding* (business) transformations. That is an important piece of the bigger jigsaw because, as Wilding explains, it is not just the products that should align with the purpose:

> The penny is slowly dropping that the people who dream up, make and sell the products would also benefit from being aligned with the purpose. Enlightened companies understand this, but don't yet know how to make it happen and agencies are starting to twig that if they want to achieve success for their clients, they ought to pay as much attention to what's happening to employee experience/sentiment inside their client as to what the external world thinks and feels about a product.

Cultivating purpose-driven culture

This loops back to the idea in Chapter 3 about a brand being a promise of an experience and the co:collective's idea of StoryDoing, where brands embody Simon Sinek's notion about 'what you do simply proves what you believe'. Wilding defines it as 'not what we say here, but what we do':

> Internally, senior leaders are the product: they embody by their actions the brand promise. And with depressing frequency, they don't realize this. Their actions are not aligned to the higher purpose nor the values that support that purpose. So what employees see is lack of authenticity and what they feel is a poor experience. If you want a higher return on experience, you need leaders to lead in a way that is clearly in step with the purpose (the *why*) and the correct behaviours (the *how*).

Hugh MacLeod, in his So What Comes After Advertising? post believes it is a tough job and that agencies may help with that new 'product' (2013):

The hardest part of a CEO's job is sharing his enthusiasm with his colleagues, especially when a lot of them are making one-fiftieth of what he is. Selling the company to the general public is a piece of cake compared to selling it to the actual people who work for it. The future of advertising is internal.

Wilding believes that factoring-in 'return on experience' (RoE) to board/management decision making could be a solution to this. Internal experience in this instance means culture, which still, sadly, too often could be defined as 'the worst behaviour that is tolerated'.

Building owned capability

There are a number of reasons for mentioning this in a book about Content and in a chapter about agencies – the simplest being that culture building represents just one of the spaces for agencies to move into. It is also linked to analysts identifying that advertisers are bringing agency capabilities in-house and/or work with independent agencies. The trust issues that the analysts diagnose are a factor, but there is another equally important one, identified in our interview with Robert Rose from the Content Marketing Institute:

> So many of the larger enterprises that I speak with are completely frustrated by the inability of their agencies to simply 'keep up' or 'innovate' (whether it is content, commerce or other digital experience development). So, the trend of moving some services in-house is just that: a move to acquire the talent and institutionalize (and centralize) capabilities.

Part of the in-house capability includes the creation of owned-and-operated (O&O) media platforms or content hubs. Hence Rose's quip about how it doesn't matter who owns what part of the customer journey internally, as long as it is 'owned'. Brand success across customer journeys needs more than just a strategy of 'build it and they will come', or the centralization of capability, integration of martech and application of one of the growing array of content-strategy frameworks. What is also likely to be required is the changing of internal culture, starting with mindset and moving on to developing the 'muscle memory'.

Changing the internal optics to build muscle memory

MTMs are also a useful way of thinking about employee experience. They are a starting place for changing the organizational mindset because they help frame the delivery of strategies through enhanced empathy and iteration. We think our EU concept could play a part in this, but our point is simply that if one wants to be successful with their external Content strategies and wider array of digital experiences, then a more empathic way of thinking needs to be baked into how the organization actually operates.

That is also another metric for internal change than just the monitoring of customer experience through the Net Promoter Score (NPS) metric (Wikipedia, 2017). Spotting symptoms is not the same as getting to the bottom of root causes, particularly when those are cultural. It is also a way to shed more light on what the IPA's report may have had in mind with the employee experience vector as part of three experience opportunities for agencies (see Figure 4.5).

Brand and customer experience are clear: it is about a fusing of the disciplines that focus on design and optimization of touchpoints and journeys with more branding-orientated objectives such as positioning, differentiation and consistency of what gets executed across those interactions between brand and customer. What was less clear in the report was how that joins up to employee experience, which we hope we have helped to clarify here.

Action capability building

The more nimble and digital-savvy agencies have already stepped in with supporting how brand and customer experience gets brought to life through the work of internal teams. Brilliant Noise's founder Antony Mayfield explains why:

Figure 4.5   Three experience opportunities for agencies

SOURCE adapted from the IPA Future of Agencies: Systems and Empathy (IPA, 2017)

> Organizations are facing an explosion of complex problems at every level, from the strategic – 'what is happening to my market?' – to the tactical – 'is app x or y the way of the future that I should bet marketing resources on exploring, or a flash in the pan?' The old partner models for solving problems will not work effectively because the gap between thinking and doing, between learning and applying, is shorter. These loops happen so fast that a consultant-led approach will take too long and deliver answers to problems that have already shifted in their nature or changed beyond recognition. Organizations need to build capability – and **the capability to build capability** – rapidly and at scale. As Louis Pasteur said, 'chance only favours the prepared mind'. Leaders should be creating prepared cultures – developing the capability to act decisively and quickly in response to complex challenges.

Brilliant Noise's action capability building (ACB) approach is informed by both design thinking and action learning. This is interesting for a number of reasons, particularly for being an agile approach where learning is facilitated by doing and solutions are built in iterative steps. The likes of Brilliant Noise and WMW are just two examples of specialist agencies that are both helping embed more empathetic and experience-orientated thinking into the organization.

Ideally, that should include the kind of 'personalization of purpose' that Professor Dan Cable talks about based on research from Adam Grant's *Give and Take: Why helping others drives our success* (2014). The idea is to get employees to make purpose their own (Daisley, 2017). One way of doing this is to go beyond desk research, analytics dashboards and hiding behind focus-group screens to actually meet customers in person to hear about their experiences of what you offer them.

Cable thinks this is important because it helps build an emotional connection with customers rather than a cognitive one. Parallels can be made with the more human-centred methodology devised by Beyer and Holtzblatt in *Contextual Design* (1998), which incorporates ethnographic research methods for gathering the 'thick data' of why we do what we do. That side of the data coin is often missing; we will explore it in Chapter 7.

We see that emotional understanding and 'thick data' feeding into Empathic Utility. That alone does not ensure that purpose and values are lived, but it is a way of thinking that can form part of that – not least by helping brands to understand how they are generally making a nuisance of themselves by bombarding consumers with messages and the cognitive smog it creates. EU may be a small cog in the bigger wheel we have been discussing here, but one we hope can contribute to the creative ethos demanded by P&G's Marc Pritchard, above, that helps deliver 'fewer and better ideas that last longer'.

References

Accenture (2016a) [accessed 11 June 2017] Accenture Acquires Creative Agency [Online] accenture.com/gb-en/company-news-release-accenture-acquire-karmarama

Accenture (2016b) [accessed 11 June 2017] Accenture Interactive Launches Its First Content Studio to Deliver Innovative and Engaging Content to Clients [Online] newsroom.accenture.com/news/accenture-interactive-launches-its-first-content-studio-to-deliver-innovative-and-engaging-content-to-clients.htm

AdAge (2016) [accessed 11 June 2017] Agency Report 2016 Index [Online] adage.com/article/datacenter/ad-age-agency-report-2016-rankings-analysis/303559/

Baer, J (2014) [accessed 11 June 2017] Why Content Is Fire and Social Media Is Gasoline [Online] youtu.be/b4J4NbGhiLc

Beyer, H and Holtzblatt, K (1998) *Contextual Design: Defining customer-centered systems*, Morgan Kaufmann, San Francisco

B&T Magazine (2017) [accessed 11 June 2017] P&G's Marc Pritchard: 'We Need Fewer Agencies and Fewer Ads', 7 April [Online] bandt.com.au/media/pgs-marc-pritchard

Daisley, B (2017) [accessed 12 December 2017] Alive at Work (Blog), *Eat Sleep Work Repeat*, 23 November [Online]eatsleepworkrepeat.fm/2017/11/23/alive-at-work/

Donaton, S (2005) *Madison & Vine: Why the entertainment and advertising industries must converge to survive*, McGraw-Hill, New York

Feldwick, P (2015) *The Anatomy of Humbug: How to think differently about advertising*, Matador, Leicester

Financial Times (2017) [accessed 12 December 2017] FT Alphaville Alphachat Podcast: Don Draper Has Been Drawn and Quartered (Podcast), 11 August [Online] ft.com/content/413879df-bf91-43cd-875f-b2c83cf2f765

Forrester (2016) [accessed 11 June 2017] Don't Confuse Media-Led and Customer-Led Content Marketing [Online] forrester.com/report/Dont+Confuse+MediaLed+And+CustomerLed+Content+Marketing/-/E-RES131044

Forrester (2017) [accessed 12 December 2017] The New Agency Operating Model for Brands: Follow a Four-Step Plan to Realign Your Agency's Value Around the Customer [Online] forrester.com/report/The+New+Agency+Operating+Model+For+Brands/-/E-RES122385

Golding, D (2017) [accessed 12 December 2017] The Big Adland Divide: Culture vs Collateral, *Campaign*, 20 February [Online] campaignlive.co.uk/article/big-adland-divide-culture-vs-collateral/1424173

Google (2015a) [accessed 12 December 2017] Build a Content Plan [Online] thinkwithgoogle.com/marketing-resources/youtube/build-a-content-plan/

Google (2015b) [accessed 15 May 2017] Win the Moments that Matter [Online] thinkwithgoogle.com/intl/en-gb/marketing-resources/micro-moments/win-the-moments-that-matter/

Grant, A (2014) *Give and Take: Why helping others drives our success*, Weidenfeld & Nicolson, London

Griffiths, J (2014) [accessed 21 December 2017] Justifying My Job – What Is Account Planning For? (Blog) *Postcards From A Planner*, 12 June [Online] accountplanning.blogspot.co.uk/2014/06/justifying-my-job-what-is-account.html

IPA (2017) [accessed 11 June 2017] IPA Future of Agencies: Systems and Empathy [Online] ipa.co.uk/Framework/ContentDisplay.aspx?id=12292

Law, N (2014) [accessed 12 December 2017] Introduction: Managing Creativity in the Connected Age, *R/GA Future Vision* [Online] cdn.space.rga.com/production/file-56c7deef6ab6dad07876ef78.pdf

MacLeod, H (2013) [accessed 12 December 2017] So What Comes after Advertising? (Blog), *Gaping Void*, 11 March [Online] gapingvoid.com/blog/2013/03/11/hughtrain/

Oakes, O (2017) [accessed 12 December 2017] Analysts on WPP: 'Expected Bad, Got Worse', *Campaign*, 23 August [Online] campaignlive.co.uk/article/analysts-wpp-expected-bad-worse/1442727

Schultz, E J (2017) [accessed 12 December 2017] Mccann's 'Fearless Girl' Is Monday's Big Winner at Cannes, *AdAge*, 19 June [Online] adage.com/article/special-report-cannes-lions/mccann-fearless-girl-big-winner-cannes/309476/

Sherwood, I-H (2017) [accessed 12 December 2017] Too Much 'Complexity' and 'Crap' Hinders Agency-Brand Relationships, Says P&G CMO, *Campaign*, 4 April [Online] campaignlive.co.uk/article/complexity-crap-hinders-agency-brand-relationships-says-p-g-cmo/1429596

Slaby, L (2017) [accessed 12 December 2017] Adland's Talent Drought Is a Real Problem and Salesforce Wants to Take the Lead on the New Agency Skillset (Blog), *Medium.com: @lasslaby*, 22 October [Online] medium.com/@lasslaby/adlands-talent-drought-is-a-real-problem-and-salesforce-wants-to-take-the-lead-72105df34838

Tan, E (2017) [accessed 12 December 2017] Unilever Marketing Boss Weed Reveals 5C Brand Strategy, *Campaign*, 25 September [Online] campaignlive.co.uk/article/unilever-marketing-boss-weed-reveals-5c-brand-strategy/1445575

Treacy, M and Wiersema, F (1997) *The Discipline of Market Leaders: Choose your customers, narrow your focus, dominate your market*, Basic Books, New York

Weigel, M (2013) [accessed 12 December 2017] 'Just Move, Me Dude': The Ancient Path to Effectiveness (Blog), *canalside view*, 11 November [Online] martinweigel.org/2013/11/11 just-move-me-dude-the-ancient-path-to-effectiveness/

Wikipedia (2017) [accessed 12 December 2017] Net Promoter [Online] en.wikipedia.org/wiki/Net_Promoter

Media agency perspective

How Content impacts creativity, process and revenue

A potted history of Content in modern electronic media

Media has since its beginning sought ways of attracting external funding for content, as well as means for filling its schedules. Already in 1929 more than 55 per cent of radio programmes in the United States were financed or produced by brands (Lehu, 2007). One of the first and more famous was *Little Orphan Annie*, on the NBC Blue Network. It was sponsored by Ovaltine, the manufacturer of a dairy dietary supplement. This radio play, based on a comic book of the same name, enjoyed great popularity, managing to attract 6 million fans to their radio sets (Harmon, 2001)! This model was considered attractive by both advertisers, for whom it was an interesting form of advertising, and stations, which found it easier to fill an all-day programming schedule.

In the 1940s, advertisers started to show an interest in the growing medium of television. Drawing on experiences from the radio – its programme-funding models and the widespread presence of sponsored content – the advertising industry in the 1940s and 1950s exerted strong pressure on commercial broadcasters in the United States (Godzic, 2010). This pressure, combined with the broadcaster's desire to develop and acquire new programmes, led to the repetition of formats and approaches from the older medium – hence the old radio favourites such as *The Colgate Comedy Hour* (Lehu, 2007) or *Kraft Television Theatre* (AdAge, 2003). These programmes were mostly produced by advertising agencies and pursued the sponsors' commercial interests.

The dominance of commercial funding was so strong that even the first American news programme was, actually, advertising content. Broadcast by the state-owned NBC, it was entitled *Camel News Caravan* and effectively served as an advertisement for a popular brand of tobacco (Godzic, 2010). The presenter reading the news smoked cigarettes on air, with the packaging always visible in the frame, while the news programme ended with a cigarette in the ashtray. The brand's influence on NBC was so great at the time that a 'no smoking' sign, or information on the fatal consequences of smoking, could not appear anywhere. Interestingly, neither would people smoking cigars, which were competition for cigarettes. Exceptions were made only for the contemporary British Prime Minister Winston Churchill – for whom the cigar was his trademark (Utley, 2000)!

It became apparent relatively soon that the radio model based on one sponsor financing the creation of a programme does not work for television in the long term because of high show-production costs. Advertisers increasingly turned to cheaper genres such as gameshows, which on one hand significantly affected the quality of the content, while on the other resulted in a series of scandals caused by quiz results being manipulated (Lotz, 2007; Carter, 2003). At the end of the 1950s sponsors made questions available to selected participants in cooperation with directors and producers. They won large sums in spectacular style and ratings grew rapidly. These scandals cast a bad light on sponsorship of television content and resulted in a significant effort aimed at curbing the practice of putting programmes financed by one sponsor on air.

Simultaneously, a 'placement black market' was developing. Increasingly, brands paid writers to place their products in scripts. Branded products were to appear on the screen in a seemingly natural way, while actors and presenters were paid by corporations to play in individual scenes (Newell, Salmon and Chang, 2006). In 1948, NBC began combating such practices via a standards and practices department, which served the role of, in essence, a censor. Soon, reports, which previously evaluated programming content for sexuality, alcohol products, racial stereotypes, violence, juvenile delinquency, religion or blasphemy, also started to report pseudo-advertising activities (Pondillo, 2003). The first mention of a product being removed by the censoring department comes from 1949. The following year brands were removed from scripts once a week, on average. However, had any illegal advertising activity escaped the attention of the censors, it was often reported to the network by manufacturers of competitive products. This resulted in NBC deciding to temporarily use bottles and packaging without labels or, in the case when the scene required a brand to be indicated, obliging the creators to check whether the brand was currently an advertiser on NBC.

Sponsoring of programmes by a number of advertisers was not the dominant form of financing until the beginning of the 1960s. In the period between 1962 and 1963, as many as 52 of the 94 programmes on air were financed using this model. Television began searching for other means and models of cooperation with brands, only to return – recently, after a number of years – to the original solutions, but in a modern guise.

It is assumed that the beginnings of what is considered today as branded content date back to 2001, when the mini-series *The Hire* had its online première. It was created and financed by the German car manufacturer BMW and is considered to be the first modern branded content campaign.

From 'Advertising in the post-network era: branded Content – case study', PhD dissertation, Izabela Derda (2017)

How easy it must have been for the early ad and media agencies, even after the big 'schism' of the late 1960s and early 1970s when the media planning and buying function got divorced from its glamorous creative sibling! In that world, brands and agencies operated in a space of only several main 'marcomms' channels: TV, radio, press, outdoor, stores – a media universe at the early stage of its development, where the 'main channels' section of the media plan did not have more than four or five rubrics.

Compare that with today's digital world of 100+ marketing (communications) paths to the consumer, a universe in which most of the touchpoints serve at the same time as advertising, PR, promotional, sales, product usage, service delivery, customer service and CRM environments. In other words, everything has gone hybrid and brands and their agencies now speak less of channels and more of 'eco-systems' for organizing overall marketing efforts. Clients, as well as agencies, are thinking hard about the role a media agency plays in this new world, and how it interlaces with creative shops.

'The world of content is definitively changing the DNA of the media industry', says Sasha Savic, CEO of MediaCom US in our conversation for the book:

The world of communications has changed more in the last five years than in the last 50. To remain relevant, every media agency must rethink the way it does business: the talent it attracts, its structure, its business model, its offering… everything.

Many of the old rules do not apply any more, while at the same time – as evidenced by the potted history of Content in the modern media above and the insights in this chapter – some still do! What seems to be afoot is an interesting reintegration of functionalities and skills separated during the big divorce of the media and creative sides of the industry. This is augmented by several new trends, particularly the need for the media agencies to become masters of two aspects of its traditional 'last mile' expertise: the *data* about how people actually consume media content, as well as the *technology* they use to consume it. The modern media agency is evolving into something its historical siblings would find utterly bewildering. The same forces that are driving Content as the new paradigm are playing an important role in that evolution.

Eco-system changes driving media agency reinvention

Tia Castagno, Global Head of Innovation at Vizeum and former VP of Maker Studios, in an interview with us offers three reasons for how that evolution happened:

On one side, there was some frustration in being the little brother in the context of the brand having two contracts when it comes to marketing: one with the creative agency and one with the media agency, where the media agency was seen as the poor relation and where the lead agency was always considered to be the creative agency. So there was a real drive to change that and wait for the right opportunity, and content marketing offered exactly that because it was a kind of 'white space' where rules could be rewritten and it wasn't so obvious who the lead agency was. So it opened up a space, where if you were opportunistic enough you could take the driving seat, coupled with insights and data becoming much more essential for making campaigns successful.

Second, as mentioned earlier, you cannot just rely on an iconic 30-second spot in content space, because developing longer-form content of multiple iterations requires very detailed audience insights and continuing to have your finger on the pulse in terms of measuring what is working for you. That has been invaluable for media agencies when it comes to making content a success.

The third variable has been the access to technology. Content marketing has proliferated so quickly as a result of the technology, which has been a driving force and effect for allowing for very quick progress, and this includes video technology or any other technology that media owners and tech companies have on the market. Because media agencies had access to media owners and publishers and were dealing with them on a daily basis, they have had access to the tech much quicker and have been able to work in partnership with publishers from day one on this, whether it was co-funded content or produced by the publisher and branded for the brand. Those three elements – in terms of being more opportunistic, having access to insights and data, and closer relationships with tech and publishers – have been the reasons for the media agencies driving content marketing to be ahead of the game.

Media planning and buying used to be fairly simple and based on a linear model with three key parts: *content* (broadly understood as all kind of forms placed in traditional media), *distribution* (media) and *audience* (viewers, readers, users). The group of producers and publishers was limited and strictly defined. But, as Izabela Derda, an academic and former Head of Entertainment at Havas, pointed out in our interview, the internet and digitalization of our world have created that 'white space' Castagno is talking about:

A relatively small media market (ads-engined) became an enormous universe with ads-free spaces. Not only did consumers get the power of choice and possibility to create their own media content, but platforms like Netflix have proven that media and platforms do not necessarily have to be under power of advertisers and be ad-supported to succeed on the market, as all their revenue comes from subscriptions.

It didn't help creative agencies that they found the new space, as well as Content, a bit threatening. Castagno observes:

The tradition of big TV ad has been very difficult to break, and the skill sets have been stuck in that old model. One of the reasons is that in content marketing insights become more relevant, and they have to be integrated with the data you have on consumers in order to make your stories more relevant. You cannot just rely on your gut feeling about 30 seconds that are going to be great no matter what the audience insight is. On the other side, for the media agencies I think it has been that moment of change that we have been waiting for, because until now we have been consigned to the number-crunching role within the chain where the creative agency would focus on creating the ad and here would be the data-people doing the data-crunching and focusing on the insights. However, with all that data and insight expertise the opportunity offered by content marketing has been huge for us because data has become much more valuable to help tell modular stories that are not just relevant to big groups of people, but also for individuals. Content marketing provides a bigger opportunity to think one on one and create modular content that is directed to niches and also at the individual level. This has definitely been seen as an opportunity by media agencies, hence all the major ones creating specialist content divisions that are now the fastest-growing part of them, including, among others, 'Story Lab' at Dentsu and 'Mediacom Beyond Advertising' at Mediacom.

Scott Donaton from Digitas is adamant that Content is both an opportunity and threat for the established agencies:

I feel the real threat is not to pay attention to it, because I think in many ways this is the future of marketing. Back to the point about labels and all of that, I am not sure there will always be a separate and specialist discipline, but as we move into a world where the audience will determine what, whether and where they will interact with any form of content, this approach of how I add value to people's lives rather than interrupt is going to be where all brands have to go, because I don't believe the interruptive mechanisms are going to be there, or be as efficient.

Obviously, there has been huge growth in things like TV upfronts despite declines in audiences, but at the same time I think the consumer has proved over and over again that they will skip advertising if they are given the opportunity, that they don't believe it adds value to their lives. I think a lot of reasons why brands even in the age of ad skipping and blocking still thought their place was safe was ultimately because the consumer would never want to pay for their own media experience and they liked that brands subsidized that experience. This is obviously still true and it becomes an economic split question, but more and more we are seeing Netflix, Amazon, Spotify premium and these other places where consumers are saying 'I will pay for content I couldn't get elsewhere, but sometimes I will pay a premium just to keep advertising out.' Not every consumer can afford to do that and I don't think we are at the point where the role of advertising subsidizing consumer experiences is going away, but I think every trend is showing you that audiences are going to be more and more in control. So I do think the answer is that brands have to figure out how what they want to say is worthy of someone's time, and adds value to their life, and is something that someone would choose to spend time with. Otherwise they are not going to get their message in front of people.

For Derda, all of this means that there is a new 'content context' in the modern media space:

Consumer journey is now increasingly content journey. Media journey is now content journey. Most of the branding today becomes 'data driven, content powered', as we used to say in Havas.

Grace Letley, Strategic Innovation Director at Vizeum, shares the sentiment:

The landscape has shifted significantly. In pre-digital media there were a finite number of places and spaces to be filled with advertising, be it radio sponsorship, six-sheet posters, 24x4 print placements or one of the 30-second spots on a handful of TV channels, for example. The introduction of digital media has changed all that. Every space is now a media space. Anyone can and everyone is creating, uploading and sharing content. Brands don't just compete with each other and the publishers for attention, they are competing with their audience's friends for attention. In this infinite stream of content, brands are fighting for a slice of consumers' finite attention, which forces advertisers to increasingly think not only about pushing messages out to consumers but instead ask what can pull them towards their brand through valued entertainment, information or utility.

In other words, these new dynamics of the media require that the approach is changing from 'campaign-led' to 'campaign-boosted'. There is an 'always on' base communications activity that is now boosted by engineered, traditional-campaign-like spikes for generating additional attention. In such a world of constant activity, more of the strategy and creative work is starting to move to the media-agency side as their business models are more flexible for charging for constant activity than a creative agency's one. Given the often quite snobbish reaction to data as a creative fuel by many advertising agencies, there is a threat that more of the conceptual thinking that is powered by data from numerous sources may also move outside of their realm. This data-powered approach is translating into a slightly different creative approach, slightly less likely to start with just one 'big idea' of the old, and more likely based on delivering tailored content to various audiences. Or, in Savic's words:

> We do not start with content formats. We start with people. Young people do not consume long-form content; they want short video created for smartphones. Older demos are still consumer long-form content on larger screens. Content and production models/monetization are customized by the audience.

The sparks with the creative agencies are already flying. In 2016, Justin Tindall, Chief Creative Officer of M&C Saatchi, complained in an article that the media agencies give creative agencies just 'a procession of buckets to fill' (Degun, 2016).

But for Castagno that also reflects some of the realities of the new media space:

> You can see this very much today in the programmatic world, everyone from creative agencies and creative backgrounds is cringing when they hear that word because it feels like a very mechanical way of dealing with media and very mechanical part of advertising, but what you can do with programmatic in terms of co-creating a format, and also timely delivery of that format, they are all dependent on deals that are done with publishers on a daily basis – that has been fundamental to content marketing at the day-to-day level. So is it being used to distribute big iconic 30-second ads,

yes, but programmatic also allows the distribution of modular content and everyday storytelling. Programmatic departments like Amnet have 10–20 people focusing on just the partnership element with publishers in terms of format creation and the development of those agreements and deals.

As if on cue, some of the world's largest advertisers seem to agree with all of the above. What amounted to a move that made creative agency people cover their mouths in shock, Unilever announced in October 2017 its intent to thoroughly overhaul its brand strategy by 2019, slashing its 3,000-strong global agency roster in half and reducing the number of ads it makes by 30 per cent! The new strategy, dubbed the '5Cs', has five revealing pillars: Consumers, Connect, Content, Community and Commerce (Gwynn, 2017). It is the wind that may push the new media agency Content-powered thinking further.

New roles for the media agency

The result of the above evolution is that some media agencies do not call themselves that any more. Some, Savic's for example, present themselves now as 'Content and Connections' agency. They are trying to be the bridge between brands and people; they are all about, what we call, the 'four rights': *the right content/message, to the right people, at the right places, in the right moments…* Tom Goodwin, EVP of Innovation at Zenith USA and one of the most followed global influencers in the industry, has posited in our conversation some outlines of a possible role for the future fully evolved media agency as exactly that kind of a bridge:

There are two parts to this. There is a huge role to represent the voice of the consumer and brand in that process of working with the content studios of media owners, because we know the topics that the audience is interested in along with examples of what we have done in the past that work, and other data about audience attributes and characteristics. This avoids commissioning work that has absolutely nothing to do with the brand whatsoever, and where the content is so generic that you could replace the brand with any other and therefore end up paying over the odds for what is effectively a banner ad. So on one hand there is a need to insert ourselves to ensure that what is created is useful for everyone, and by that I mean it has to serve the media owner, their readers and the brand. The second part is that you are measuring the right things, so not just reach and level of engagement but also levels of association, and attribution of sales uplift.

It could be argued that performing the role of the voice of the consumer could or should be conducted by a creative agency, but someone needs to do that and it is debatable about whether it is a role that creative agencies want to perform. That provides media agencies with an opportunity to do so instead and also because it involves a relationship with a media owner. When it comes to evaluation, there is a more obvious fit for the media agency because of our role in how media budget gets allocated on what, along with the data we have on why those decisions are being made.

Faris Yakob, one of the industry's leading consultants and authors, explains in our interview why creative agencies may not want to be that conduit:

Creative agencies don't want to do it because it is a planning, not a creative job. Agencies get briefed by a... brief. Creative directors don't particularly like that and creative agencies are largely structured around creatives. Also, as far as the research for the strategy goes, creative agencies don't really do it any more, they have outsourced it to research agencies or consultants.

For Derda, this process of 'insertion' means that Content cannot be defined any more just as a media form, as traditional advertising was, but that it has become a *process of exchange* between consumers, brands and a medium, with the media agency as a catalyst, or in Yakob's words, 'an enzyme' that makes this process possible (see Figure 5.1).

Last but not least, the new kind of media agencies – almost as a natural consequence of their evolution – should also be much more commerce-friendly to brands and help them turn the whole of the media eco-system into a commerce system, says Goodwin:

Generally speaking we have not been very imaginative when it comes to digital transformation. We take analogue devices and make smaller digital versions. But if we thought more imaginatively, we would realize that things could be bigger and more interesting. Part of this includes every digital screen that exists being a shoppable service, including those you pass when travelling on the underground or subway. If you think about every screen being the opening of the purchase funnel, and if you think about how technology can help move you through that purchase funnel more quickly, then there is an opportunity to think of commerce in a different way where you get this thin shoppable service everywhere. So ads on TV should be something you can talk to and buy the product directly, and even hover your phone over a print ad to buy what is on offer using Touch ID. Content has a part to play in this as it can be more interesting and engaging, so it will be interesting to see how shopability and content will work together.

Figure 5.1 Content as process

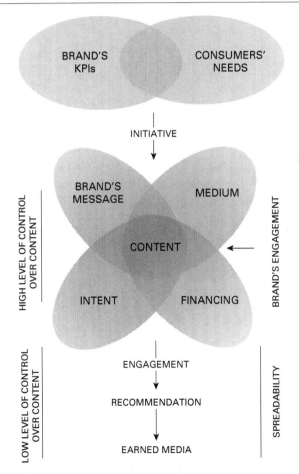

SOURCE used with kind permission (2017) of Izabela Derda

Impact of Content on the business model

The relentless diversification of revenue streams underfoot in the marketing services industry, as a response to the pressures and opportunities of the digital space, is probably most visible in the media-agency world. Savic is precise:

> In 2016, we had 26 different revenue streams in our agency. Content is just one of them. Nothing more, nothing less. Content has two opportunities: production (fees) and licensing (where content is produced not for a specific brand, but for a specific audience and it can be licensed to various brands). Investing in content creation is riskier than the traditional product set of a media agency, but has the potential to deliver higher revenue.

However, for some agencies – depending on the size, business history, legacy skills and personal styles of the top management – Content is potentially the main focus for driving new revenues. Derda sums it up as:

> Content marketing can be now the foundation of driving business growth and delivering a standalone source of revenue. It is no longer a marketing model, it is a business model. It has forced media agencies to restructure internally to be able to make best usage of the redefined relationships with media outlets and flood of data.

CASE STUDY   Dentsu

Japan's Dentsu is often quoted as a prime example of how a once-traditional ad agency is reinventing itself around Content-based intellectual property (IP) approaches.

First, the agency works with film studios both in Japan and in Hollywood in the early stages of film development as an investor. Both *Les Miserables* and *Jurassic World* benefitted from its investment. Second, the agency is active in developing TV content, both regular and one-off, with various approaches to monetizing it. In addition, it is involved in financing and creating various music industry and live event tie-ups, artist development, exhibitions, musicals and other entertainment products.

Finally, Dentsu is also famous for its various animated characters, many of them wildly popular in Japan, such as Mameshiba. These characters are then deployed, on a licensing base, to various clients (see Dentsu, 2017).

Castagno agrees with Derda that this is a welcome opportunity to re-engineer the way the business was done in almost every aspect: skill sets, internal organization, ways of charging clients and evaluating efforts:

It has been a great opportunity for agencies to get a little bit out of the loop of media becoming a commodity in this procurement-led world where we all race to the bottom. That is because of the normal ways of dealing with media, which are commission-based, and those do not apply in the content world. That helps to open conversations that are based more around talent and the skills that they provide, and moving away from that race – especially for those agencies that have been able to leverage content marketing as a new offer to clients.

In terms of skill sets and how you would set up an agency today, considering all the big competition out there for creative talent – not only from start-ups, content studios, tech companies, the likes of Facebook and Google – we have learnt that it is less important to have talent that is full-time and more important to have a flexible environment where you work on an ad hoc basis on more project-based collaborations of around three to six months. People are more focused because projects are fresh, and because you get the best talent for the task you have at hand. With media, you needed media experts, but that skill set was pretty much the same whatever brand you worked on, whereas in Content you need specific experts depending on the topic you are working on. From a revenue perspective it has moved us away from the commission-based model and put much more emphasis on the actual talent and the skill sets they provide to make sure the clients actually value the work the agency can do for them from a strategic perspective.

This heightened business edge, data expertise and technical savvy, internally and externally, means that digitalized media agencies are increasingly taking the role of a business partner responsible for the end-conversion of a digital user into a brand consumer. New media agencies often pride themselves for 'trackability' and 'attribution' chops they can bring to the table. Derda sees in this a specific role for Content too:

> The 'system' of media planning and buying became very spread, complex and fragmented. Buying high-reach media with good affinity does not work any longer. As the digital world became 'trackable', agencies need to keep in mind more of brand's end key performance indicators (KPIs) (eg sales), so use the data and technology to target not broad audience, but the audience that will convert to sales. Agencies are becoming close partners to brands – they help understand audiences, their habits (not only in the media sphere) and what makes them tick. So (in a perfect world) the content that is delivered to them does not intrude and doesn't turn them off, but makes them want more and can elevate brands to the sphere of 'meaningfulness'.

Creative and media agencies as agents for contextualizing choice

The last word in Derda's quote, derived from Havas's flagship research into how brands can become 'meaningful' for consumers (Havas, 2017), is a potent one and opens up one of the key roles for Content thinking today. It does not negate the existence of advertising, but builds on it and works alongside it. That role is in how Content can create 'context' for consumer choice, how it may frame it.

Although we will talk about context in more detail in Chapter 6, dedicated to the role of Content across the customer journey, here are some initial thoughts on how more nimble media agencies may use this opportunity to also make their mark. Sasha Savic summarizes the challenge neatly:

> A brand's success today is less about spend and more about how relevant it is to consumers and how engaging its story is. Some of the most successful brands of our time never spent more than their competitors; they just expressed their purpose in a more human way through content, experience and good old storytelling. Given the continuing fragmentation

of media and competition for consumer attention, the need for more differentiated stories will continue. Given that we are marching into a world where an algorithm will know when to offer us a product that we need, want and are willing to pay for, your question begs a much larger one: what, if anything, will be the role of brands in the future?

One possible answer to that question may be linked to time. In one of our previous interviews with Ogilvy UK's Vice Chairman Rory Sutherland, he pointed out that there are some problems that can be solved only by long-form communication (Kirby, 2014). He cited QVC, the televised home shopping network, as an unfashionable example of how a fortune has been made out of this discovery – there are things that you could never sell in 30 seconds, but in 20 minutes. For Sutherland, the problem that advertising is trying to solve may not be simply to increase sales, or even increase saleability, but to reduce 'unsaleability' – 'to overcome those hurdles to purchase that are preventing people from confidently buying something whose ownership would ultimately justify the cost'. As with QVC, he thinks that sometimes this requires more than a six-word headline, or a 30-second spiel:

> Take British Airways (BA) India 'Go further to get closer' film (2014). You can't achieve that in 30 seconds – and it was doubly effective for me because I watched it on a BA flight immediately before the film *The Lunchbox*. But, equally, include an ad my old boss Drayton Bird wrote for the first LCD digital watch for sale in the UK in which, over 900 words, he basically wrote – in a double-page spread – the complete instruction manual for the watch and all its features. By the time you had finished reading the ad, you knew how to use the watch, so you felt silly not owning it.

Interestingly, Tom Goodwin has mentioned something along similar lines when he was elaborating on the need for the new commercial chops that media agencies should start developing. His example was that an integrated 'omnichannel' retailer such as Argos could become a Content commerce brand where their catalogue becomes more of a magazine than just a dry directory of products. This kind of creative approach, not necessarily based on the traditional 'big idea' but more on the kind of thinking mastered by publishers, is clearly within the grasp of the media agencies.

Another way to answer Savic's question above is by applying a paradox – and a little of the, often impenetrable, new French philosophy of the Michel Foucault kind: *make brands more culturally relevant by making brand communications less brand-focused*. Until recently, it would be considered pure nonsense. But in the media environment where scarcity of attention is the rule and where an increasing number of consumers are blocking 'ads as usual', it seems that brands can do better if they focus on becoming a relevant part of their audiences' cultural repertoire, not just purveyors of hardcore 'buy' messages. In other words, brands have to become less narcissistic, less vain, less intrusive, as vividly portrayed in the quote by David Beebe, former VP, Global Creative and Content Marketing, and Founder, Marriott Content Studio (2015):

> Content marketing is like a first date. If you only talk about yourself, there won't be a second one.

This approach was famously outlined by Adam Arvidsson in his book *Brands: Meaning and value in media culture* (2006):

> Brand management is not a disciplinary practice. It does not seek to impose a certain structure of tastes or desires, not even a certain manner of relating to goods… Rather, brand management works by enabling or empowering the freedom of consumers so that it is likely to evolve in particular directions. In its present form, brand management recognizes the autonomy of consumers. It aims at providing an environment, an ambience, which anticipates and programmes the agency of consumers. Brand management says not 'You Must!' It says 'You May!'

The role of data and media agencies in creating 'empathic media'

The digital world is trackable. Thanks to data we are able to follow an entire consumer's path: from seeing the ad or product for the very first time, through all digital touchpoints, to an e-commerce visit. We know how long consumers spend on a particular site or watching content. The trick is to use that data well. Sadly, it seems not many brands are there yet. Proprietary global Havas research 'Meaningful Brands' indicates that if 74 per cent of brands disappeared tomorrow, no one would care (2017). It is quite powerful, if we understand that this is about 300,000 people globally, giving their opinion on 1,500 brands in 33 countries. The data is even more shocking if we take a look at developed markets: 60 per cent of consumers think that content coming from brands is of poor quality or irrelevant. As the title of this book advises, **content marketing must be strategic**. According to the research, 84 per cent of consumers today expect to receive brand content with four strong sides:

Four strong sides of branded content

- Entertains.
- Tells stories.
- Provides solutions.
- Creates experiences and events.

In other words, the consumers would like brands, and their media choices, to be more – what Prof. McStay names in Chapter 11 – 'empathic'. None of this is possible at scale and, often, in an 'always on' manner, without utilizing wisely the vast universe of data signals we leave behind as we pursue our needs and wants in the endless digital space.

We now know that such real-time cleverness is going to be nigh impossible without the further deployment of artificial intelligence (AI) in those algorithms. The first signs of that tide are already lapping at the feet of the media agency's business as usual. As widely reported in the trade press in 2017, the lingerie brand Cosabella had deployed an AI 'media planner' named 'Albert', by a company Adgorythms, with spectacular results in optimizing the client's media budget, response and conversion rates (Martin, 2017). A similar exercise was repeated in late 2017 in the Philippines with the Dole Seasons brand, with the year-on-year increase in sales by 87 per cent (Pathak, 2017). It is very debatable whether we can talk about 'empathy' here yet, at least in the sense the creative agencies would like to. But business results based on personal relevance to consumers speak for themselves.

The last frontier in creating empathic media and in defining the media agency of the future is the impact AI may have on the definition of the very words 'media' or 'interface'. Probably the biggest question for both media and creative agencies – and, admittedly for brands and their whole agency eco-system – is: when clever voice becomes THE interface, how are we going to ensure we still have the attention of the consumer, if the access is supervised by an intelligent virtual assistant? How do we optimize for the age of targeting marketing to the machine, not to the actual user – and whether the machines will have their own 'cognitive biases' that could be gamed? Data signals that consumers leave behind like breadcrumbs are certainly going to be even more important, but this has strong ethical implications.

There may be another, more positive development for good storytellers: even in the 'stronger' AI age, people are still going to seek time-killing fun, transformational experiences, knowledge and skills. They will still watch films and videos. They will laugh and cry. That will certainly include branded content, but it seems more likely that one of the ways to bypass the AI filter could be to actually make the consumer deliberately tell it to go and fetch something specific. That something will, therefore, have to be very good, very famous, or recommended by a lot of people we trust in order to get registered on our attention radar. In other words, it has to have *pull*. It may spell the end of advertising as we know it and bring about new and unexpected mergers of disciplines such as advertising, entertainment, PR and CRM; 'cultural context', planned across the customer journey. The following chapters will explore some of those potential scenarios, but no one, yet, knows exactly how they will pan out. That is why, for media agencies especially, but not exclusively, the quote by Alan Kay, who, again, quoted the Hungarian scientist Dennis Gabor, may be very apt: 'The best way to predict the future is to invent it.'

We have made the important client and publisher perspectives freely available as online chapters, as a flavour of the extensive contributions made by those we interviewed for this book. It helped (re)shape our thinking and conclusions (see Acknowledgments for full list). You can read these at the following URL: **www.koganpage.com/strategic-content-marketing**.

References

The section about branded content history is based on the fragment of the chapter 'The TV is dead, long live the TV!', 'Advertising in the post-network era: branded content – case study', PhD dissertation, Izabela Derda, University of Social Sciences and Humanities, Warsaw, Poland, 2017

AdAge (2003) [accessed 30 December 2017] Kraft Foods [Online] adage.com/article/adage-encyclopedia/kraft-foods/98739/

Arvidsson, A (2006) *Brands: Meaning and value in media culture*, Routledge, London

Beebe, D (2015) [accessed 30 December 2017] Why Content Marketing Is Like Dating, *LinkedIn*, 27 April [Online] linkedin.com/pulse/why-content-marketing-like-dating-david-beebe/

British Airways (2014) [accessed 30 December 2017] British Airways India – Go Further to Get Closer [Online] youtu.be/ixbLMsVlpes

Carter, B (2003) Skipping ads? TV gets ready to fight back, *The New York Times*, 10 January

Degun, G (2016) [accessed 30 December 2017] Transparency Concerns Could Lead to Clients Hiring Separate Planning and Buying Shops, *Campaign*, 14 June [Online] campaignlive.co.uk/article/brands-split-media-planning-buying/1398068

Dentsu (2017) [accessed 30 December 2017] Entertainment Content: Japan Is Brimming with Entertainment [Online] dentsu.com/business/japan/contents/entertainment.html

Godzic, W (ed) (2010), *Media Audiowizualne: Podrecznik Akademicki*, Wydawnictwa Akademickie I Profesjonalne, Warsaw

Gwynn, S (2017) [accessed 30 December 2017] Unilever's '5C' Strategy Heralds 'Functional' Shift in Marketing, *Campaign*, 9 October [Online] campaignlive.co.uk/article/unilevers-5c-strategy-heralds-functional-shift-marketing/1446647

Harmon, J (2001) *The Great Radio Heroes*, McFarland & Company, Jefferson

Havas (2017) [accessed 30 December 2017] Meaningful Brands [Online] meaningful-brands.com

Kirby, J (2014) [accessed 30 December 2017] Rory Sutherland on Long-Form Branded Content (Blog), *BOBCM*, 20 August [Online] bobcm.net/2014/08/20/rory-sutherland-on-long-form-branded-content/

Lehu, J-M (2007) *Branded Entertainment: Product placement and branded content in the entertainment business*, Kogan Page, London

Lotz, A D (2007) *The Television Will Be Revolutionized*, New York University Press, New York

Martin, C (2017) [accessed 30 December 2017] Cosabella Lingerie Balances AI With Humans, *MediaPost*, 24 September [Online] mediapost.com/publications/article/307725/cosabella-lingerie-balances-ai-with-humans.html

Newell, J, Salmon C T and Chang S (2006) The hidden history of product placement, *Journal of Broadcasting & Electronic Media*, 50 (4), pp 575–94

Pathak, S (2017) [accessed 30 December 2017] Who Needs Media Planners When a Tireless Robot Named Albert Can Do the Job? *Digiday*, 9 May [Online] digiday.com/marketing/needs-media-planners-tireless-robot-named-albert-can-job

Pondillo, R J (2003) Censorship in a 'golden age': postwar television and America's first network censor – NBC's Stockton Helffrich, unpublished doctoral dissertation, University of Wisconsin, Madison

Utley, G (2000) *You Should Have Been Here Yesterday: A life in television news*, PublicAffairs, New York

PART THREE
Data, new formats and the role of Content in the consumer journey

Content distribution and its role in the consumer journey

In March 1996, it was none other than Bill Gates who declared that 'content is King' (1996). The internet as we know it today – social, collaborative, mobile and fast – was just a glimmer in the futurists' eyes and it would take another three years for the name that introduced it to the masses – Web 2.0 – to be coined (Wikipedia, 2017).

For the publishers, gaming companies, YouTube stars and a very selected band of traditional brands, it turned out to be true. Not so much for the rest of the brand and advertising community, deep into copying old interruption formats from print and TV into the new digital space. For them, something else was always key: placement. It took more than a decade for the new clarification of this interesting dynamic. In 2012, the now equally widely famous Gary Vaynerchuk observed that 'if content is King, than context is God' (Faeth, 2012). The arms race in metaphors has not abated since then, adding various new versions: about how context is actually King Kong (Dzamic, 2016), or, according to some, even the Queen (Chan, 2015) – and she's wearing the pants!

It's a simple, yet often neglected message: a great piece of content offered to a wrong consumer, put in a wrong place or at the wrong time, making it irrelevant or annoying, will fail; a creatively decent, not necessarily revolutionary, unit of content in the right context may feel like THE answer to the consumer's need. In other words, creativity – in whatever form – should be matched with great contextual placement in order to be efficient and effective. Content is like water, to quote Josh Clark's maxim from 2011 (inspired by none other than Bruce Lee): it flows across the whole of the customer journey (Myers, 2011). As Izabela Derda echoed in Chapter 5, customer journey is now Content journey.

Figure 6.1 Context across the customer journey © Brian Solis

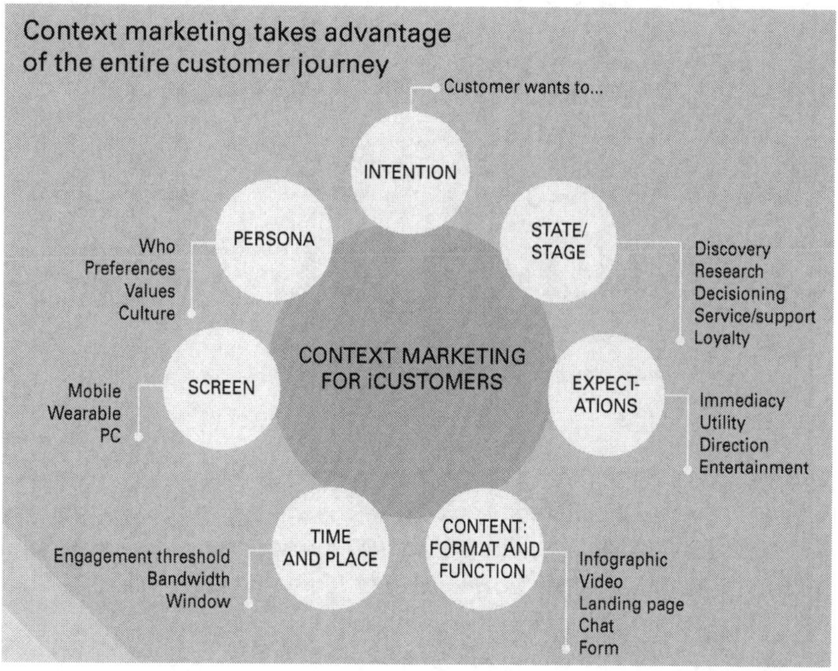

Context marketing takes advantage of the entire customer journey

Customer wants to...

INTENTION

PERSONA
Who
Preferences
Values
Culture

STATE/ STAGE
Discovery
Research
Decisioning
Service/support
Loyalty

CONTEXT MARKETING FOR iCUSTOMERS

SCREEN
Mobile
Wearable
PC

EXPECT-ATIONS
Immediacy
Utility
Direction
Entertainment

TIME AND PLACE
Engagement threshold
Bandwidth
Window

CONTENT: FORMAT AND FUNCTION
Infographic
Video
Landing page
Chat
Form

SOURCE used with kind permission of Brian Solis, www.briansolis.com (2016)

What does that mean in practice? Predominantly that Content can now be used for increasing the impact of all the key elements of the journey, from acquisition to winback activities, and everything in between. It mitigates the tendency, as evidenced in various places in the book, to pit Content against only advertising. That simply is not true. The role of Content is much broader. It now has the chance, if applied correctly and with integrity, to reach new heights of imagination, precision and relevance.

But, what is context? A well-known consultant and author Brian Solis has schematized the elements of context across the customer journey, as shown in Figure 6.1 above.

CASE STUDY TUI contextual content – post-booking

Once a traveller has booked, TUI – one of the world's leading travel operators – activates a sophisticated sequence of messages full of useful and relevant content. It includes details about where to check in at the departing airport, how to enhance the in-cabin experience, destination information such as temperature and cultural events at the time of visiting, additional services that may be useful such as car hire and excursions, money, visa and other information. All of it is packed into a personalized microsite as the one-stop hub for the trip. The system uses millions of variations of various content sources and customer data to power a very effective approach.

Gary Vaynerchuck (2016) helpfully offers three ways for making context the God, echoing principles of designing for 'time and place' from Chapter 2:

1 Respect the platform and the psychology of the audience that spends time there.

2 Avoid interrupting the experience the audience wants to have on a platform: 'Meet consumers in their day in authentic ways.'

3 Be consistent and self-aware, which means having a consistent story, tonality and personality.

Knowing your purpose as a company, as discussed in Chapter 3, will help too.

In his interview with us, Scott Donaton from Digitas stresses this critical need to understand the role of Content across the journey:

I think in terms of return on investment (ROI) for brands, a lot of the time we are asked what is content best at and where does it deliver the best value to brands. Is it awareness, is it perception, is it intent, is it loyalty? I think what we are finding is that it is not the right way to look at that question. We are actually finding that custom content can outperform traditional advertising at almost any point along the customer decision journey. So, it is better to think about what you are trying to accomplish and once you have established that KPI then it is going to change the kind of content you create and how you distribute it. I think it is less about how you get a return on content and what it is best at, and more about what are you trying to achieve and then what kind of content you create and how you distribute it.

Just as another thread on this, it doesn't have to be content versus advertising, or content versus product messaging. To go back to the people-first versus brand-first, I still believe that if you are driving people to

> look at a video that is people-first rather than something more traditional, it doesn't mean you don't provide the hooks to go further into the information, to take actions, etc. So I think it is going to be about how this comes together in one eco-system, rather than content is better than advertising.

Ana Andjelic of Fashion Tech Lab, and a former Havas strategist, shares a similar sentiment in our conversation:

> Content design needs to start from the entire service and experience that a brand delivers, rather than from a single channel or device. Content mix should be driven by the architecture of the customer journey through this service and experience, which links individual interactions in a way that creates new value for an end customer. This value-adding journey becomes central to the way customers experience a brand and its products. Currently, campaign-centred media buys favour brand messages instead of content that creates and delivers value. It is hard to change this media planning rhythm. Brands are big and change is expensive. But in the long run, the costliest thing imaginable may turn out to be focusing on media, not customers.

The concept of consumer or customer 'journey' is not new. From E. St. Elmo Lewis who devised AIDA in 1898, through McKinsey's 'spiral' (Court *et al*, 2009), to MillwardBrown's 'predisposition' and 'heuristics' decision path (Staplehurst, 2016), brands, consultancies and agencies have been trying to bottle that particular magic that happens on the path to purchase and beyond.

In that effort, we have started moving from a largely linear journey (Acquire > Convert > Retain > Win back) to the already mentioned Google's 'Moments that Matter' (MTMs) paradigm (Gevelber, 2015). Brands should talk to their prospects and consumers all the time, everywhere, in exactly the moments where they reveal intent, need or desire, not just in neatly composed campaign windows. As the new saying goes, 'Every time is now primetime.' This creates several philosophical, business and organizational challenges for the main industry players, as discussed in various parts of this book.

Main conceptual and organizational challenges with context

CRM is merging with advertising – and is now everyone's game

CRM used to be, historically, just about two things: data and platforms. However, both were internally looking and *ours* (owned). It is all about control. This picture is now becoming too simplistic and, increasingly, not a full reflection of the reality. Consumers now leave a vast amount of data 'signals' behind them in the digital space and those signals could be picked up, analysed and acted upon by clever marketers. We now may know that someone is our customer, or in the conversion phase, even if they are on other people's digital properties. In which case, we may use programmatic advertising as an extension of CRM – converting, upselling, cross-selling and stimulating relationships – wherever they are. This is also one of the reasons for the rise of the new super-paradigm – Customer Experience Management (CXM/CEM) – a holistic way, when executed well, of looking at all the key touchpoints in the customer journey. This is, sadly, still more an attempt than the rule, as explored in detail in the next chapter.

There is another challenge. As we have seen in Chapter 4, the industry is binarily divided: advertising agencies focused on the top of the 'funnel', while various integrated and specialist agencies diligently beavered away on the rest. With the more 'liquid' nature of today's consumers' purchase behaviour, that does not really work any more, particularly from the point of view of Content. It is driving a new kind of integration: not just a new way to do advertising, but also a new way to do CRM. Looked at through the Content lens, nothing now stops advertising agencies, media agencies, management consultancies, publishers, various production companies and all kinds of specialists from credibly pitching for Content-based solutions across the whole, or just part, of the customer journey. CRM has become everyone's game. If you have ever wondered why Accenture bought Karmarama and its associated integrated agency Crayon, look at this space.

Customer funnel is not dead – but belongs to consumers

The 'funnel' is one of the perennial controversies in the industry. Many claim that the old workhorse is on its last legs, mostly due to the rise of MTMs. Professor Mark Ritson disagrees:

The funnel is being used ever more and ever better in many organizations, as it has become more important than ever in planning. The beauty of it is that you don't have to separate one part of it against the other part because it is by definition a journey. The real problem is that digital marketing is focusing exclusively on the middle to bottom end of it because that is the bit it can attribute and that is the bit it targets. What is missed is the context that the funnel has that flowing movement and that one needs to achieve the first bits in order to move to the next. We have seen this materializing in companies who have done a good job with digital communications and then discovered that their numbers are rapidly diminishing in terms of performance and whatever other attribution metrics they have because, as the IPA has nicely demonstrated, **it's fantastic to use your robot to pick the fruits efficiently, but if you're not feeding your tree at the top of the funnel eventually the fruit starts to disappear**.

The whole point of customer experience (CX) comes down to market orientation: **it's not what the company thinks or does, it's what the consumer goes through**! Again, it is replete in many organizations: they all have a digital sales funnel; but there isn't a digital sales funnel, there's just customer experience and then there are various tactical tools that we can use, but the funnel itself and the customer journey is a customer's journey and it has nothing to do with the company.

The tactics we use in order to move that customer in our direction is a very interesting, but very late-in-the-day question; the first question is 'where do we want to focus our resources strategically on that journey irrespective of the tool or device?' I do agree that CX is increasingly important but I'm also seeing first-hand that it is again something that is not rapidly associated with marketing because we tend to see it as purely the comms thing. If NPS is not playing a role in the funnel then something has gone horribly wrong. It is the ideal tool to use at the back end of it to see what is going on, almost as the final catch. CX seems to be spinning into its own little tribe with its language and systems and not the spine of marketing planning as it used to be – which again does not bode well for marketing down the track. One of the great ironies is that the funnel has been derided in the last five or six years because it is all changing and it is all done in real time, but that is a classic error because the funnel still exists and what may be changing is the tactics of how we move the consumer through the funnel, digitally or otherwise. Just don't use the generic one from some textbook, use your own based on the category you're in where different segments have different funnels and different numbers!

Intent trumps identity; immediacy trumps loyalty

In this new 'fluid' space, as thoroughly understood by Google and Facebook, some new thinking helps (Gevelber, 2015). Take the staple of marketing, 'segments' or 'personas', used for decades to target advertising and CRM, as well as website build projects. They have not gone away fully yet, but it is increasingly recognized that in the fast-moving digital world **intent** is often becoming a stronger currency than identity. This trend is known as 'post-demographic' marketing (Trendwatching, 2017). Given the myriad ways and touchpoints consumers have during the day, or within a purchase cycle, being 'there' becomes critical. What is the use of knowing that your typical consumer for a luxury car is a 50+, mostly male, a senior manager or a well-off 'empty nester', who lives in suburbs and prefers cruising holidays and playing golf – if they just bought that car a month ago? Identity could be used for creating the tonality of the message (eg classical music or talking about how many golf clubs can fit in the boot), but the timing and context, being there when it counts, is becoming critical. In the thought-provoking statement by the AI and contextual marketing agency Sentiance: 'There's no such thing as a customer segment, there's only customer context' (Vandendooren, 2016).

It is not a huge leap of imagination to make that resonate with Professor Byron Sharp's assertion that in any particular category, within the period of measurement, about half of the consumers are in the switching mode (2010). If this is true, does that mean that the whole of marketing can now be divided into only two parts: talking to switchers (immediacy) and talking to your own customers (longer term)? This means it would be critical to distinguish between the two. Mass marketing is not dead, just needs to become smarter.

Organizing for the 'fluid' Content experience is not easy

These new ways are now widely discussed, but doing something about it in practice is still difficult. Legacy business models, organizational structures, operational siloes, cultures of compartmentalized skill sets – it is the whole 'muscle memory' and the need to move at different speeds that Mark Runacus from Karmarama talked about in Chapter 4. However, our experience tells us that there is a slow, but noticeable movement towards more conceptual and operational unification based on the concept of the customer journey as the 'glue', internally and externally. Customer journey

(CJ, in the industry parlance) thus becomes, particularly on the client side, one of the key factors in achieving digital transformation, more agile ways of working and financial gains.

So, in what ways does Content play a role across the customer journey, from acquisition to winback?

Content as advertising

Again, Google's 3H framework comes in handy. In it, Content could fulfil its full Empathic Utility (EU) role: emotionally engaging people (Hero) and providing them with what they want in that moment (Help).

CASE STUDY   Unibet – passion points as the route to success

The Grand Prix at the DMA Awards in 2016 was this Content-based approach seizing the tent-pole moment of the Euro 2016 tournament. Punters were targeted based on their interests in specific games. The campaign strategy, counter-intuitively, played on helping them win through a better understanding of the basic elements of the game such as possessions versus kicks, or whether weather conditions may favour particular teams. Instead of dry statistics, the brand partnered with YouTube stars S2freestylers to perform a six-part series of entertaining experiments around the specific game conditions, supported by experts such as ex-players and managers. For the brand, ethical questions aside, it was also a clever ploy to overcome restrictions on gambling advertising in some countries through creating buzz and the content Hub in social media and on YouTube (DMA, 2016a).

It would come as a surprise to some that one of the most ubiquitous advertising formats around, AdWords, is also perceived as Content. That is the view of Omaid Hiwaizi, Global Head of Experience Strategy at Blippar and a veteran of several prominent integrated agencies, in our conversation:

Content may be a better promise if we look at the interruption model of the old; if we look at AdWords, it is Content because of the quality score that Google applies. It is an ad unit, but no one sees it as an ad unit, not even advertisers themselves. It is so well targeted and people click on them happily because they fulfil that specific need, as Google has the privilege to know what someone is curious about at that particular moment, and the advertisers have the opportunity to fulfil that need. It is the mindset of Content. It doesn't mean to say that it cannot be broadcast, and AdWords are in some ways broadcast, but because it is so well targeted they are not seeking to distract you from what you are interested in, they are seeking to help you with that.

Programmatic is, of course, the word of the moment, sitting firmly in this particular paradigm. Creative agencies hate it because it does not allow them to really stretch their wings. Crude, templated ads, where the machines contextually change the background image, headline, copy and offer based on the consumer intent are a far cry from the polished storytelling master-pieces that creative agencies are known for.

Also, for Bob Hoffman of *Ad Contrarian* fame, programmatic has become almost a dirty word. Fraud, waste, public annoyance and the issues of brand safety and transparency are rife and the big clients have now started shaking things up, to the embarrassment of the industry (2017).

However, some of the recent award-winning campaigns, such as the one for *The Economist* (DMA, 2016b), point out the new ways of thinking about how programmatic can evolve to cover both sides of Empathic Utility. For *The Economist*, programmatic was used across the spectrum, including the social networks, to contextually target the millennials who were not consid-ering the venerable magazine as their source of information about the world. Ads were matched to the content delivered at the destination and the free relevant content was the key draw. The campaign has generated more than 50,000 variants, an excellent ROI, long-term subscription value – and awards.

Another often-quoted example, 'Romeo Reboot' for Axe/Lynx deodor-ant, comes from Brazil and is, still, a rare experiment (Neff, 2015). Programmatic was here redefined as 'dynamic video', an approach that was not new on a website, but is in the ad network space. Consumer signals were grouped into several profiles based on interests and then six of the scenes ('vignettes') in the retelling of the celebrated Shakespeare's story were automatically replaced to create a version of the branded film that will best resonate with those consumer interests. So, a sci-fi fan who listens to heavy metal or hip-hop will get a different version of the story than someone who loves romance and prefers Celine Dion. The approach allowed a claimed total of about 100,000 variants – but the results and eventual improvements on the business as usual, at the time of writing, are still to be revealed.

Ultimately, the bone of contention that the creative side of the industry has with programmatic may be in that it is difficult to see their role in it. It is, deep down, the question not just of business models, but optics. It may even be the matter of *fame* and the ways to earn it. This is why we believe that with changing the optics, and the cleaning up of bad practices in the space, the creative teams may find a new lease of life in programmatic, even on the utility part of the spectrum.

If Hero content is like a Hollywood blockbuster kind of fame, Help could be like the BBC documentary kind of fame, if executed well. And with Hub, it is all about packaging Content into an episodic form, echoing what HBO does with its series. There are opportunities for the smart brands and agencies to become the BBCs and the HBOs of their respective categories, across the customer journey, if they deploy the technology to its full empathic, customer-centric advantage. In that sense, what we used to know as 'advertising' has a chance to transform into a new, Reithian, form of 'inform, educate and entertain', which, strangely, quite reflects the structure of content one can find on YouTube...

The role of Content in search

Although Intent Utility addresses a big part of this dimension, there are a few specifics that we want briefly to mention here.

For many industry experts, Content and SEO are two sides of the same coin. It was probably best encapsulated in one blog post by a popular social media and SEO blogger Neil Patel (2015). He compares it with a conversation between two people: SEO makes demands, Content fulfils those demands. There is no such thing as SEO without backing content. SEO demands keywords, Content uses and allows for keywords and phrases that people actually search for. SEO demands linkbacks, Content introduces linkbacks, particularly if it is good and gets connections from domains that give it more 'link juice'. Finally, says Patel, SEO demands consistent output and good Content is all about consistently producing relevant and fresh content that resonates with what people want. In all of this, Patel is keen to point out that it is the depth and quality of Content that matters (and to Google), not the thin, shallow 'stuff' crammed with keywords for maximum optimization.

Today, a video, a map, an infographic, a guide, a list or a presentation, may often be what consumers get in search results and what they need. One of the most mentioned Content-based SEO case studies around is again Unilever's 'All Things Hair' on YouTube (Shorty Awards, 2015). It deployed all three 'Cs' of Content generation to maintain quality, credibility, diversity and reach:

- **Creation** – content produced by the brand itself, on a particular topic.
- **Collaboration** – content created in collaboration with some leading YouTube stars in that category.
- **Curation** – existing content by the YouTube creators that was 'imported' into the brand channel.

The role of Content in conversion

If advertising – or whatever unit of communication that brought the consumer into the brand's 'gravitational field' – has harvested consumer attention, it is in the phase of conversion that this investment is lost or realized. It could be lightning-short, where the initial attention-allocating action leads to the checkout; or longer, where the same action ends up in the lead-generation pool, to be followed up with another message or a sequence trying to generate a sale. In this step, where the consumer may show a degree of 'warmth' towards the purchase or data capture, a spot-on piece of content can have three roles:

Roles for Content in conversion

1 Nudge a brand on to the consideration list during the phase of 'active consideration' (to borrow the phrase from the McKinsey's model).

2 Turn a browser into a prospect by revealing to a brand a deeper piece of contactable data.

3 Give additional reasons to close the sale against the competitors.

In many categories, it is the relevant and, often, personalized detail that counts. Three prominent marketing concepts, as set out below, may be considered as the main fields of activity for the role of Content in conversion: *shopper marketing, conversion rate optimization* and *value exchanges*.

Shopper marketing

This is one of the hottest new areas of marketing today. It is intrinsically linked to the concepts of customer journey and 'path to purchase'. Omaid Hiwaizi is a big believer in the role of Content in this phase:

First of all, shopper marketing is about understanding how people buy, it is not about interrupting people to sell things to them. The insights are based on what the shopper wants, not what the brand wants. The trigger is usually a need, as opposed to 'I saw a TV ad'. In that context, shopper marketing is about helping them understand that need and then help them navigate to the product or service solution for that need. 'What do I need?' 'Where do I get it from?' 'How do I choose?' Well-placed content is the answer to all of these. In the cosmetics category, for example, when you stand in front of the shelf there is a lot of category complexity about what to choose, what looks you can get and so on, and that is why a lot of brands employ people to stand there to help customers, at the moment when they are ready to purchase, to make the product selection. My view is that this is the content play. It is about the brand or a retailer having the right content at a key moment. And that is shopper marketing. It is typically not what advertising agencies make. We are talking beyond advertising and the longer version of the TV ad; Content could be 'Which of these three cough sweets will help me with my particular cough?' I think that the default conversation about Content comes from people who are not traditional copywriters, or are filmmakers, and the issue with advertising agencies is that great content in these contexts is not about telling the brand story, it is about the brand helping the shopper.

CASE STUDY   Max Factor – 'Make-up Artist in Your Pocket'

A Blippar project where customers can scan, using the Blippar AR app, any of 500 stock-keeping units (SKUs) at the shelf to get information to help them choose the right product. They can see the 'before' and 'after' photos, customer reviews and professional make-up tips, different colour palettes and similar, all for the product they scanned. They can even purchase through the phone, if that is a preference. Then, they can scan again at home to get help from an expert in how to apply the product and buy another one (Blippar, 2016).

Hiwaizi also warns that in this space we may get used to measuring things differently:

> People are increasingly making decisions to buy stuff based on content they encounter: recommendations from a friend, googling a random blog, or it could be an ad. Brands are largely not involved in making most of that content at the moment, but they could be – creating and placing it using various techniques. Whether it be AR, brand packaging, ads, or other brand platforms... just make sure it is visible at moments when people need it. Native advertising is an interesting middle area, a half-way house, but only if the KPIs move from brand advertising metrics into shopper marketing: from measuring brand equity and unprompted awareness (a cultural sticky point in the category, a default when the category is entered) to more shopper-marketing KPIs such as navigating value and complexity barriers once people are engaged in the category; it is more about behaviour than recall. It also impacts on what we should test based on those KPIs, for example A/B tests for Content interventions in a store such as walkaway rates, conversion rates, weight of purchase and similar.

Conversion (rate) optimization (CRO)

Another hot area and a huge moneymaker for brands who are paying attention to it. It could be defined, in a nutshell, as a systematic approach for trying to increase the rate of visitors to a website (or another transactional digital destination) who are converted to buyers. It is a sort of the digital equivalent of shopper marketing.

Testing different variables for maximum optimization is one of the staple approaches of CRO. Content often plays a prominent role in this, for example by changing the page assets to correspond to the consumer profile or intent, or by offering a unit of content as a 'value exchange' for a consumer action that is valuable to the brand.

Many categories sell products and services with complex features and any additional help in the transactional space may sway the decision towards those helping us make better choices. Buyer's guides to everything from TVs to washing machines are such examples. Tutorial videos, e-books, podcasts, white papers and infographics are others. Amazon, TripAdvisor and a few others really got it very early on when they introduced one of the most powerful forms of content as an additional help in evaluating products (although not without initial validation hiccups): customer reviews – other people's opinions as free, self-generated, influential content...

CASE STUDY   Lowe's and IKEA YouTube playlists

Lowe's is one of the largest US DIY chains (Lowe's, 2017). IKEA is a global phenomenon (IKEA, 2017). Both brands have understood that YouTube is the place billions of people flock to for answers about DIY or home furnishing. Both brands have dozens of playlists with videos explaining hundreds of different concepts, actions and needs. The videos are watched both before and after the purchase, making this content work across several steps in the journey.

Creating enticing 'value exchanges' (VEs)

VE is a concept very familiar to all who had spent some time in direct marketing and CRM. It is a cornerstone of the prospect-pool building and data capture. VE is the reason why a consumer should give us something – particularly contactable data such as an e-mail or postal address, or a mobile phone number – and expect or request to get something in return; good VE gives the answer to the question 'Why would I enter your brand's world?' Why would I read your white paper, subscribe to your newsletter, join your club or otherwise let you pester me? Bad VE is one of the key reasons why a lot of Content (and marketing communications overall) is bad, annoying and ignored.

In our set of optics we talked about in Chapter 4, VE is how a great Empathic Utility (EU) will be expressed. It is what makes it tangible.

The usual approaches to VE and reasons for consumers to enter into a brand's world

1 Because you are giving me something for free or discounted.

2 Because you are giving me something exclusive that money cannot buy.

3 Because you are giving me something personally relevant.

4 Because you are giving me something interesting or entertaining.

5 Because you are giving me something useful.

6 Because you are giving me something I can share or enjoy with others.

7 Because it is essential for using the product or service.

One of the tools we have developed over the years was always helpful in deciding what kind of VE and what kind of Content could fit the strategic objectives. It consists of three layers of considerations (see Figure 6.2):

Three wheels of value exchange (VE)

1 **The positioning wheel (WHY)** – all of the strategic inputs that need to be considered in order to shape the right kind of feel, dimensions and mechanics for the VE (key insights on brand, category, consumers, culture, competitors, etc).

2 **The dimensions wheel (WHAT)** – key possible territories, individual or in a mix, for approaching the actual motivational architecture of the VE experience, based on the insights in the previous wheel (eg exclusivity, financial rewards, co-creation, entertainment, tools).

3 **The mechanics wheel (HOW)** – the exact tactical mechanism(s) that will turn dimensions into a specific delivery system in a profitable way and in the manner that is simple for consumers (eg points, coupons, club, exclusive content, social rewards, competitions, events and so on).

CASE STUDY IKEA Family Club

It has millions of members globally, who are also some of the most loyal and frequent customers. The VE is a combination of exclusive products, discounts on selected products from the main programme, restaurant freebies, a magazine, free transport insurance and replacement for goods damaged in members' own transport and various other perks (DMA, 2016c).

The role of Content post-sale and in customer service

Probably the biggest canvas for continuous deployment of Content is the part of the customer journey that many equate with 'hardcore' CRM – everything that happens after the purchase. This is particularly valid in categories with longer purchase cycles, with higher-ticket or more complicated products and services. After all, having a gap of several years between

Figure 6.2 Value exchange wheels for a local beer brand

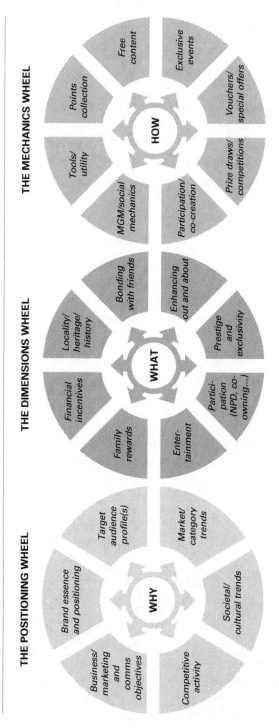

THE POSITIONING WHEEL

THE DIMENSIONS WHEEL

THE MECHANICS WHEEL

WHY
- Brand essence and positioning
- Target audience profile(s)
- Market/category trends
- Societal/cultural trends
- Competitive activity
- Business/marketing and comms objectives

WHAT
- Locality/heritage/history
- Bonding with friends
- Enhancing out and about
- Prestige and exclusivity
- Participation (NPD, co-owning...)
- Entertainment
- Family rewards
- Financial incentives

HOW
- Points collection
- Free content
- Exclusive events
- Vouchers/special offers
- Prize draws/competitions
- Participation/co-creation
- MGM/social mechanics
- Tools/utility

SOURCE authors

car purchases (in developed markets, much longer in developing ones) is an awfully long time to rely just on the vagaries of top-level advertising messaging to keep the brand flame alive at the point of repurchase.

There are so many opportunities for a brand to talk to consumers in the meantime in relevant ways, making the ownership or usage experience more fulfilling. Content could play a big role here in turning that efficient marketing 'robot' that Ritson was talking about above into a 'brand tree' watering agent as well. For that to happen, clients and agencies have to adopt Empathic Utility thinking, that, again, goes above and beyond the 'campaign' mindset. Mark Runacus of Karmarama stresses the importance of this new, richer, approach:

The example I am going to give you is from one of our financial services clients, about mortgages. In the traditional CRM way, we wanted to understand the journey, so we mapped it and identified the moments of truth to find out where Content can help from an earned perspective. We had a strong focus on utility, but did not rely on it. This decision was driven by an understanding of the Content purpose, which itself cascaded down from the brand purpose. Then we defined the important customer touchpoints, and we identified items of Content that should draw customers through the journey and towards bigger pieces of content. Little social snacks may lead them to the YouTube channel, or e-mail if we captured the data.

In summary, the approach was to create a Content eco-system mapped across the entire journey. Looking back, I realize we still treated this exercise like a campaign. We had not yet developed the mentality to realize that this is a living, breathing, always-on activity – it is like painting the Forth Bridge: you have to keep doing it all the time. But the agency business model gets in the way – we were focused on pricing to do it, not to maintain it. Integrated agencies can be really credible players in this space, particularly because we understand measurement and results, plus all the other elements I had mentioned before. However, we can sometimes be too measurement-focused and 'systems first', to the detriment of a good story. That is probably the only hurdle that good integrated agencies need to overcome: to be able to tell bigger, more consistent stories.

Zappos would agree, as it is famed for its excellent and authentic customer service. Much virality had ensued several years ago when one of their representatives sent an e-mail to a complaining customer not just to resolve the problem but, through the sheer tonality of the writing and additional rewards to the customer, turn the problematic situation into a brand celebration (Copywriting Tips, 2011). It was Empathic Utility in its purest!

The utility nature of Content really comes to the fore in this part of the journey as well, by turning brands' digital channels into self-servicing FAQs. To a large extent, YouTube could be regarded as 'The World's FAQs', given the prevalence of the problem-solving, educational and advisory content on it, much bigger in volume than just entertainment. The examples of Lowe's and IKEA above show that leading brands are starting to understand this truth.

Finally, with chatbots as the newest addition to the customer journey and service-brand arsenal, the notion of their tonality will rise with the increasing sophistication of their language processing. We expect brands soon to have chatbots with 'personalities' that reflect the tonality of the brand, although, admittedly, this is already happening with Facebook's alleged deployment of real people to power its chatbots (Simonite, 2017). We should expect to see these new platforms, surprisingly, turning into Content hubs in their own right – effortlessly connecting, contextually and with great EU, various content assets residing on the brand side for maximum empathy.

On this point, Ana Andjelic introduces one interesting new concept that may help brands think and behave in this space:

> From a customer's point of view, brands are valuable only when they respond to their motivations, barriers and goals. Superior brand service and experience has since become a given: it is noticeable only when it is missing. Content plays a critical role in good service, and consumers want content that meets and exceeds their expectations and adds value to their lives, in a manner that is not unlike the Japanese principle of *omotenashi:* by being intuitive, effortless and flexible. To deliver on this expectation, content creators need to understand how their customers move through the experience their brand provides, and to connect these steps into a customer journey. They need to move away from their single-minded focus on individual interactions between a customer and the brand and understand how these interactions form a relationship. *Omotenashi*-based content design allocates and sequences investments across steps in this relationship that are most desirable from the customer's point of view and critical in their decision-making process.

The whole industry, it seems, *has* to become more '*omotenashi*'. As Ben Jones, of Google Art, Copy & Code fame once said, 'we shouldn't be thinking about how to avoid being tuned out, we need to figure out how to get chosen' (Twitter, 2017). Context is key for that. In powering the more relevant and empathic customer and Content contexts, data will play an increasingly critical role, which we will talk about in Chapter 7.

References

Blippar (2016) [accessed 30 December 2017] Blippar & Max Factor: The Future of Retail Is Here (Blog), *Blippar*, 21 April [Online] blippar.com/en/resources/blog/2016/04/21/blippar-max-factor-future-retail-here/

Chan, N (2015) [accessed 30 December 2017] Content Is King, But Context Is Queen, *ClickZ*, 21 May [Online] clickz.com/content-is-king-but-context-is-queen/25867

Copywriting Tips (2011) [accessed 30 December 2017] Why Zappos Is Awesome (Blog), *Copywriting Tips: The Belligerent Copywriters' Guide*, 10 December [Online] copywritingtipsguide.com/447/zappos-customer-service-letter/

Court, D, Elzinga, D, Mulder, S and Vetvik, O J (2009) [accessed 30 December 2017] The Consumer Decision Journey, *McKinsey Quarterly* (June) [Online] mckinsey.com/business-functions/marketing-and-sales/our-insights/the-consumer-decision-journey

DMA (2016a) [accessed 30 December 2017] 2016 Gold Travel, Leisure and Entertainment [Online] dma.org.uk/awards/winner/2016-gold-travel-leisure-and-entertainment

DMA (2016b) [accessed 30 December 2017] 2016 Gold Best Use of Programmatic [Online] dma.org.uk/awards/winner/2016-gold-best-use-of-programmatic

DMA (2016c) [accessed 30 December 2017] 2016 Gold Best Loyalty or CRM Programme [Online] dma.org.uk/awards/winner/2016-gold-best-loyalty-or-crm-programme

Dzamic, L (2016) [accessed 30 December 2017] King Kong Rules: Redefining What Content Is and How It Shapes the Future of Advertising (Blog), *BOBCM*, 7 April [Online] bobcm.net/2016/04/07/king-kong-rules-redefining-what-content-is-and-how-it-shapes-the-future-of-advertising/

Faeth, B (2012) [accessed 30 December 2017] Gary Vaynerchuk: If Content Is King, then Context Is God (Blog), *Inbound Marketing Blog*, 1 September [Online] inboundmarketingagents.com/inbound-marketing-agents-blog/bid/214177/Gary-Vaynerchuk-If-Content-is-King-then-Context-is-God

Gates, B (1996) [accessed 30 December 2017] Content Is King, *Microsoft*, 1 March [Online] web.archive.org/web/20010126005200/http://www.microsoft.com/billgates/columns/1996essay/essay960103.asp

Gevelber, L (2015) [accessed 30 December 2017] Why Consumer Intent Is More Powerful than Demographics, *Think With Google*, December

[Online] thinkwithgoogle.com/marketing-resources/micro-moments/
why-consumer-intent-more-powerful-than-demographics/

Hoffman, B (2017) [accessed 30 December 2017] Top 10 Reasons Online
Advertising Must Change (Blog), *The Ad Contrarian*, 24 October [Online]
adcontrarian.blogspot.rs/2017/10/top-10-reasons-online-advertising-must.html

IKEA (2017) [accessed 30 December 2017] Playlists [Online] youtube.com/user/
IKEA/playlists

Lowe's (2017) [accessed 30 December 2017] Playlists [Online] youtube.com/user/
Lowes/playlists

Myers, C B (2011) [accessed 30 December 2017] Josh Clark Debunks the 7 Myths
of Mobile Web Design, *The Next Web (TNW)*, 7 November [Online] thenext-
web.com/dd/2011/11/07/josh-clark-debunks-the-7-myths-of-mobile-web-design

Neff, J (2015) [accessed 30 December 2017] Axe Remakes Story of Romeo –
100,000 Times: Brazilian Programmatic Creative Campaign Takes
Customization to New Level, *AdAge*, 10 August [Online] adage.com/article/
see-the-spot/unilever-s-axe-remakes-story-romeo-100-000-times/299888/

Patel, N (2015) [accessed 30 December 2017] Why SEO Is Actually All About
Content Marketing (Blog), *Kissmetrics*, 19 February [Online] blog.kissmetrics.
com/seo-is-content-marketing/

Sharp, B (2010) *How Brands Grow: What marketers don't know*, Oxford
University Press, Melbourne

Shorty Awards (2015) [accessed 30 December 2017] From The 7th Annual Shorty
Awards All Things Hair – Big Hair Meets Big Data [Online] shortyawards.
com/7th/all-things-hair-big-hair-meets-big-data

Simonite, T (2017) [accessed 30 March 2017] Facebook's Perfect, Impossible
Chatbot, *MIT Technology Review*, 14 April [Online] technologyreview.
com/s/604117/facebooks-perfect-impossible-chatbot/

Staplehurst, G (2016) [accessed 30 December 2017] How Consumers Buy Brands:
The New Decision Journey, *MilwardBrown* [Online] millwardbrown.com/
Insights/Point-of-View/How_Consumers_Buy_Brands_The_new_decision_journey/

Trendwatching (2017) [accessed 30 December 2017] 5 Consumer Trends for 2017
[Online] trendwatching.com/trends/5-trends-for-2017

Twitter (2017) #4AsTransformation ben jones [Online] twitter.com/
search?q=%234AsTransformation%20ben%20jones

Vandendooren, T (2016) [accessed 30 December 2017] 6 Reasons Why Context
is the New King in Marketing Land, *Sentiance*, 28 April [Online] sentiance.
com/2016/04/28/6-reasons-why-context-is-the-new-king-in-marketing-land/

Vaynerchuk, G (2016) [accessed 30 December 2017] Content Is King, But
Context Is God, *The Next Web (TNW)*, 11 April [Online] thenextweb.com/
insider/2016/04/11/gary-vee-content-king-context-god/

Wikipedia (2017) [accessed 30 December 2017] Web 2.0 [Online] en.wikipedia.
org/wiki/Web_2.0

Content and storytelling in the age of user data abundance

If Content is considered, as highlighted in this book, a part of the better promise of the new marketing decoupled from the shackles of the traditional interruption model, it seems that data sits at the heart of that promise. Particularly *digital* data, all the signals we leave behind in the digital space.

In the now truly famous aphorism – allegedly first coined by the 'father' of the Tesco Clubcard Clive Humby, then attributed to the consultancy Gartner – 'data is the new oil', while analytics is the new combustion engine (Haupt, 2016). The phrase has a lot of evangelists and a few rejecters, but it was obvious that a lot of leading names we interviewed for the book look at data as a potential advantage in the new Content game. The truth is always more nuanced, as data could be a friend or a foe depending on who is using it and how. Examples of the ethically challenging data practices highlighted in the Chapter 11 are a good warning. Also, looking at the relevance and fraud problems the marketing communications industry is fighting recently, it seems the new oil is spilling everywhere, polluting everything.

At the same time, examples of great contextual resonance, business efficiency and effectiveness, as well as data fuelling more interesting creative stories, are also all around us. Not to mention the hugely profitable CRM programmes of the Tesco, Target and TUI kind, sophisticated value-creation machines that are constantly evolving and whirring smoothly on the same oil...

The role of data in Content and brand storytelling in the age of data abundance is, therefore, the story of balance.

The promise of data

First, the good promise. As mentioned in Chapter 4, 'Moments that Matter' (MTMs) or 'Micro-Moments' (focusing on the mobile space specifically) pioneered by Google, is rapidly becoming THE leading framework for modern marketers with a potentially huge impact on Content thinking. No wonder, as Google has for years been 'the world's homepage', processing nearly 1.7 *trillion* search queries per year according to the last count on 'Internet Live Stats' in November 2017. That is already four to seventeen times bigger – depending on the approach to calculations – than the number of stars in the Milky Way! It is a universe of wonders, the largest library of intentions ever – if only one is able to read it...

'Moments' marketing as the new fuel for Content

The first cluster of this framework is driven by the four main consumer needs largely conditioned by the dependence on the mobile phone and the evolution of mobile services into voice assistants with more sophisticated predictive capabilities (Lawson, 2017):

- 'I want to know' moments (information).
- 'I want to go' moments (destinations).
- 'I want to do' moments (actions).
- 'I want to buy' moments (transactions).

At each of these archetypal moments a brand could be present with the right solution that will often involve some sort of content. As the moments evolve, so does the reading of the consumer behaviours. Several newer trends identified by Google shed light on potential approaches that Content marketers could adopt. One of them is the rise of the 'well-advised consumer' who now researches everything regardless of the category and price. For example, searches for 'best' have shown higher growth among the low-consideration products than the high-consideration ones in the period 2015–17. The other one is the 'right here consumer' pursuing local interests and needs – while at the same time revealing less of where they are through location blocks! There is also the 'right now' consumer who is making decisions faster than ever before and acting upon those decisions instantly too. For example, travel-related searches for 'tonight' and 'today' have grown over 150 per cent on mobile, over the same two-year period above (Gevelber, 2017).

Roles of data for Content: define, target and optimize

The 'Moments' framework opens up three specific roles the data may play in Content thinking – as well as in the overall strategic and creative process:

Define

One of the traditional roles of data was to inform better creative and Content ideas – what good agency planners and data scientists have known all along. Data is here one of the ingredients – or the sole engine, depending on the circumstances – of the insight or of the idea.

Buzzfeed is using data both for finding interesting new things to talk about, but also to optimize everything to achieve best engagement rates. Social listening company Brandwatch has the same approach: turning what their tools pick up in the digital sphere into interesting blogs and articles on their website that acts not just as a sales and marketing vehicle, but a content hub for the prospects as well (Brandwatch, 2017).

'YouTubers' are the new masters of digital narratives and also masters of turning any current trending data – such as film launches, fashion events, memes and 'challenges' – into fodder for new episodes or even series. They don't do Big Data, but are very clever and nimble with the 'small data', usually via free tools from YouTube and Google (eg Google Trends or Google Correlate).

'Tent-pole' moments are another example, also used by many YouTube 'creators' and sophisticated brands. During the year, there are many important moments in particular categories, or society at large, that may be an opportunity to create content that will resonate with a larger audience. Big sport and cultural events, either regular or occasional, seasonal tides such as the hayfever season or the celebrations and holidays – and the accompanying flurry of various current search terms and moments – are all 'creative briefs' of a sort for relevant contextual Content.

Then there are the actual interesting patterns in the user data that may inspire a good creative idea. Spotify marked the end of 2016 with a global outdoor campaign that generated a lot of publicity (interestingly, created by an internal team), based on intriguing behavioural insights from its global user base. The campaign that went under the slogan of 'Thanks 2016. It's been weird.' punched hard using real behavioural insights such as 'Dear person who played "Sorry" 42 times on Valentine's Day, what did you do?' or 'Dear 3,749 people who streamed "It's the End of the World As We Know It" the day of the Brexit vote, hang in there' (Nudd, 2016).

Rob Blackie, a distinguished digital business consultant with extensive experience on both the agency and the client side, points out in our conversation another interesting angle on how the consumers' data – in this case the user-generated content (UGC) – could be used for insight and creative aesthetics purposes:

> The key rule is to understand what your customers find interesting or, perhaps, delightful, about you. UGC only works if you're a high-engagement brand, for example, in fashion, where UGC is proven to have increased the conversion rates. However, there aren't that many high-engagement B2C brands really, as opposed to B2B where people are betting their career on buying your product or service. The UGC could harness a useful insight or a creative prompt, rather than garnering some meaningful volume of excellent work in its own right. Not a lot of people may respond, but it may be of high value. If you're a hotel chain, very few people post photos of your hotel on TripAdvisor, but it's pretty influential to your customer journey.

The examples of this low complexity/high engagement approach to insight are fairly common. Lego is very good at it, turning its annual competition for the best new Lego set idea coming from its users into a huge engagement drive matched only by the launches of the biggest film franchise such as *Star Wars*! It works because the audience is already very engaged and because they can see their idea turned into a tangible product, with a profit-share deal as an additional reason to get excited.

Observing what and how people do things may impact not just the content of the communication, but its aesthetics too. Content could borrow the actual tone of voice from the brand's users. This is particularly important, as flagged up in the chapters on purpose (Chapter 3) and the publisher's perspective (Online Chapter 2), from the point of view of authenticity and avoiding the clichéd visual language of traditional advertising. Rob Blackie has been involved in several projects where observing user behaviour led to new creative approaches:

> Two things make the UGC work, aesthetically: one is a product demo and the other is when it makes it obvious that real people use it. We as consumers are very good at filtering the stock-photo kind of aesthetics prevalent in today's advertising.

One research I've done for the fast-food category showed that people who go to Burger King post photos with their friends in there, while the KFC ones post just photos of food. Or, people on holiday who often post a shot of a drink in their hands, but it is the compositional approach that you rarely see replicated by brands. I worked with a big pub recently and they realized that one of the strongest stories is that they are full of attractive young people. When they had a look at what people are posting on social media where the pub was referenced, it was selfies from the pub… So they embraced that fully, for example their Instagram feed is that they go around and do that themselves and they also repost customers' content on the pub's official feed. So, it does create the feel of community, but it also amplifies what customers are doing anyway. I think that a lot of brands have not really looked at how people are using them, how they are doing UGC and then copying it.

Target

As discussed in Chapter 6, context of a consumer touchpoint can make or break a piece of content. The 'Moments' approach, in theory, offers huge potential for the brand to be where it counts, with spectacular intent and emotional resonance. Here are two examples:

CASE STUDY Airbnb 'Hosted Walks' gives tourists the local experience

To demonstrate the principle of contextual relevance, Airbnb, in collaboration with Google, has created an audio guide synchronized with the map of the hotspot places in particular locations. When users insert the destination point in a city they want to walk to, the app maps out the route that also brings up audio clips of local Airbnb hosts that offer visitors a first-hand account of their favourite shops and places on that route. The clips are not ads, but advice, and the feeling of authenticity is what makes it different and useful (Think with Google, 2015).

CASE STUDY 'Pedigree Found' – a lost dog alert via geo-targeted mobile ads

A great case of marketing-as-a-service. Dog owners register their dog on a mobile app and, if it gets lost, they press just one button. Immediately, a set of geo-targeted mobile ads – paid for by the brand – gets triggered, containing the name and the picture of the dog lost in that area. The chances of finding it rise exponentially if more people in the area are aware of it more quickly. A true 'Moment that Matters' and a true role of the relevant brand in it (RedazioneBrandNews, 2015).

But, looking at the numbers and the prevailing tendencies of the digital marketing space, examples like these are still just an exception, as evidenced below.

Optimize

When it comes to using data to optimize Content, Buzzfeed has pretty much written the rulebook, putting the old CRM and publishing testing on steroids. They have established sophisticated feedback loops where constant flow of data analysis via internal data scientists feeds content creation, which then gets tested, the data flows back in, content is optimized and so on.

First, there is the pre-publishing optimization, for example an A/B test on the title of an article, a thumbnail, the number of items that should be used in a 'listicle' ('16 things…') and so on – all done as live tests on their platform, with live audience. This helps the editors 'surface' the elements or combinations that work best and the editorial efforts are then focused on these to increase the chances of content stickiness and engagement. For example, one of the findings was that the number in a listicle shouldn't be too big (as people are not inclined to wade through too much), but also not too small (as that may indicate lack of substance).

On top of that, writers also get a bit of conditioning through 'trending badges', which are a combination of the number of views within a time frame and that indicates to writers whether their content is performing well in the initial phases.

Finally, the post-publishing dashboard tells the editors how much of the total views were discovered due to Buzzfeed pushing it themselves as opposed to the organic discovery via sharing (the 'virality' of the content), giving it the score for the internal metric called the 'social lift' (Looker, 2016).

Admittedly, this kind of optimization may favour a popular online publisher more than long-term brand planning. If everything is optimized for immediacy, where is the role for content that should last for longer and may not be subjected to the vagaries of trends? Also, there is the question of the brand fit, as whatever may be popular this instant may not be a good match with every brand's purpose, mission or tonality, nor the audience. As a direct marketing principle, though, applied rigorously in the field of Content, it is a valuable evolution in thinking compared to just the gut feel of the editorial team.

Problems with data – hype, waste and narrow-mindedness...

There is, of course, the other side of the story. Data is still an unfulfilled promise and, in its worst manifestations, an active ingredient in the current demise of large parts of the digital marketing. This goes for all badly used data, big or small. The data promise in the marketing industry was always bordering on utopia: being able to make sense of everything the consumer touches that is related to the brand and leaves signals behind, all the structured and unstructured data, sensors from the products and services themselves, even mood states – all offering unparalleled opportunities to be more relevant, to turn the wretched, despised advertising of old into a service bonanza! The Big Data paradigm is often quoted here, immediately counter-weighted by the formidable challenges due to its famous '4Vs': Volume, Velocity, Variety and Veracity (IBM Big Data Hub, 2013). But, it is the less often quoted fifth 'V' – Value – wherein lies the crux of the matter.

Problems with data – the big hype

At the moment, personalization is the elusive ideal. It is a great story waiting to be told in practice, particularly in Content, but, in the mesmerizing phrase by Ben Jones of Google Art, Copy & Code fame: 'Data is still waiting for its Scorsese' (Twitter, 2017). Not just big data, almost any data... Certainly, there are a decent number of individual cases of data being used in the traditional media targeting and CRM space using more traditional data sets, often several pots of creatively connected 'small data' – but, saying that the majority of organizations are fully data-literate and maximizing use of data in marketing, is an exaggeration. We are, indeed, still waiting for the data Scorsese.

Probably no one recently has summed it up as precisely as Rob Blackie in his 'Three Laws of Technology Hype' (2017). It is a prescient warning and a call for sanity, a manifesto for focusing efforts where it matters the most. For many, it still means mastering the data and tech basics first:

There still are not very many examples of good personalization. The pieces of structured data, such as one's name, are not that engaging in themselves and the unstructured data, which is much more interesting, is much harder to manage. Facebook and Google are probably the only ones who can do it in a high-quality way with their tools. Joining up the pots of data on people is hard; most visitors to most destinations are anonymous most of the time, cookies degrade, people use multiple devices or multiple people use the same device (iPad as the frequent example)...

The pool sizes we often get are too small for lots of purposes. When I was trying to target a specific subset of pub landlords in the UK, about 5,000 people, it was impossible to do it via social. Also, a lot of pots of data tell you the same thing, meaning that adding some more info on top of a few key pieces of data does not give you a lot of predictive power (eg if I know who bought a BMW in cash, then knowing their mortgage size or whether they bought any luxury clothes doesn't add much). So, unless you are some huge-scale e-commerce site like Amazon, that can use their own vast amounts of data, the only realistic option is to take your own data and pair it up with Google or Facebook. It comes down to the creative use of just those two platforms.

The second issue is that most organizations do not have enough data of the right sort to do personalized content for more than a fraction of their audience. That makes it really difficult to change your market share if you reach only 10 per cent of your market. For my money, the most neglected channel for personalization, or for almost anything, is SMS, but hardly anyone does anything interesting. You can generate enough first-party data yourself, but it takes time and there is the category attrition issue (people coming in and out of the category) and it needs a constant flow of good content. The biggest issue is that your organization needs to commit to it for years at a time, and very few are capable of doing that. Even if you do that, is it a better use than the alternatives? Does personalization matter in the category? For FMCG, baby milk is good for that as it has a use case, washing powder not so much...'

Rob Blackie's three laws of technology hype

1   Impossibility – the technology doesn't exist or is impractical:
    –   Mass scraping of data is usually impossible.

- The vast majority of data is either private, anonymized or just not very useful.
- Impracticality beyond the hype...
- Legal challenges around privacy.

2 Value – new technology is not worth the effort:

- Cheaper and easier alternatives are often equally, if not more, effective.
- Have you exhausted all your testing and optimization options?
- Even tech companies do not always use cutting-edge technologies.

3 Reach – technology doesn't reach enough people to work:

- Penetration: what proportion of the target audience encounter your technology?
- Time use: how long does your audience spend with the technology?

Based on the three laws, what is the most hyped technology?

- Anything with not enough reach, and not much evidence of impact in many cases.
- AI that is implied to be fully automated. If you recast these claims as 'software tools making people smarter' then there are plenty of sensible cases. But implying that you have an artificial intelligence, when you just have programmatic media buying, you are pulling a con.
- Almost all discussions of social media that don't mention reach.
- 'Data science' that claims to know people better than they know themselves.

Problems with data – privacy and ethics

As explored in detail in Chapter 11, there is an enormous worrying side to personalization and the promise of data omniscience: message opacity, filter bubbles, atomization of modern societies, addictive architecture of the user experience and empathic manipulation. Data is here not just hyped up, but practically dangerous.

Much noise in the trade press has been made around the introduction of new EU data protection rules, the General Data Protection Regulation (GDPR) (Wikipedia, 2017a). In a nutshell, it aims to give back control to citizens and residents over their personal data and to simplify the regulatory environment for international business by unifying the regulation within the EU. The marketing industry is already huffing and puffing about the increased cost for business and marketing that these new rules will require, but given its track record so far, consumers may actually look upon it with a more favourable eye.

Problems with data – waste

In a hard-hitting article mentioned in Chapter 6, Bob Hoffman (*aka* The Ad Contrarian), exposes quite shocking levels of waste, negligence and even worse, that the industry seems plagued by (Hoffman, 2017). Quoting Marc Pritchard from P&G who said that only 25 per cent of his programmatic budget ever reaches the consumer, Hoffman also mentions research showing that of those ads that do reach the consumer less than 10 per cent are even noticed! In his words, 'a waste factor that is beyond belief'. On top of that sits the question of effectiveness, hilariously reflected in the fact, also quoted by Hoffman, that P&G had cut about $140 million from its online advertising budget from their second quarter of 2017 – during which period their sales grew by 2 per cent, with minimal impact of that cut on business! If there were a deliberately designed showcase to demonstrate exactly the opposite of what the promise of data-based automated digital advertising could be, current programmatic practice would be hard to beat!

Mark Higginson, from Twenty Thousand Leagues, one of the fiercest critics of the modern ad industry, including Content, in our conversation also strongly challenges the industry's record on the clever use of data for targeting and relevance:

> It seems idiotic to point this out, but the fundamental, foundational need of any marketing activity, before we even consider the psychological effect of a message and whether it prompts any action, is: was it seen or heard? I would start with that. I would especially focus on this because measurability is what we were promised by digital marketers. Yet, here we are, years into this project, and still no one agrees on any kind of standard for measuring the impact of this stuff, nor can anyone produce any independently verifiable results confirming this is not wasted time and resources. Forget labelling content, packaging it, creating teams at agencies or in-house to produce it. Look at what is being made already that is similar to what you might produce and simply ask:

- Where is it appearing?
- How often does it appear and to how many people?
- How is this independently observable and verifiable?
- Does the form fit the context?

Towards a better data promise

Are there any potential solutions for the almighty irrelevance glut witnessed in the modern media and marketing space, despite all the sophisticated technology? The answer has several parts.

One of them is a bigger focus – for many companies forced by the demands of the market and consumers – on the organizational purpose, as explored in Chapter 3. As a corollary, it should lead to the production of more responsible and relevant marketing messages, including Content, disseminated across more contextually relevant touchpoints.

Another is the emergence of the sharper-toothed regulation, as an answer to the clear and present danger that the main digital platforms present as a disruptor not just of the outdated business practices, but our civilization as well. Consumers voting with their wallets and regulation still seem to be two of the most powerful mechanisms for changing the behaviour of companies.

Finally, part of the answer may come from the current industry soul-searching and the admission of data overhyping and questionable practices. In this space, key roles could be played by the world's biggest marketing clients and the agencies who may realize that obsessive relevance, not just obsessive budget optimization, may be a better answer. If the vast and currently unmanageable data sets are not giving us the most relevant answers – and ad blocking, fraud and the overall drop in trust in the digital advertising industry seem to support the case – what may give us relevant answers? What are the ways to introduce increased levels of both Emotional Resonance and Intent Utility across the spectrum, and even a better merger of the two, currently antagonistic, schools of thinking?

Merging 'small,' 'big' and 'thick' data into 'rich' data?

A potential answer comes from anthropology and its use of the concepts of 'thick' and 'thin' descriptions of human behaviour. The 'thick' description explains not just the human behaviour (what), but also the context that generates and frames the behaviour (why) so it could become meaningful even to an outsider (Wikipedia, 2017b). It is a more qualitative way of describing and explaining human behaviour as opposed to more mechanistic approaches for understanding cultures, organizations and various human environments. The market is one such. Given the already described shift of many leading brands towards building or maintaining their cultural relevance, it seems that our data-inundated industry consumed by a desperate chase of ever sharper machine intelligence could start correcting its mechanistic excesses by becoming a bit more 'thick'.

Careful clients and agencies have always made sure to have a raft of quality insight inputs from various sources, both quantitative and qualitative. Think the UGC-led approaches mentioned above by Rob Blackie – it is a great example of the 'thick' approach. What seems to have happened recently, with the rise of programmatic and our self-induced belief in the automatization of human understanding, is that the 'library of intent' based on Google's MTMs becomes the only library in town. By accepting that, we have become too narrow-minded and 'thin'. People, in order to understand them fully, still have to be studied 'in the field' too, with 'thick' descriptions. Those calls for balance – in the venerable tradition of the industry mavericks that we have always, luckily, had – are forcefully put forward by the consultants and thinkers such as Christian Madsbjerg and Mikkel Rasmussen of ReD Associates (2014) or Tricia Wang (TED, 2017), for example.

Bizarrely, a potentially winning exploration of the amalgamation of the new and the old, of the emotion and the data, was articulated as far back as 2007 by one of the industry's leading strategy thinkers, Russell Davies, in his seminal article on 'Rich Ideas' (Davies, 2007). Building upon a thought by another stalwart of the planning world, Richard Huntington of Saatchi fame, Davies calls for a new kind of idea, more tailored for the rich digitally powered environment, against the flashy, but 'flat' big advertising ideas of old:

> I prefer to think about rich ideas. Richard Huntington describes this kind of idea as 'generous' meaning it is something that every agency and partner around the brand management table doesn't just 'get', they can immediately think of a dozen great ways to bring it to life in their particular medium.

Could the ultimate creation of a more balanced data-interpretation space fusing small, big and thick data sources create a new 'rich data' playing field – beyond the current utterly functional and, frankly useless, definitions of the term (Colman, 2015)? Could it produce more relevant and 'rich' ideas and finally resolve the current crisis of marketing communications? It remains to be seen, but the future of the marketing profession depends on it.

References

Blackie, R (2017) [accessed 30 December 2017] Three Laws of Technology Hype (Blog), *Rob Blackie Digital Strategy*, 20 March [Online] robblackie.com/technology-hype-three-laws/

Brandwatch (2017) [accessed 30 December 2017] Brandwatch Blog [Online] brandwatch.com/blog/

Colman, M (2015) [accessed 30 December 2017] Rich Data Vs. Big Data, *Digital Thing*, 29 September [Online] digitalthing.com.au/rich-data-vs-big-data/

Davies, R (2007) [accessed 30 December 2017] Big, Rich and Green (Blog), *Russell Davies*, 22 April [Online] russelldavies.typepad.com/planning/2007/04/big_rich_and_gr.html

Gevelber, L (2017) [accessed 30 December 2017] 3 New Consumer Behaviors Playing Out In Google Search Data, *Think With Google*, July [Online] thinkwithgoogle.com/data-collections/micro-moments-consumer-behavior-immediate-expectations/

Haupt, M (2016) [accessed 30 December 2017] Data Is the New Oil (Blog), *Medium*, 2 May [Online] medium.com/twenty-one-hundred/data-is-the-new-oil-a-ludicrous-proposition-1d91bba4f294

Hoffman, B (2017) [accessed 30 December 2017] Top 10 Reasons Online Advertising Must Change (Blog), *The Ad Contrarian*, 24 October [Online] adcontrarian.blogspot.rs/2017/10/top-10-reasons-online-advertising-must.html

IBM Big Data Hub (2013) [accessed 30 December 2017] The Four V's of Big Data [Online] ibmbigdatahub.com/infographic/four-vs-big-data

Internet Live Stats (2017) [accessed 30 December 2017] Google Search Statistics [Online] internetlivestats.com/google-search-statistics/

Lawson, M (2017) [accessed 30 December 2017] 4 Things You Need To Know About the Future of Marketing, *Think With Google*, May [Online] thinkwithgoogle.com/marketing-resources/micro-moments/future-of-marketing-mobile-micro-moments/

Looker (2016) [accessed 30 December 2017] How BuzzFeed Uses Data to Optimize Content Publishing #JOINData 2016 [Online] youtu.be/eZoSpBvmdB0

Madsbjerg, C and Rasmussen, M B (2014) *The Moment of Clarity: Using the human sciences to solve your toughest business problems*, Harvard Business Review Press, Boston, MA

Nudd, T (2016) [accessed 30 December 2017] Spotify Crunches User Data in Fun Ways for This New Global Outdoor Ad Campaign: Music Service Gives Thanks for a 'Weird' 2016, *Adweek*, 29 November [Online] adweek.com/creativity/spotify-crunches-user-data-fun-ways-new-global-outdoor-ad-campaign-174826/

RedazioneBrandNews (2015) [accessed 30 December 2017] Pedigree – Found: Case Study Film [Online] https://youtu.be/rttMkbO7hQk

TED (2017) [accessed 30 December 2017] Tricia Wang: The Human Insights Missing From Big Data [Online] ted.com/talks/tricia_wang_the_human_insights_missing_from_big_data

Think with Google (2015) [accessed 30 December 2017] Micro-Moments: Airbnb Hosted Walks [Online] youtu.be/dgYt2Fn4fn4

Twitter (2017) [accessed 30 December 2017] #4AsTransformation Ben Jones [Online] twitter.com/search?q=%234AsTransformation%20ben%20jones

Wikipedia (2017a) [accessed 30 December 2017] General Data Protection Regulation: Pseudonymisation [Online] wikipedia.org/wiki/General_Data_Protection_Regulation#Pseudonymisation

Wikipedia (2017b) [accessed 30 December 2017] Thick Description [Online] wikipedia.org/wiki/Thick_description

The evolution 08
of Content formats
From text to video to AR/VR to AI...

One of the best sci-fi books no one knows of is Sam J Lundwall's *No Time for Heroes*, a brilliant satirical dystopia in which a very reluctant army 'hero' Bernhard Rordin is shot off to strange worlds accompanied by a commercially sponsored intelligent 'Robofriend'. In times of great stress, what Bernhard gets from the metal spider-like creature are brand jingles, upbeat marching music, a snitch on his behaviour to his military superiors – and various product offers.

The future of the tech looks amazing, but one of the fears, based on the current experience, is that the newest media paradigms are, again, going to be trivialized by the old ways of thinking. After all, the first thing brands did when 'in-game advertising' became available was to plaster scenes with their billboards and virtual versions of their high-street shops... The first digital iterations of the popular Content formats were also replications of the old. Blogs were newspaper columns by unknown people; infographics were public service and commercial newspaper ads and public-service posters; articles were, well, articles.

A raft of new technologies are changing our notions of the traditional split between the 'physical' and 'virtual' spaces and what a 'story' is. They tend not just to replicate the reality, but to augment and even create it in ways never before seen. All of this has huge ramifications for brands, publishers, agencies and other players in the entertainment, media and marketing sectors as they go about trying to stay relevant in this new world. It is also revolutionizing what we mean by Content and how we create it and consume it.

The new age of affectiveness

The whole evolution of the media and technology space could be, in some ways, observed as a progression from lower- to higher-empathy means of engaging the audience. Professor Andrew McStay of Bangor University, in our chapter about ethics (Chapter 11) refers to this aspect as the 'creative branding affective space'. New creative and media paradigms such as augmented reality (AR), virtual reality (VR) and artificial intelligence (AI) could power solutions that are some of the most immersive, most affective, most impactful environments we have ever created.

It is a far cry from the paper paradigm that has ruled the world so far: a text read from a surface; first, the paper, then a screen. That was the reason that Content used to mean, and still does to a large extent, 'text' in various forms. An analysis of 1 million Google search results in 2016 had found that the average Google first-page result contains 1,890 words (Dean, 2016). Blogs, articles and white papers are still some of the most common Content formats for many companies.

The main characteristic, though, of almost all the content we have created so far, with the exception of games, was its 'linearity': the narrative, the 'story', was unfolding in a sequence set up and controlled by the creator. Skip some parts and you may lose the sense of it. This particularly applied to films as, essentially, THE content format of today. But, an affective revolution is coming. What the new immersive environments are beginning to do to narrative experiences is to lend them the immediacy and viscerality of an actual presence that make the linear, 'flat' 2D and pseudo-3D formats comparatively less inspiring. Chris Milk, a respected video creator and 'immersive storyteller' described film as 'a series of rectangles played in a sequence'. As a contrast, he famously referred to VR as the 'ultimate empathy machine' and described his approach as 'breaking through the rectangle window of the film frame... VR is not a video-game peripheral, it connects humans to other humans in a profound way that I've never seen in any other form of media' (TED, 2015).

As one performance art project called it, it is 'The Machine to Be Another'. That very program has been used by psychologists, neuroscientists and researchers in six countries to explore issues such as mutual respect, gender identity, physical limitations and immigration. Stanford University's Virtual Human Interaction Lab is literally turning this technology into a way, through its 'Empathy at Scale' project, to teach empathy, towards ourselves and towards others. For example: does seeing a 65-year-old avatar of yourself prompt you to save more for retirement? It does (Stanford Alumni, 2014). It is a different kind of the affective beast...

Our first taste of these new more immersive ways of processing content – apart from the computer games as the global phenomenon that marketing so far failed to properly utilize – was the introduction of the

180-degree and 360-degree videos. Chris Milk's 360-degree film for the United Nations, 'Clouds Over Sidra' (Within, 2016), managed to change perceptions of the refugee crisis and inspire action from some high-profile political personalities at one of the recent Davos gatherings.

But, now, things are getting elevated by several orders of magnitude through AR, VR and intelligent real-life ambients. Google's seminal 'Storyliving' ethnographic study from mid-2017, a joint effort between the Google News Lab and their ZOO creative team, explored how audiences experience VR and what that means for journalists (Google, 2017a). The findings then got its marketing-focused expression in a set of recommendations for brand storytellers, 'Humanizing VR' (Google, 2017b), revealing the blueprint for revolutionizing the way we tell stories. It is the result of the VR research, but the paradigmatic shifts captured by it apply to any of the new deeply immersive spaces.

CASE STUDY Disney *Jungle Book* VR experience

To celebrate their latest version of the popular story, Disney allowed VR users to experience three scenes in the film from the point of view of Mowgli. In one of them, Mowgli meets the giant snake Kaa, who hypnotizes and tries to eat him. The scene is rendered in such exquisite detail, based on the actual video and audio film assets, that some people found it too much: they were quickly getting anxious from standing on a thick branch high above the ground or from the movement of a massive serpent's body through the tree crown, ducking and covering their face when the snake 'pounced' on them, and even falling on the floor in panic! Although basic in player's interaction, the experience was a powerful visceral demonstration of the primal force that a good immersive experience could have.

New rules of storytelling

What Google found in its research was striking (Google, 2017a, 2017b):

- All-encompassing experience: gear and stimulation filter the user out of the real world, no more multi-tasking...

- Open-sourced experience: user is in control and tends to actively explore, instead of just watch; but without a single point of view (POV), every user may get a different takeaway, reducing predictability of the experience.

- Momentary and often non-linear: as Google's Abigail Posner from ZOO explained: 'It might be about a moment in time, and then that moment is slowed down so users can absorb every single detail. Users now have the chance to look under the hood, and feel the nuances of a story in a new way. Imagine, for instance, getting to explore some of the immaculately composed spaces in a Wes Anderson movie' (Berkowitz, 2017).

- Triggering the 'beginner's brain': totally focused in this new world, our brain tries to find any moorings and patterns to make the environment more familiar; in this state of the 'beginner's brain' we tend to be more open to ideas and concepts that challenge existing beliefs.

- 'Embodied knowledge': combining physical, emotional and visceral cues connects us to the story in ways that make it more authentic.

- 'Inhabiting the stories': immersive experience gives our brains the feeling of capturing the *essence* of place, person or thing. We feel we 'know', versus simply 'imagining'.

- 'The fourth perspective': not just the sense of the three-dimensional space, but also of the lasting emotional perspective; a feeling of new 'selflessness', 'shapeshifting' into any other person or object and assuming their point of view...

The bottom line of this crucial set of insights is that users responded to content that was developed outside the traditional frame of characters, plot points and value messages. They had the impression of 'living' the story, not just 'receiving' it as in the traditional channels. It is a visceral experience. As this new space grows, it is breaking through Chris Milk's 'window of a film frame'. In time, user preferences will require us to re-engineer the way we conceive brand work.

New storytelling models for immersive spaces

The biggest challenge for brands and their agencies is going to be how to approach this new space in a strategic way and not as a gimmick where the technology itself is a hero. The much-maligned and braggart-liked industry phrase 'media first' is an example of the wrong focus. PR is here confused with true innovation. That kind of thinking has become a trap for a significant part of the marketing industry. There is another one, potentially even bigger: are these spaces going to be just new and richer canvases for delivering interruption advertising, or new models of brand communications more akin to a product or a service?

As one recent Forrester report wisely observes: 'interruption only works if consumers spend time doing interruptible things on interruption-friendly devices' (McQuivey, 2017).

As our modes of using the media move from communications to experience, and as the very ways we interact with the systems change (from navigating the screen to navigating our lives via intelligent assistants through voice, for example), brand interruption, particularly out of context, could become a brand killer. Context, then, as explored in Chapter 6, becomes the universal, unbreakable law in the new marketing universe. We may, finally, move to marketing as experience.

As we explored in Chapter 2 (about the Experience Economy), designing for time and space – with time and attention now being the only scarcities we have to think about – then also becomes mandatory. The world without discrete boundaries and 'edges' we elaborate on below offers infinite possibilities for both brands and audiences, but the nature of its consumption disadvantages blunt interruption.

CASE STUDY Ivyrevel 'Coded Couture': personal data-designed fashion

Many brands in the fashion and retail space have experimented with interactive and AR technologies, usually in the shopper marketing space. Ivyrevel pushed the concept of data into the personal story space. Consumer's data about various daily activities are collected by the app: daily runs, commuting to work, check-ins into restaurants and public spaces, weather info... Then, when the user needs an item of specific clothing, their mobile phone designs it for them based on the data collected. Data is turned into visual patterns that are then turned into design patterns. Totally unique, as they are uniquely yours. Each item is also a story (Ivyrevel, 2017).

Ivyrevel is also an example of a narrative that is not under the total control of a brand. As Posner highlights above, users may decide to freeze a moment in time within an immersive space for a personal experience that is unique to them. They may also decide to go in any direction they fancy. They may even enter the story at the end and travel backwards. It takes getting used to this way of thinking if we are the ones architecting such experiences.

Chris McCarthy from Google ZOO builds a new angle that may be a bit difficult for traditional brands to digest yet, but is a case for the new and braver reflection of the incoming realities:

I think there is a point here to make that it is often a journey that brands are going on rather than any single claim or point in time that matters – and content can clearly help narrate this journey. Single claims or tent-pole events can provide focal points, for example the REI activist stand against Black Friday, but I feel there is a new storytelling paradigm at work where we set off on a journey without first knowing the end point. This creates authenticity and trust when done right and huge problems when it is not. We have a new ability to create powerful, engaging brand experiences via content that involve the user in a way that wasn't possible before. I often call out three clear groups: stories based on context through data signals (for example the personal data-based clothing design patterns); stories based on immersive experiences (for example BMW's 'Visionary'); and cognizant stories with AI built in (for example Google Assistant's role as the Westworld's 'concierge' Aeden). In all cases, people really drive the experience themselves and also create the content as they go through it. Proof: if I ask you to navigate through a VR/AR experience twice in exactly the same way, you can't – by definition it is a unique, one-time experience. Here technology is really solving problems for brands: they struggle with the tensions of 'control' between the brand and the user and the issue of 'scale' between the unique and the mass. VR for instance can solve both issues: stop thinking brand-controlled content versus user-generated content and get used to user navigated-experience – UNE. The brand controls and creates a brand universe with all the aesthetic demands of the brand equity, then allows users to navigate through it in a unique way. But this can sit on global platforms such as YouTube, with a massive reach.

Hypertelling

In 2016, at the C2 event in Montreal, one of the founders of the Google ZOO creative think-tank, Mike Yapp, used the word 'hypertelling' to great acclaim, to explain the 'new evolution of storytelling' (Sherwood, 2016). He was echoing another talk by the former Google ZOO strategist Eric

Solomon, from 2014, where he described how he coined the word with the help of his Mum (AListDaily, 2014). Mike Yapp explained the approach as user-directed, non-linear and a marked departure from the ways the story was told before. The promise was intriguing, in Yapp's words:

> We are at the cusp of a new era of storytelling in which the user is now the author. The experience is immersive. Scripts are going to look more like decision trees. Directors are going to direct remotely. The user is going to be part of the cast.

The most often-cited example of 'hypertelling' is 'This Exquisite Forest', a project created in 2012 by Chris Milk and Aaron Koblin for Tate Modern, in collaboration with Google's Chrome Experiments program (Google, 2012). Following in the tradition of the French Surrealists who invented a creative word game called 'The Exquisite Corpse', This Exquisite Forest allowed the public, the users, via their browsers, to contribute to the joint narrative initiated ('seeded') by the creators. They added animations, films and any other formats that may be connected, or not at all, with the idea of the main seed narrative. The concept of 'hypertelling' is that the users create their own narrative trees with, theoretically, an infinite number of narrative and directional possibilities; branches and twigs forming their own trees and so on, taking the user consuming it into myriads of unexpected directions. As inspired by Solomon's Mum, a bit like hyperlinks...

Theoretically, the approach offers significant benefits compared to the traditional linear storytelling:

- participation of and co-creation by users;
- a potentially endless number of story element variations;
- a broader inspiration map of manifold creative souls;
- democratization of the story;
- story co-ownership;
- a place and a cause to create a community;
- unlimited duration of the narrative;
- savings by outsourcing production resources;
- celebration of human diversity.

However, since the Tate project, not a lot has been heard about this particular approach, probably because of the equally various difficulties with executing it in practice. Some of the challenges are obvious:

- uncertain, unfocused product of indeterminate shape;
- copyright and IP complexities;

- potential abuses of the space;
- competitive undermining through guerrilla spoilers;
- resources needed to moderate content for legal protection;
- the lack of the skilful, professional storytelling;
- analytics and attribution;
- brand incoherence and tonality challenges;
- quick novelty wear-out;
- need for constant promotional investment to keep it going.

It seems that 'hypertelling', the word that got many buzzing a few years ago, is still just a possibility. Like the data, it is still waiting for its Scorsese...

Storydoing

The other word of the moment got a lot more traction, most likely due to a less obscure founding concept and a broader set of implementation use cases, some of them quite famous.

Originated, as far as we know, in Ty Montague's book *True Story: How to combine story and action to transform your business* (Montague, 2013), the word could mean different things in different contexts. In the organizational strategy space, it is sometimes used to stress the difference between strategy as a 'noun' (storytelling) and a 'verb' (storydoing). Or, from passive broadcast of strategic brand messages, from 'telling' to active behavioural expressions of what a brand is all about, to living and 'showing' the organizational purpose in all touchpoints (Ryan, 2014; co:collective, 2014).

Another definition stems from the advertising space and points to the stronger narrative element in the unit of branded content, making it a story in its own right (Vallance, 2016). They are pieces of drama or experiences of various kinds, including service, replacing the mere 'message'.

CASE STUDY   Glade 'Museum of Feelings'

What used to be considered as the 'mere' experiential marketing is nowadays getting its new digital expression and amplification through projects like this. Glade used one of its scented candles as the platform to visualize and bring to life, in a physical experience, how scents impact our moods. A special interactive and immersive gallery was set up in New York, giving visitors a multi-sensory opportunity to experience the invisible power of scents, reading out their emotions in various biometric ways and collating them into the overall real-time mood map of New York that was then displayed in the gallery (even changing the colour of its walls) and amplified via various social platforms connected to the experience (RedazioneBrandNews, 2015).

Finally, there is an interpretation of the term that is slowly gaining prominence and centrality: a difference between a passive consumption of brand messages by a consumer, usually via traditional channels, and the heightened state of immersion brought about by the 'mixed reality'. So, content, even when done in new ways and in new spaces such as YouTube, even if they are stories in their own right, if they do not have the reality-enhancement elements of 360-degree, AR, VR and AI, would constitute 'just' storytelling.

CASE STUDY Lockheed Martin 'Field Trip to Mars'

A collective VR experience often mentioned as a great example of 'storydoing' (Unreal Engine, 2016). A school bus in the United States was fitted with special windows, dual-purpose glass that turns into a screen. During the ride that was supposed to be just an ordinary school trip, at one point the windows would dim and instead of the familiar street scenes of Washington, DC the kids would see Mars! The experience is powered by the virtual rendering of an area of Mars coordinated with the street grid of Washington, DC, so when the bus turns in real life, it also turns on Mars, matching the speed of the bus, the turning angles and everything else that makes it real. It is one of the best examples of branded 'storydoing' so far, especially because of the collective immersive nature of the experience; everyone was in it together, experiencing it communally, sharing the wonder, instead of through the cocooned separation of the VR visor.

AR at the moment is probably the strongest candidate for rolling out 'story-doing' for the masses. Not just because of the decision by the major platform owners such as Apple or Google to make AR part of the 'native' functionalities on its devices, thus reducing the barriers, but because it has a vast number of genuinely interesting potential use cases (Moren, 2017; Cragg, 2017).

Do you remember the Pokemon GO craze? Another one is Google Expeditions, showing the potential of 'storydoing' for transforming education, or any learning experience.

Omaid Hiwaizi from Blippar has been at the coal face of the AR revolution for some time and, in his discussion with us, is a big believer in the transformative contribution that AR could bring to Content:

> AR has so far largely been a bolt-on to advertising campaigns and that is one of the reasons it still hasn't achieved the traction it could have. However, brands and agencies are now realizing its potential and the power of attaching content to every branded touchpoint and unbranded object in the world and every location. That is when it will actually and truly deliver its value, including societal value. For example, providing help in locations, opportunities for learning languages, finding a way around complexities in areas where expertise isn't immediately available, such as medical help in countries where there isn't a doctor – all of that could be delivered beautifully with AR. Frankly, I think that AR delivering knowledge and expertise to all of society is a much bigger play than providing remarkable help in shopper marketing for brands. For me, that's the stickiest use case for AR.

Storyliving

This is where the lines begin to blur. As mentioned above, 'storyliving' is a new coinage emerging from the Google News Lab ethnographic study, with some radical new rules for constructing stories (Google, 2017b).

The difference between 'storydoing' and 'storyliving' could be perceived as just the semantics, but two things make the latter the emotionally stronger candidate for being taken up as THE label for the new approach to Content. One is the question of the subject: 'storydoing' implies more of something a *brand* would do in its way of engaging consumers; the 'living' part suggests a stronger, deeper, more all-encompassing experience, the people's way of living in which AR and VR have a permanent role, above and beyond occasional 'campaign' messages. In which case, Hiwaizi's use cases can easily sit within the 'living' space too.

'Storyliving', once it becomes ubiquitous, will pose some truly gargantuan challenges for brands and marketing, as well as the overall media and cultural space. As one of the punchlines in 'Humanizing VR' says, brands have to move on 'from message making to meaning making'.

The full 'meaning making' comes to life with how our reactions to the physical space around us will change once this heady combination of AR and VR, called 'mixed reality' (MR) becomes ubiquitous (Wikipedia, 2017). Graeme Devine, Chief Game Wizard at Magic Leap, has a powerful way of putting the point across in one of his lectures, describing the world in which the physical presence of anything is no longer the key determinant of reality: 'just photons, atoms are no longer required… It's the world without edges' (Games for Change, 2016a, 2016b).

A screen, sadly, still gives us the world with edges. It is limiting us. Devine gives a very good example of the worst aspects of the current screen paradigm, especially on mobiles: distracting us from and impeding on real life, blocking us from living in the moment. Take, for example, a visit to a concert. A forest of hands, holding smartphones, recording the gig in front of them – but actually not watching the gig! Just getting a pitiful 2D representation of it. That is not 'storyliving'.

Neither is the vision of the everyday reality imagined in Keiichi Matsuda's short film 'Hyper-Reality', a garish holographic nightmare of AR banners and promotional offers cluttering our visual field as we walk down the street (2016).

It's Devine's worst nightmare come true, the first days of the WWW replayed in real life, screaming for a StreetView equivalent of an ad blocker. If, in Devine's words, people's reaction to the promises of the MR is not 'thank God', we are doing the absolutely wrong thing. The marketing industry has been warned. Purpose has never been more needed than in the next several years.

Mika Tasich, a creative technologist from several digital hot-shops, also with Google experience, makes a very interesting point in our interview on what may be considered 'Content' in the MR world:

It is quite likely that in this space the very definition of it will broaden too, way beyond the immersive films or fully rendered artificial VR or 3D environments. The majority of it may not be 'media' content at all. With MR, the whole space around us becomes the carrier of content, Graeme Devine's world without edges. We may be able to choose new 3D wallpapers in our apartments, digital ornaments for our mantelpieces or walls, or embodied virtual assistants that may change their form depending on how we feel that day, or moment. In this space, IKEA, graphic and interior design studios and Swarovski may become credible players too. We could choose screensavers for our life and, yes, 'brandblockers': any logo, billboard or bus shelter poster we don't want in our viewing field, if we chose so, may be replaced with photos of my dog, cat or family.

It is a terrifying prospect for the interruption ad industry and, if it sounds like sci-fi, think about the current 'adblocalypse' of programmatic and why Google and several other prominent companies have invested heavily in Magic Leap… It should sober us up. On the other hand, says Tasich, there is an opportunity for brands and organizations to enhance and brighten our lives by providing virtual architecture, and furniture, mapped onto the real environments:

We can, for example, walk to work not through a drab London suburb, but through Westeros! And I don't have to be nose-deep into a mobile screen, I can still see people around me. It's the same on public transport, we can actually now look at each other and see a better version of the world, if we choose to. So, if I come to work refreshed and upbeat because of it, instead of miserable and dull, the technology is being the agent of optimism. Also, we may, very probably, not need a lot of physical products any more, things like watches, clocks – TVs and mobiles! – anything that functions through our visual field may be replaced by this one optical-electronic device, feeding into our environment infinite product design and functionality choices! There are many roles for brands in that world, for sure, but unlike the current advertising, and even physical product, paradigm.

What Tasich describes is the Empathic Utility principle on steroids. That kind of thinking, though, we can start practising already in smaller ways, in our world full of edges, while we wait for the magic leap…

AI-powered virtual assistants and smart home environments

The brand relevance challenge particularly applies to the AI-powered virtual assistants such as Alexa, Siri and Google Assistant – the screenless 'Robofriends' of our times. They offer yet another kind of immersiveness, more like having a companion with us than escape from the real world. The usage data is already showing strong trends, as about 20 per cent of all Google searches from mobile and Android devices in the United States – according to Google's own data in 2016 – came by voice (Sterling, 2016). Voice has arrived and is looking for its physical use cases.

Probably one of the biggest around is going to be what Simon Gosling, a futurist from Unruly, called in our interview the 'Ambient Era':

Connected cognified home is going to be the most powerful advertising and marketing canvas that we have ever seen! It is totally immersive, it is familiar and it has got a very low behaviour change threshold, people don't need to learn new kinds of behaviour nor go through the process of firing up a VR set, as currently, to experience the benefits. They would just do whatever they already needed to do, only easier and cheaper. As the home of the future in the 1950s was all about reducing the amount of labour, our home of the future is all about smart assistance. It's only that it's bigger than just our home, as it applies to our car and other spaces we touch in the universally connected world of the internet of things (IoT). The Ambient Era connects all of our 'living' into a central system and is activated by voice in both directions. 'Presence' becomes THE thing, especially for brands. As MR could be considered part of the Ambient Era, 'holograms' that are part of our lives will have to deserve their presence too, it's the hyper-contextual marketing of the highest order. Saying that, there still may be the case for the 'opt-in' approach as we know it: we may still be able to go into the 'Offers On' or 'Offers Off' modes, giving brands a chance to push contextual messages to us for a minute. Saving money and time are still the main reasons quoted by consumers as the reasons to consider such technologies. But, it could also give us an added value in a relevant new discovery; Spotify's Discover Weekly is a great example of applied machine learning: I have started with the music I listened to regularly, only to now move to a completely new set of artists in the genres and moods I like, based on my listening data. The system has started to 'get' me.

But, as we mentioned before, optimizing marketing for an intelligent assistant is a completely different, and still unknown, game. The rules are not yet defined, let alone practised. Brands may create 'skills' – voice-powered assistant 'apps' – for Alexa, but that is just replicating what happened on mobile phones. How the overall media embedding of messages is going to work in the MR world is ours to be discovered. This may even lead to a shift in disciplines, for example from customer relationship management (CRM) to product relationship management (PRM). If the product IS us, it makes sense. What seems a given, though, is that another age, even more than the 'ambient' one, is properly arriving, in the user behaviour, advertising and Content channels and formats: Richard Saul Wurman's 'The Age of Also' (Kolawole, 2011).

Some possible Content challenges with the new affective spaces

It would be foolish to assume that this new paradigm will arrive without challenges beyond technological complexity and the ancient muscle-memory of the industry. They will manifest themselves both at introduction and with the longer-term effects of the new affective spaces on people, business and society.

Probably the first that comes to mind is how to avoid the 'Sam Lundwall/ Hyper-Reality' effect that has plagued the current web: how to protect the new spaces from being spoilt with the crude 'push' thinking that will eventually trivialize it and turn people against it? It could be, for once, that the word 'protect' is not needed here, as any dilettantic effort to try to force and keep the user inside the mixed reality field will most likely be immediately rejected. 'Ambient Era' spaces are even more 'binary' than, say, film: they will either have empathy, or not.

Omaid Hiwaizi agrees:

AR, for example, is a huge challenge for brands if you treat it as a literal layer on everything you see, and people have zero appetite for 'push' in that environment. It's in your eyes, it's in your line of sight, you want to just rip the glasses off and throw them away if they are invaded with crude ads. Should that situation happen, and I think it will, brands will only be able to be successful if they act as great content, finding the places in people's life journeys where they will be welcomed. Then, work with whomever is providing content networks so that their stuff appears on the wider internet, not just on their touchpoints.

In addition to crudeness, the mixed reality introduces a whole new box of worries, for the individuals and for the brands.

One is potential individual isolation introduced by the VR headsets – at least until they are replaced by the more advanced glasses-like devices that Magic Leap is working on. What to do when people become even more strongly separated from their real life, if they prefer the VR worlds? How many brands would like to be associated with it?

Another one is the potential emotional exhaustion from so many intense, immersive experiences 'storyliving' will make a reality. How will the schools, workplaces and our relationships suffer because of it? Are we going to create a new generation of Content zombies?

Related to that, and mentioned in the Google research, how will we take into account the heightened vulnerability of users when constructing a brand experience, due to the 'beginner's brain' and 'embodied knowledge' effects? Various 'Black Mirror' scenarios seem ever more plausible...

Then there is the question of addictiveness that we explore in our chapter about the ethics of Content (Chapter 11). The issue is getting some serious traction in society and MR will just pour petrol on the fire. Omaid Hiwaizi recognizes the challenge, although in a more balanced manner:

I don't think we need to look to the future to answer that question. VR isn't new, it has existed for a long time – the biggest VR use case so far was Second Life, with tens of millions of users, with Second Life marriages, scandals and businesses built on it... Many people got addicted to that. Some people's psychology will lead them to prefer the existence in VR more than in 'R'. With 'mixed reality', which I consider as AR with better visuals, it is still a layer to what is actually going on around you. Thinking of headsets as a form of wearable, what is the profile or the functionalities of it that one would be willing to wear all the time or most of the time? Clearly it will have to look like a set of spectacles, with a holographic projection, that you may order from a local optician, as a future development. We will not be totally separated from the world.

A big challenge is the business model: if users start getting immersed into a particular brand or publishing space for a longer time, they will inevitably be consuming less horizontal content; other contextual stories, clickbait and revenue streams based on the number of page views will potentially evaporate. That will require new business models – borrowed from gaming, publishing, entertainment, e-commerce and consultancy industries – but the industry is currently unused to it.

Given how immersive the new space is, and how adaptable people are, are we going to see an incessant escalation of the emotional intensities in order to keep attention and engagement? Will the space become too extreme at one point? Sam Gregory from Harvard University describes the scenario where 'dropping viewers into a violent experience that is too shocking or horrific might alienate them and make them not want to return, or get involved. Or, if people have no way to take action and help after seeing another's plight, then virtual reality could end up being just another form of poverty tourism. It is confusing immersion for empathy' (Greenwald, 2017).

An interesting and potentially beneficial challenge for the whole industry is the question of whether the more rational, product-attribute-oriented brands will suffer in this space. Will 'storyliving' in the mixed reality space force them to find more creative ways to show (not just to talk about it) why they deserve to exist? Will the FMCG category suddenly undergo a purpose tsunami of a sort, above and beyond carbonated water, chocolate bars and crisps-image fluffery?

Finally, the new immersive, ambient and empathic spaces will produce, collect and analyse even more vast quantities of data in order to create that deserved 'presence' in our new exciting world without edges. The potential for the misuse of that data is also rising exponentially. How we will be affected – as well as protected – in the media future is suddenly gaining yet another, more sinister, dimension.

References

AListDaily (2014) [accessed 30 December 2017] Eric Solomon – Hypertelling Keynote [Online] youtu.be/vnABfK1LWIc

Berkowitz, J (2017) [accessed 30 December 2017] You Are There: Google and TBWA On How VR Will Change Storytelling, *Fast Company*, 24 October [Online] fastcompany.com/40483203/you-are-there-google-and-tbwa-on-how-vr-will-change-storytelling

co:collective (2014) [accessed 30 December 2017] Storydoing: Idea [Online] storydoing.com/#idea

Cragg, O (2017) [accessed 30 December 2017] Google Will Bring AR Apps to 'Hundreds of Millions' of Android Devices in 2018, *Android Authority*, 9 September [Online] androidauthority.com/google-ar-apps-android-arcore-813595/

Dean, B (2016) [accessed 30 December 2017] We Analyzed 1 Million Google Search Results. Here's What We Learned about SEO, *Backlinko*, 2 September [Online] backlinko.com/search-engine-ranking

Games for Change (2016a) [accessed 30 December 2017] Keynote – Into the Future, with Magic Leap's Graeme Devine [Online] youtu.be/_x_VpAjim6g

Games for Change (2016b) [accessed 30 December 2017] Keynote – Into The Future: A World Without Edges with Graeme Devine [Online] youtu.be/QVFkPEqQX-0

Google (2012) [accessed 30 December 2017] This Exquisite Forest: Introduction [Online] youtu.be/nnhJ1841K-8

Google (2017a) [accessed 30 December 2017] Storyliving: An Ethnographic Study of How Audiences Experience VR and What That Means for Journalists [Online] newslab.withgoogle.com/assets/docs/storyliving-a-study-of-vr-in-journalism.pdf

Google (2017b) [accessed 30 December 2017] Humanizing VR and quick Takeaways for Marketers [Online] inventours.com/wp-content/uploads/2017/07/Humanizing-VR.pdf

Greenwald, M (2017) [accessed 30 December 2017] Storytelling To VR 'Storyliving': Future Marketing Communications, *Forbes*, 31 July [Online] forbes.com/sites/michellegreenwald/2017/07/31/from-storytelling-to-vr-storyliving-future-marketing-communications/

Ivyrevel (2017) [accessed 30 December 2017] Coded Couture By Ivyrevel – Introducing the Data_Dress [Online] youtu.be/PUlF3rW8flU

Kolawole, E (2011) [accessed 30 December 2017] Richard Saul Wurman and Living in a World of 'Also', *The Washington Post*, 30 September [Online] washingtonpost.com/national/on-innovations/richard-saul-wurman-and-living-in-a-world-of-also/2011/09/14/gIQA37wx7K_story.html

Matsuda, K (2016) [accessed 30 December 2017] Hyper-Reality [Online] youtu.be/YJg02ivYzSs

McQuivey, J (2017) [accessed 15 May 2017] The End of Advertising, the Beginning of Relationships (Blog), *James McQuivey's Blog: Forrester*, 2 May [Online] blogs.forrester.com/james_mcquivey/17-05-02-the_end_of_advertising_the_beginning_of_relationships

Montague, T (2013) *True Story: How to combine story and action to transform your business*, Harvard Business Review Press, Boston, MA

Moren, D (2017) [accessed 30 December 2017] Analyzing Apple's Next Moves OPINION Apple: Betting Big on AR, *Macworld*, 10 November [Online] macworld.com/article/3236717/iphone-ipad/apple-betting-big-on-ar.html

RedazioneBrandNews (2015) [accessed 30 December 2017] Glade – Museum Of Feelings Case Study [Online] youtu.be/t6_TllTf7-A

Ryan, R (2014) [accessed 30 December 2017] Forget Storytelling, Try Storydoing. There's a Difference between Living Your Brand's Story and Simply Talking about It. Here's How to Distinguish the Two, *Inc*, 27 August [Online] inc.com/rosemarie-ryan/forget-storytelling-try-storydoing.html

Sherwood, I-H (2016) [accessed 30 December 2017] How Long? 2–3 Minutes Forget Storytelling. 'Hypertelling' Is the Future, Says Google Zoo Founder, *Campaign*, 25 May [Online] campaignlive.co.uk/article/forget-storytelling hypertelling-future-says-google-zoo-founder/1396454

Stanford Alumni (2014) [accessed 30 December 2017] Jeremy Bailenson, 'Infinite Reality: The Dawn of the Virtual Revolution' [Online] youtu.be/1jbwxR8bCb4

Sterling, G (2016) [accessed 30 December 2017] Google Says 20 Percent Of Mobile Queries Are Voice Searches Voice Search Growing as Virtual Assistant Market Heats Up, *Search Engine Land*, 18 May [Online] searchengineland.com/google-reveals-20-percent-queries-voice-queries-249917

TED (2015) [accessed 30 December 2017] Chris Milk: How Virtual Reality Can Create the Ultimate Empathy Machine [Online] ted.com/talks/chris_milk_how_virtual_reality_can_create_the_ultimate_empathy_machine

Unreal Engine (2016) [accessed 30 December 2017] Field Trip to Mars: Framestore's Shared VR Experience | Project Highlight | Unreal Engine [Online] youtu.be/e0XNlsXnKp0

Vallance, C (2016) [accessed 30 December 2017] Storytelling Is Dead. Long Live Story Doing, *Campaign*, 22 August [Online] campaignlive.co.uk/article/storytelling-dead-long-live-story-doing/1405760

Wikipedia (2017) [accessed 30 December 2017] Mixed Reality [Online] wikipedia.org/wiki/Mixed_reality

Within (2016) [accessed 30 December 2017] Clouds Over Sidra [Online] youtu.be/mUosdCQsMkM

PART FOUR
How to measure and evaluate Content marketing

Key measurement issues relating to Content marketing

Content works. Content doesn't work. Sometimes it works, sometimes it doesn't.

These are all familiar tropes we are hearing on a daily basis. As with many other debates in our industry, either side is rarely completely right or completely wrong.

The basic logic with any Content activity is that there is *something* that was created and placed *somewhere* for public consumption, ideally with some specific business-related *objectives*. As such, it *can, should* and, if we want to pursue accountability to the end, *must* be measured. In that sense, Content is no different from any other business and marketing activity.

Why the confusion, then? In our experience, part of the answer lies in the breadth of strategic, media, creative and production use cases and expressions that Content has unleashed on the industry. It is a much more 'liquid' space for thinking through, which is mirrored in the evaluation debates. Another reason is the muscle memory of the industry: Content does not have its archetypal format(s) with a solidified set of usual metrics attached to it. It requires constant contextual evaluation. But, there are other structural internal issues and just plain wrong questions asked about the role of Content in marketing activities.

This chapter outlines some of the key debates around Content evaluation in its broadest sense.

Key strategic challenges

Measurement starts with asking the right questions

As Scott Donaton from Digitas pointed out in Chapter 6, it is wrong to ask 'what is Content best at?' as it can outperform traditional online advertising across the whole of the customer journey. It is more useful to first determine:

> ... what you are trying to accomplish and once you have established that KPI then it is going to change the kind of content you create and how you distribute it.

In other words, strategy comes first and, with it, a set of strategic objectives and metrics. We should always try to measure the success factors for our specific strategy. Joe Pulizzi from the Content Marketing Institute calls it 'ROO: return on objectives' (2012). They may, and will, vary across the customer journey and various touchpoints and need states.

Joe Lazauskas from Contently, summing up their experience with working across a large client portfolio, highlights several reasons that contribute to Content often not being well measured:

A lot of folks threw themselves into Content without thinking about how it relates to their larger business goals. They were doing Content for the sake of it, because that was that hot thing they thought they should be doing without actually thinking about the business problem that it was addressing. Without it, it becomes impossible to measure its effectiveness because all you are doing then is grabbing arbitrary metrics that don't mean a lot to the CEOs. I believe that is where this notion that Content is not measurable comes from. If you have the business cases for using it, it is actually fairly easy to prove the impact that Content had. There is nothing inherent in Content that makes it harder to measure.

Integration is another big factor: in many companies Content is developed as a siloed operation, not integrated in the overall marketing strategy as it is seen as this magical 'other' thing that is just put aside with the experimental budget. There is this magical thinking that Content is, somehow, just supposed to work! You just make it and people somehow just arrive there. No promotion, no push, no discoverability efforts. That is not how it works. You have to market it via all your relevant channels. I think we are seeing this shift to the strategic view of Content more these days, particularly among the market-leading companies, not isolated but integrated into the overall marketing functions. That is where the industry is heading now. Content is becoming a fundamental part of all brand communications.

Magical Content thinking

This magical thinking about the power of Content influences the expectations of its potential success as a cultural, 'mimetic' product. From what we have observed, it creates a very peculiar cycle of overexcitement and inflated expectations at the beginning, followed by the disappointment and confusion afterwards. We believe it is a remnant of another early web phenomenon, 'viral marketing', with the assumption that brands can suddenly replicate massive successes of various unbranded web content phenomena; that just having a great idea is enough to be widely spread. Sometimes it is, but very, very rarely. Purchasing a lotto ticket is the precondition of a possible win, but how many times does it actually happen? It is the same with great brand creative ideas. It is a table stake for success, but the odds are against it. To start with, they are not that easy to create, even by the best agencies; even more important, the noise in the modern media space is such that even an organically strong idea will not have a long cycle of sharing. The 'social diffusion curve' by Unruly, based on the speed of social sharing of the 100 globally *most shared* branded videos in 2013 and 2014 shows that the 'viral window', defined as 65 per cent of all shares the piece of content has received, happens by the end of the launch week (Waterhouse, 2014).

The industry is in a desperate need for a 'viral myopia' correction. A robust post by Gartner L2 about the myth of the viral video (Rosen, 2015), and many prominent industry names we have interviewed for the book, agree with our personal experience that the majority of the views a good piece of branded content will receive in its lifetime will have to be paid for – particularly if aimed at the beginning of the customer journey, trying to generate brand awareness and buzz resulting in a large number of views. Even for the most iconic ones, of the Always '#LikeAGirl' or Dove 'Real Beauty Sketches' calibre, that ratio will rarely go below 50:50, or half of it will be paid and another half earned (and is reported for 'Real Beauty Sketches' in the Gartner L2 piece above as 75 per cent paid). For merely 'good' ones, that ratio is usually closer to 70:30 or 80:20 paid/earned, as a rule. An officially uncorroborated estimate for the average paid/earned ratio across the whole of the branded Content spectrum on a global platform such as YouTube puts it as high as 90:10. So, Content HAS to be promoted, admittedly in smart and dynamic ways depending on the organic strength of the creative idea, and that additional promotional spend has to be planned in advance and contribute to the overall ROI calculation and the expectation management.

The internal integration puzzle

Joe Lazauskas flags up another layer of assumptions that are often missed when thinking about evaluating Content, this time relating to the internal operational and process-driven considerations:

> A centralized Content operation, supported by appropriate technology, allows a company to organize, surface and optimize content, as well as have a strong Content strategy, so that it can utilize it across the functions, markets and even the globe. That is another way to look at ROI that people don't usually talk about, a hidden area of ROI: the joint production costs, savings in time needed to conceive it because it was done in a unified workflow, saving from reusing the content and, ultimately, money saved by making 95 per cent, instead of 25 per cent, of your content usable.

This is one of the most important points to be made when Content is benchmarked against other parts of the marcoms mix. At the moment, for all the reasons mentioned above, a lot of organizations are wasting money – even before they send out a single piece of content! The biggest problem with the effectiveness of Content is internal, not external; at the point of origin, not delivery. This fact was highlighted quite powerfully in an often-quoted research by the international B2B consultancy Sirius Decisions. As reported in a Contently blog post, 65 per cent of content never goes public because it is either unusable (37 per cent) or internally unfindable (28 per cent). Sirius Decisions reports that enterprise B2B organizations spend roughly twice what they think they do on Content. No wonder, as the same research flags up a disturbing fact that 75 per cent of the marketing teams in this space do not have a formalized approach to the Content eco-system (Baker, 2017).

'The martech tsunami' – explosion of integration and evaluation platforms

Modern marketing, to the chagrin of the creative side of the industry, is rapidly getting 'platformized': marketing technology ('martech') is becoming the engine of the industry, in a myriad of different ways. The number of software companies providing some sort of a marketing solution is exploding, as evidenced in the staggeringly complex 'Marketing Technology Landscape Supergraphic' created by Scott Brinker of Chiefmartec.com (2017a): it has 5,000 logos in it! Some estimates posit that by 2027 we may see around 1 million software companies providing marketing solutions (Brinker, 2017b)! The industry is, undoubtedly, changing beyond recognition and these new shiny 'delivery systems' are, apparently, contributing to the Content 'digital landfill' that bothers Dave Trott so much (see Chapter 10).

It is the consequence of several trends. Digitalization of the world has grown the scope of marketing as we know it. It blurred the lines, as we mentioned elsewhere in the book, between the product itself, the place of sales, the communications and the customer service. In other words, Experience (ideally with a capital 'E') becomes critical and for that we need better (and better unified and accountable) customer and business intelligence, as our actions will sprawl the whole of the customer journey. To complicate further, parts of that journey are also going to be offline. The question of context, as explored in Chapter 6, looms over all marketers. It goes without mention that this new marketing universe runs on data, bringing the challenges of Big Data's 5Vs, as we have seen in Chapter 7. Only technology can provide the solution for that. Being able to deliver strong Empathic Utility in all key touchpoints is the new battleground. This is also the reason for other trends mentioned in the book, particularly the shift of budgets to more measurable modes of marketing, consultancies coming downstream to compete for the share of the brand marketing spend, advertisers buying media and even creative services directly from big platforms, or creating those capabilities in-house. The martech tsunami is also one of the reasons for both proliferation of the measurement metrics, and – as explored below with Content in mind – for the creation of some new ones.

Measuring the right things: evaluation 'canvases'

These are big conceptual 'levels', or sets of optics that an organization could apply to look at the role of Content and subsequently measure. They often sit above the specific evaluation frameworks and sets of metrics and should provide the answer to the 'why?' question: why deploy content in the first place?

Measuring the effects across the customer journey

This is probably the most common conceptual 'canvas' for defining evaluation frameworks not just for Content, but for the whole of the marketing activity. As explained in detail in Chapter 6, the role of Content across the journey spectrum could be manifold. Due to its flexibility and ability to work across the whole of the Empathic Utility spectrum, Content evaluation should be guided by contextually specific, to quote Joe Pulizzi again, return on objectives.

This is the broadest evaluation canvas and presents significant challenges for strategic unification between different organizational functions. It is complicated enough to make various comms siloes work together, even more difficult across various disciplines. Although individual metrics are not difficult to define against specific objectives, setting up technology, tracking, attribution and reporting across different functions is still a formidable management challenge. When our washing machine packs up, we don't want marketing content, we want to have that problem solved. That may include a Content solution: a diagnostic utility (even better if it is empathic) to tell us if our washing machine is *kaputt*, or an agent, or a chatbot, or some kind of decision tree to work out if the problem is fixable by ourselves, or by someone at a cost that is less than getting a new one. Because if we don't get that Empathic Utility, we will not be buying another product from that vendor regardless of how well they measure their content.

Measuring short- and long-term effects

One of the most influential analyses of the impact of marketing communications on the long- and short-term effects in building a brand and achieving business success are Les Binet's and Peter Field's studies for the UK's Institute of Practitioners in Advertising (IPA). They are based on the Databank of the IPA's Effectiveness Awards – great creative campaigns with a proven business impact. For a decade now, it has influenced how clients and agencies – deeply divided along the binary world view of 'emotional' and 'rational' explored in Chapter 4 – weigh their budgets and prioritize media channel mixes. Its newest iteration, 'Media in focus – marketing effectiveness in the digital era' (IPA, 2017), brings confirmation of the already proven principles, and a few surprises.

For example, long-term communication strategies, usually based on emotional resonance, are more than 10 times more likely to generate market-share growth. Similarly, they advise brands to focus on profit growth versus return on marketing investment (ROMI), in other words less on efficiency of the budget and more on the impact. To do that, they advise dividing the budget long-term 60:40 between the brand-building and activation efforts. Most surprisingly for some, they demonstrate that broad-reach campaigns are still the best way to drive market share, which is in turn a key driver of profit, as well as that TV is still the most effective medium and has been getting more effective in part due to synergies with online video. Binet's and Field's work is still the industry standard that cannot be missed in any serious analysis of the effects of marketing communications, including Content. However, the potential downside is that it is communication- and advertising-centric, which leaves an open question: can we apply the same principles on other marketing areas, such as experiences? Will this sturdy piece of analysis stand in the immersive world of MR, intelligent agents, IoT and Ambient Home?

Measuring the organization's 'storydoing'/'storyliving' capabilities

As we have seen in the previous chapter, the nature of what we call 'story-telling' is going to be transformed with the arrival of the more immersive media platforms with 'experience' instead of 'message' at the heart of it. This would require an unusual blend of external and internal evaluation approaches that support several concepts – such as Experience Economy, 'return on experience' or the hybrid Empathic Utility that we have discussed elsewhere in the book. This touches upon several criteria that consultant Ty Montague calls 'storydoing', as mentioned in Chapter 8 (Montague, 2013). This is a virgin territory for most brands, but Montague gives six useful thinking points to define 'storydoing' and potential ways to measure it:

1 Do you have a story?

2 Does it define an ambition beyond commercial aspiration?

3 Is it understood and cared about by the entire company?

4 Is it used to drive action throughout the company?

5 Have you defined a few iconic transformative actions to focus on?

6 Are people outside the company engaging with and participating in the story?

It remains to be seen in the years to come in what ways the new rules of building immersive brand worlds will correlate with business success, internally and externally – and how they will be measured…

Measuring things right: key metrics debates

In our experience, organizations always measure three key things in marketing communications: emotions, behaviours and financials. However, there are myriad ways that these could be packaged in various canvases and frameworks to be made useful for various stakeholders in the company, for various purposes. These are the 'what?' and 'how?' questions: what exactly to measure for a specific 'canvas' and objective, and how to track it and benchmark it. These measures are a mix of the old and new, metrics that have been used for decades in advertising and some new ones that reflect the hybrid nature of the Content space and various formats and objectives it could address.

As mentioned above, the key skill here is to choose and set up metrics that will allow us to measure specific goals we are trying to achieve, instead of measuring only what is easy or simple to measure. This really has a very strong impact on the analytics deployed for providing evaluation, tracking put in place and interdepartmental roles and responsibilities, and mechanism in order to make it happen. That is one of the reasons that many companies still opt for the easy route.

There are several metrics worthy of spending more time on, as they highlight various facets of the Content evaluation spectrum.

Brand outcomes

One of the most discussed charts relating to Content in the last few years was Unruly's 'social diffusion curve' mentioned above. It used the metric of sharing a video, in this instance based on the 100 most shared branded videos globally, to assess the strength of its viral quality. However, the reason for not having updates of the chart was summed up in our interview with Ian Forrester from Unruly:

> Sharing is only one by-product of a really strong video. There are others, such as brand recall, purchase intent, intent to discuss, tendency to find out more or video rewatch. We saw a shift towards measuring key brand

> KPIs so the clients can compare likes with likes. Also, what we have seen in our research is a strong correlation between the emotional power of the video and brand outcomes, which then correlate with business outcomes, so we tend to focus on those.

What about the 'eyeballs'? Should the views be an important metric? Not according to Jonah Peretti, founder of BuzzFeed: 'The primary thing we look for with news is impact, not traffic' (Martinson, 2015). Matthew Barby from HubSpot, in his high-impact blog piece on Moz, agrees (2016):

> Just because you've managed to get more eyeballs onto your content doesn't mean it's actually achieved anything. If that were the case I'd just take a few hundred dollars and buy some paid StumbleUpon traffic every time.

Sales funnel metrics

One of the running jokes in the industry is the set of acronyms for evaluating different parts of the customer journey funnel. They sound funny, but actually save time to the professionals and go under the monikers of TOFU, MOFU and BOFU, each focusing on a specific part 'of the funnel' (OFU): top, middle and bottom.

These approaches reflect frameworks used by many organizations to measure the effects of their communications activities across the customer journey canvas. So much, in fact, that they are very often considered THE ways to measure marcomms, especially on the client and agency side. It makes sense, as Content in the marketing context usually means driving various brand and business indicators, some sort of an action, not just aggregating 'eyeballs' so that they could be sold to advertisers, as would be the case with a publisher.

An example of that, in the Content area and with a slight B2B slant, is proposed by the Content Marketing Institute (CMI) and uses four 'buckets' of metrics (Linn, 2012):

1 **Consumption** (views, downloads and similar, indicating how users consume our content).

2 **Sharing/engagement** (all the actions indicating further engagement with the content such as likes, comments, shares, e-mail forwards or inbound links generation).

3 **Lead generation** (a broad bucket containing everything from downloads and various subscriptions, to brochure orders, enquiries, trials, test-drive bookings and similar).

4 **Sales** (online and offline, if it can be attributed).

Testing emotional impact

As mentioned in Chapter 6, various organizations try to reduce the risk of producing and promoting content by using various techniques for measuring and optimizing desirable aspects of the work. BuzzFeed is one of the most dedicated to it, but a raft of new approaches try to bottle that particular emotional magic.

One of the newer and rapidly deployed is 'face tracing' or 'coding'. It relies on face and mood-states recognition patterns via a camera, while the typical prospective user recruited for the research exercise watches the content. Eye-pupil dilations, face-muscle movements and archetypal emotional expressions are all recorded and interpreted via, usually ML-trained, algorithms. It is an exciting prospect for content creators, if its promise gets fully realized over time, to measure these involuntary and, hence, unbiased levels of emotional engagement – providing an entirely objective response that can identify the strongest points within the content, as well as overall. As such, it has a potential to become THE creative and story optimization tool.

Ian Forrester makes an important point about how this kind of creating an 'emotional profile' of the user may help with increasing the predictability of effects:

The cumulative emotional response of our test group, typical for the audience we are trying to reach, allows us to predict how the video will perform for the same 'bull's eye' audience 'in the wild'. The granularity of some of these techniques help us to see how a video may behave in a fast-scrolling sound-off environment such as Facebook: the need for fast-paced cuts or overacting and exaggerating the action in the first few seconds – all in an attempt to attract attention and avoid being skipped. It is also interesting to mention that emotion can happen even without a story, for example, as a shock, which we would be able to capture too. The market has massively moved in this direction now.

This seems to be corroborated by the amount of effort various other leading industry players are putting into proving the correlation between emotions and effects on brand and even sales. The IPA, Nielsen, Ehrenberg-Bass Institute and big ad testing houses such as Millward Brown or Ipsos have all published extensive research on this topic.

Finally, a concept that hogged most of the limelight in the last few years when the 'future of marketing' was discussed: neuromarketing. Seeing people with EEG headsets or lying in an MRI-scan 'doughnut' watching ads is also becoming a more common sight in the research rooms. However, the approach was not without its challenges (Dooley, 2015). Many neuroscientists disagreed with claims that what was so far tried only in labs could be brought into the commercial testing environment with a purpose of predicting the effectiveness of ads. It culminated in a famous incident where a well-known business writer and consultant Martin Lindstrom published an op-ed in the *New York Times* purporting that, based on fMRI data, the way iPhone owners felt about their phones was akin to romantic love – only to be strongly rebuked by a group of 45 academics (Poldrack, 2011)!

Some recent developments seem to be a point where science meets marketing half-way, as more robust academic assessment of various techniques did show that some of them can have predictive power, but not all of them (Dooley, 2015). However, variations in the procedures by vendors and a few other factors may complicate the picture for the time being, but one important thing has been achieved: the gap between the claims of the marketers and the academics seems to have begun to close.

It is relevant to mention here an already existing approach developed for the purpose of predicting the potential resonance of advertising. This is Professor Robert Heath's Cognitive Emotive Power (CEP) Test, attempting to measure, still based on what consumers say, the emotional and cognitive reaction to ads (and content, in this instance). Heath is the author of one of the industry's seminal books, *The Hidden Power of Advertising* (2001), one of the first to build a compelling scientific case for the emotional impact of ads. The CEP system tries to measure two sides of the impact (Brandt, 2015): the information power (the perceived value of the message to the consumer) and the emotive power (not which emotion is triggered by the ad, but whether it is going to influence feelings about positive brand perception). It remains to be seen how this stalwart of adland's emotive research is going to sustain the onslaught of the neuro-measurement armada.

However, CEP is just one iconic example in a very broad and very rich field of research by many well-known industry names, encompassing a raft of academic disciplines in trying to increase the robustness of the answer to that magical question: 'will it/did it work?' As Raymond Pettit, the VP of analytics at comScore, explains, it is an eclectic mix of approaches:

> Neuroscience supports the use of psychophysiological methods to assess the unconscious response to branding moments in content. This gets at the inherent implicit processing of the brand by the viewer. Aesthetics provides mostly theoretical frameworks for how people respond to and find meaning from signs/symbols (eg brands) and, more importantly, the structural analysis of aesthetic form (the familiar terminology says branded content has to be organic and seamlessly fit in the storyline – there are aesthetic concepts). In addition, we have used research on quantitative information theory and aesthetic response, which is quite useful to quantify content impacts. Finally, semiotics is a research discipline that looks at how people create 'meaning' from stories, narratives, associations and symbols – again very relevant to the brand's appearance (moments) in content that are measurable. You hear a lot that 'emotion' drives behaviour, we actually believe it is 'emotion and meaning' that drive behaviour. Thus the extension in these other areas of science and research to ensure a holistic perspective in the measurement of brands in content.

As always, there must be a fly in the ointment. Effectiveness debates aside, here it is ethics. Some may fear that all the findings from the emotional response and neuromarketing tests, and the wider deployment of the learning, will eventually build the theoretical and practical apparatus for what Andrew McStay calls 'empathic media'. The learning we glean from predicting emotional responses of the population in certain situations may also be appropriated for more nefarious purposes than selling holidays, crisps and shampoo, producing bigger and more disturbing consequences. The outlines of that are already visible in our public sphere in recent years and pose a question of the ethical robustness (or relativism) of the whole marketing industry regarding the overall impact it has – or will have – on society.

Total time read (TTR)

The main contester, in the last few years, to 'page view' as the clunky workhorse of digital marketing analytics has been this composite metric borrowed from the digital publishers and getting more sophisticated by the day. In a nutshell, TTR measures the total time a piece of content, in this case a text-based one, has received from either an individual user or all the users who have visited its page. It is a more qualitative and nuanced metric than just the page view (that could be defined in at least four different ways), particularly because the measurable actions that go into the metric include regular readings of the scroll positions on the page, across the period of time. That way, a publisher can spot when users are taking a break, only to return to the article later – sometimes after a few days! Given that TTR reflects the quality of the engagement through the proxy of time spent, it puts the page view into a different light: a piece of content may receive only 1,000 page views, but accumulate more TTR than one with 10,000. From the quality point of view, TTR works better. It is a favourite metric of the publishers such as *Medium*, who are often described as 'content matchmaking' platforms (Davies, 2013). They want people to write – and others to read – great posts and TTR is the weapon to achieve that.

Dejan Nikolic from Content Insights, one of the newer analytics providers used by a raft of well-known brands, explains another side of such quality-based metrics:

The tension in the publishing world regarding measuring is that the sales are looking at building the inventory, management is keen on delivery and the editorial, well, it is now quite confusing for them... Metrics should not be used just to rate and benchmark the internal performance of people, the 'Jack Welch-ian' approach to analytics, but – when we start introducing more reader-experience-based metrics, instead of just browser-based for such a page view – we get a different view of what works. Pinging the page every five seconds gives a raft of data to assess the attention time given by the user to the piece of content. We can now measure loyalty of audiences by a topic, an author and even the contribution of individual articles to building an overall loyalty to the publisher, with impact on the business model and the sales. This can now spill over into a different incentive model for the editorial too.

'Watch time' and 'average per cent completion' – key video metrics

Both for YouTube and Facebook – and brands who want to operate well with video content on these platforms – these two may well be the most important metrics to consider. So important, actually, that YouTube has replaced page view report from its analytics with watch time (YouTube Creators Academy, 2016). Watch time is measured in cumulative minutes watched (all viewers of the video), and each video uploaded – as well as every channel on YouTube – is prioritized by watch time. Channels and videos with higher watch times are likely to show up higher in search results and recommendations. For a brand, it is a signal that content is resonating with the audience.

Even more interesting and important for the video creators is the average percentage of the whole video that the audience bothered to watch. It is stating the obvious that the ideal outcome would be 100 per cent, but not a lot of branded videos reach that level, if any. However, this is the key pointer about the overall length of the video and its optimization, as well as about the strength of the overall story and its structure. Facebook is hot on this metric and uses it to prioritize videos in the news feed, with a particular weighting given to the completion percentage of longer videos (Bapna and Park, 2017).

Social lift

One of BuzzFeed's secret weapons, social lift is a split of a total number of views received for the piece of content between the views that came from the 'Seed' traffic (that owned and promoted by BuzzFeed, for example in their news feed) and the 'Social' traffic (originating outside of BuzzFeed, such as social media, e-mail and blog shares). It points to the 'virality' of content, its energy for being shared on the web (Barby, 2016). It does not require huge leaps of imagination to see how it may help editors create more popular solutions. Whether it helps develop better-quality content is a moot point because *quality* is in the eye of the beholder and *popularity* has become the default proxy for it, particularly from the point of view of a publisher. In a more tightly focused brand world, this metric may be a good benchmark for the overall shareability of the brand content, historically, with an aim of improving and optimizing strategy, messaging and targeting over time.

Advertising value equivalency (AVE)

A favourite of PR agencies in the early phases of the web during the 'viral' craze, this metric is now much reviled, although, surprisingly, not completely abandoned. Like the page view, many practitioners in our industry are questioning its usefulness, mostly because they deem it too imprecise to reflect the reality of the 'organic' reach a piece of content may have achieved. But a lot of people are sticking with it as it is such a simple and intuitive concept to grasp, particularly to non-communications people, and often at no additional cost. Never mind its often shoddy reporting methodology. Data from media-measurement company Kantar Media reveals that of the company's 1,000 analysis clients, most of them in-house professionals, 25 per cent are still requesting AVE figures (Baker, 2016). It is a strangely comforting metric, deceptively showing how the client's money and the agency's idea had worked harder and, because it has the feeling of 'saving' imbued in it, it works strongly on our 'loss aversion' biases. The informed debates these days advocate, first, a strategic approach to defining project objectives and, second, paying more attention to behavioural change metrics instead – the 'outcome' metrics versus 'output' ones such as AVE – as a better gauge of the efficiency of the budget.

Lifetime value (LTV)

This is a metric cherished by start-ups and app managers (Sahni, 2016). It reads out the quality of the customers an organization is recruiting over time and as such is an example of the 'outcome' metric: things that really make the difference to the bottom line. Although not very difficult to understand (total value realized from a typical customer during their 'lifetime' with a company, calculated in various ways), it is surprisingly rarely used by brands. However, various evidence points to a shift from measuring just an immediate ROI on acquisition channels to this metric as a more reliable long-term measure of how marketing budget, and media mixes, are performing. As a basic example, a channel that provides more TOFU traffic than others may be proven to also recruit lower-quality customers long term and smart companies may want to change that. Also, in the new world of immersive environments, which may be expensive to create, keeping the customer for longer may become one of the key tasks, increasing the prominence of this metric in the future.

References

Baker, D (2017) [accessed 30 December 2017] The Problem That's Quietly Sabotaging Your Marketing Budget, *Contently: The Content Strategist*, 8 September [Online] contently.com/strategist/2017/09/08/quietly-sabotaging-marketing-budget/

Baker, H (2016) [accessed 30 December 2017] Measuring PR: What Comes After AVE? (Blog), *CIPR Influence*, 31 May [Online] influence.cipr.co.uk/2016/05/31/measuring-pr-comes-ave/

Bapna, A and Park, S (2017) [accessed 30 December 2017] News Feed FYI: Updating How We Account for Video Completion Rates, *Facebook Newsroom*, 26 January [Online] newsroom.fb.com/news/2017/01/news-feed-fyi-updating-how-we-account-for-video-completion-rates/

Barby, M (2016) [accessed 30 December 2017] Measuring Content: You're Doing It Wrong (Blog), *MOZ*, 27 April [Online] moz.com/blog/measuring-content-youre-doing-it-wrong

Brandt, D (2015) [accessed 30 December 2017] Uncommon Sense: The Emotive Power of Marketing, *Nielsen Newswire*, 6 November [Online] nielsen.com/us/en/insights/news/2015/uncommon-sense-the-emotive-power-of-marketing.html/

Brinker, S (2017a) [accessed 30 December 2017] Marketing Technology Landscape Supergraphic (2017): Martech 5000, *chiefmartec.com*, 10 May [Online] chiefmartec.com/2017/05/marketing-techniology-landscape-supergraphic-2017/

Brinker, S (2017b) [accessed 30 December 2017] 1 Million Software Companies by 2027? We're Gonna Need a Bigger Chart, *chiefmartec.com*, 11 November [Online] chiefmartec.com/2017/11/1-million-software-companies-2027-gonna-need-bigger-chart/

Davies, P (2013) [accessed 30 December 2017] Medium's Metric That Matters: Total Time Reading, *Medium: M Data Lab*, 21 November [Online] medium.com/data-lab/mediums-metric-that-matters-total-time-reading-86c4970837d5

Dooley, R (2015) [accessed 30 December 2017] Neuromarketing: Pseudoscience No More, *Forbes*, 24 February [Online] forbes.com/sites/rogerdooley/2015/02/24/neuromarketing-temple

Heath, R (2001) *The Hidden Power of Advertising: How low involvement processing influences the way we choose brands*, NTC Publications, London

IPA (2017) [accessed 30 December 2017] New IPA Report from Binet and Field Reveals Key Ways to Drive Campaign Effectiveness [Online] ipa.co.uk/news/new-ipa-report-from-binet-and-field-reveals-key-ways-to-drive-campaign-effectiveness

Linn, M (2012) [accessed 30 December 2017] A Field Guide to the 4 Types of Content Marketing Metrics #eBook, *Content Marketing Institute*, 5 November [Online] contentmarketinginstitute.com/2012/11/a-field-guide-to-the-4-types-of-content-marketing-metrics-ebook/

Martinson, J (2015) [accessed 30 December 2017] Media Interview BuzzFeed's Jonah Peretti: How the Great Entertainer Got Serious, *The Guardian*, 15 November [Online] theguardian.com/media/2015/nov/15/buzzfeed-jonah-peretti-facebook-ads

Montague, T (2013) [accessed 30 December 2017] Good Companies Are Storytellers. Great Companies Are Storydoers, *Harvard Business Review*, 16 July [Online] hbr.org/2013/07/good-companies-are-storyteller

Poldrack, R (2011) [accessed 30 December 2017] The iPhone and the Brain, *The New York Times*, 4 October [Online] nytimes.com/2011/10/05/opinion/the-iphone-and-the-brain.html

Pulizzi, J (2012) [accessed 30 December 2017] How to Attract and Retain Customers with Content Now, *Content Marketing Institute* [Online] contentmarketinginstitute.com/wp-content/uploads/2012/09/cmi_attractandretain.pdf

Rosen, E (2015) [accessed 30 December 2017] Why the Viral Video Is a Myth, *L2 Gartner*, 21 August [Online] l2inc.com/daily-insights/why-the-viral-video-is-a-myth

Sahni, D (2016) [accessed 30 December 2017] School of Ad Tech Part 2: ABC's of LTV (Blog), *AppLift*, 3 November [Online] applift.com/blog/Why-LTV-Matters

Waterhouse, D (2014) [accessed 30 December 2017] Speed of Social Video Sharing Almost Doubles in 12 Months, *Unruly*, 21 May [Online] unruly.co/news/article/2014/05/21/speed-social-video-sharing-almost-doubles-12-months/

YouTube Creators Academy (2016) [accessed 30 December 2017] Lesson: YouTube metrics that Matter [Online] creatoracademy.youtube.com/page/lesson/impact-metrics#strategies-zippy-link-2

PART FIVE
Content marketing: not such a new and better promise?

The rejecter's manifesto

10

Key arguments against the Content marketing 'mirage'

Is content marketing a load of bollocks?
The emergence of content marketing as a separate discipline has
distracted marketers from their real job of communicating with customers
and selling stuff.

PROFESSOR MARK RITSON, *MARKETING WEEK* (2016)

The phrase arrived from a different area of expertise, but very quickly caught on in adland and became a synonym for all the 'viral' delusions, sloppy strategies, uninspiring creative ideas, useless apps and other assorted collective misses the industry entering the digital age has become notorious for. 'Digital landfill' was an apt way to describe what happens with our ideas (Mancini, 2008) when we don't think, don't empathize, don't use the data well, don't tell a good story – don't provide a great experience.

Criticisms of Content are manifold, from a lot of different angles. Some are related to terminology and definitions (or the lack of); some deny Content any novelty and there is also despair about the lack of substance and too much focus on new tech delivery systems; some are meticulous demolitions of exaggerated claims and confused models, using robust analytics.

The feelings of many involved in the industry are mixed. On one hand, any constructive and informed criticism is welcomed to prevent the industry getting into one hype too many, as it is usually prone. Keeping the focus in the uncertain times of paradigmatic shifts is crucial.

On the other hand, to some, the critics sound like laggards, fogies who yearn for the good old times where pints of beer were the fuel of creativity and advertising still relied on TV-watching humans to make a difference. Then, there are careers to be made in this sexy new field, technology to sell, revenue streams to be diversified and reputations to be built on the new points of confusion. There is a whole new evangelical industry that energetically defends its newly found commercial hunting ground against any naysayers.

As with many other things in this book, the truth is somewhere in the middle and hugely depends on the optics. The people who are pointing to the emperor's new clothes, or at least the partial exposure of sensitive parts, are not laggards, bur some of the wisest and bravest people in the industry, putting their professional heads above the proverbial parapet in the battle for truth, sanity and perspective. In order to prosper as an industry, we owe it to them to listen seriously as they try to save us from our own worst excesses, particularly as they seem to have the data on their side.

However, do we also want to throw the baby out with the bathwater? As this book has also shown, convincingly we hope, Content IS one of the ways brands could think and behave in their move away from the troubles of online advertising and the challenges of the new immersive spaces that do not tolerate 'push' actions well. It could also become an important stepping stone towards the more empathic media space and the more developed Experience Economy, if only done with more thought and care – if we manage to separate the hype from the truth.

In the next few sections we explore some of the main thrusts of objecting to Content as a paradigm, or at least some of its aspects.

Content marketing is nothing new

Never mind John Deere's *The Furrow* agricultural journal, the *Michelin Guide* or the very beginning of branding in electronic media such as radio, as highlighted at the beginning of Chapter 5 – the argument that Content doesn't deserve even a separate name, let alone a discipline, goes all the way to our present days.

It was rubbed in the industry's face by the article that caused much stir, quoted above, from the columnist and marketing professor Mark Ritson. He compared content marketing to Theodore Levitt's famous phrase about 'marketing myopia' and accused content marketers of thinking that the only reason for their existence is creating content, not talking to customers and selling.

In the two legendary examples mentioned above he sees only long-established approaches that could be useful to consider as valid marketing thinking, but nothing new:

> Both are amazing marketing tactics but I see them as examples of direct mail and nascent advertising respectively, not something in need of a new name.

In our conversation for the book, Professor Ritson – with an extensive experience of working with some of the world's biggest and most successful companies – warns against some excesses related to the way the marketing industry thinks of Content:

It certainly pays these days to invent the trademark term and a different approach. With the long tail, one can make quite a significant amount of money by then marketing that term as something legitimate and distinctive. It wasn't the case with some previous stuff like 'integrated marketing', on which Professor Don Shultz never wrote dumb insulting textbooks on the subject and never made a dime on it. It was a more realistic concept, rather boring and humble in its scope. That doesn't pay now. Content marketing certainly isn't the only area where we pushed the boat out, and then some, because there is a financial incentive to try and claim a bit of a territory, whether that territory actually exists or not.

If it exists, it is not something truly distinctive. There are two issues here. One, it reflects the ignorance of people coming into marketing without training and, therefore, thinking they are genuinely discovering a wheel and not realizing they are reinventing an old one because they never studied a wheel in the first place. Marketing is full of thought leaders and gurus who really should go and study it first before they start writing books on it, give video series on it and similar. As a professor of marketing I do have an inherent axe to grind, but it doesn't stop me from being true; if everyone had been taught marketing reasonably well, somewhere, whether at a company or a business school, much of this would already fall into place. It's like we've got basic biology and suddenly all these people have started practising medicine without a fundamental knowledge of biology, so they rename the lungs as the 'breathing apparatus' and it doesn't occur to them that someone had discovered that 150 years ago and just called it something different. So, it's a reflection of the naivety and ignorance that goes on in the corners of marketing at the moment.

Then, there is the issue of the inflated self-importance. By my brutal averages, I think we can award 8 per cent of the total marketing challenge to all forms of communication, including Content, all forms of digital, PR, promotional advertising and so on… It would certainly not break 10 per cent in terms of the overall role and function of what marketing should be doing. Let's acknowledge that content marketing does exist as a very minor part of communications, let's give it 1 per cent. That is a very small tactical box, it has got nothing to do with strategy at all, and certainly it has nothing to do with research, nor with pricing, nor product development (although it can link to product development), no link to distribution strategy whatsoever… none of the real strategic challenges. If I want to be generous I would give them a percentage point from marketing, but they are trying to argue they are a big part of this and I don't think it is a part of anything. Even if it were, it would be a small part in a minority part of communications, itself a small part of tactics, which in itself is a smaller part of marketing.

The issue of the 'importance delusion' was flagged up by Professor Ritson in our Introductory chapter too, with some quite stark realizations about the view senior managers in big organizations may have about their marketing teams.

The view of Content as nothing really new is seconded by another highly respected name in the ad industry, Mark Wnek. As the creative force that shaped the success of agencies such as Ogilvy & Mather, Euro RSCG and Lowe, he has an ear finely attuned to the skills of creating something that will deserve the attention of the audience:

I have always had a problem with the idea of 'content' as a term.

All the best creative people have always approached every single brief as an opportunity to create content: never forget that most agency creatives are would-be long-form creators: novelists, film and TV show creators and such…

Great creatives would say that there is only content. In a world where the millennials and now plurals see through so very much, I believe that current scepticism around values for money, as opposed to value for money, will fade. Brands will increasingly need to stand for something and thus longer-form content will become the norm.

This will indeed impact the world of creative people. But it will not impact the world of great creative people one bit. They always sought to subvert norms – be they media norms or anything else. The only crucial question is how many of these great creatives there will be: in a disastrous and suicidal bid to save money, while seeming to pay lip service to some millennial panic among clients, agencies have jettisoned much of their stellar talent on the grounds of money and non-digital nativity.

To bring up that famous quote by 'the Socrates of San Francisco', Howard Gossage:

> Nobody reads advertising. People read what interests them, and sometimes that's advertising. (Gossage and Goodby, 2006)

Of all the new industry voices that the rise of the blogosphere had introduced to the collective professional attention, almost none resonated so strongly as Bob Hoffman's *Ad Contrarian* blog. Perennially on the lookout for hype, vacuousness and snake-oil peddling, Hoffman has become the scourge of the industry. It wasn't much different with Content (or, in his acerbic interpretation, the 'C-word'). His criticism delivers straight between the eyes in his two famous blogs from 2014, 'Why I Hate Content' and 'Hiding Behind The C-Word':

> 'Content' is a meaningless term – a media contrivance – invented by bullshit artists to add gravitas and mystery to mundane marketing activities.

Hoffman has several charges to deliver to the industry, from pulling the wool over our collective eyes in order to have a new thing to monetize, to spectacular ineffectiveness.

The first is the sheer vastness of the term, with no specific definition and, thus, the temptation to sweep under it almost any action, independent of its quality (2014a):

> Content is anything you can upload to the web. In other words, it is pretty much anything.
> It is a Shakespeare sonnet and a picture of my cat's ass.
> It bestows value on anything, and in so doing, debases everything... It is an excuse masquerading as a resource.

In our interview, Hoffman brought up another Gossage quote to drive home this point:

> Gossage also said 'I don't know how to speak to everybody, only to somebody.' I don't know what 'content' means, other than it's a catch-all phrase for what I think of as 'web litter'. Sometimes it's a nice adjunct to what you do in real marketing, but if you can't point to a major brand, or anything, that was built by content, then I have to say that all content is a footnote to marketing. It may have helped a few brands, but I don't think of it as a major opportunity for most brands.

Then, there is the charge of ineffectiveness in a world drowning in content, echoing what Mark Higginson and the consultancy Beckon are exploring below in more detail, about how attention works on the web. Hoffman here used a funny thought experiment. In July 2014, Google has indexed about 38 *trillion* pages on the web. Hoffman reminds us that each of them is 'content'. He then pulls out the chalk and calculates that if one were to spend only one minute on each of those pages, it would take, on average, 72 *million* years (2014b) to:

> Get around to your page of 'content'. If your content is **below** average... gosh, it could take a long time.

This is a credible and powerful challenge and reflects many things said in this book. The discussion about the 'peak content' is gaining traction, as if we seriously believe that we have reached the peak of the content production frenzy precisely while we are just warming up.

Tom Goodwin, from Zenith USA, has a more down-to-earth explanation of this collective obsession with the 'new':

The kind of reason that this all happens is because you want to be something more interesting, or to get some press for it, or because your boss expects you to do something new, or because you are bored, or because someone sold you in on the idea, or because you got a bit happy on a Friday afternoon one week.

Content is still far from mainstream. There are a few notable examples that almost use content marketing as their strategy, such as Casper beds, Allbirds shoes, Brooklinen sheets or Dollar Shave Club. But if you are a big telco, retailer, FMCG or utility company, then this is not likely to be what you do. It is more likely to be a bit of garnish on the side, so it hasn't really changed how we work with brands that much. Bear in mind that this is a specific combination of being at a very a big agency with big clients in a traditional market. If you go to China you would find that things are different. If you go to Brazil then things would be very different.

Content is about hyped-up delivery systems, not ideas

The other challenge came with a huge sigh from another legendary name in adland, Dave Trott. A much-admired creative director and blogger, in one of his posts he recalled a situation where he participated in a panel of big industry names who all gushed about content. When he asked if they can explain to him what content actually is, he was none the wiser and got the impression that it wasn't important at all. It was just (2015):

> The unimportant stuff that gets delivered by efficient, exciting new delivery systems?

He thought that it signified a huge shift in the marketing communications business:

> Previously, the most important thing was to solve a business problem.
> Then to work out what contribution marketing could make to that.
> Then have advertising deliver that solution in the most impactful way.

But not anymore. It's not about the idea, he says. It is all about the delivery systems, who create a vast space that has to be filled. It doesn't matter with what, it just needs filling. For Trott, it is like a massive lorry and once we acquire it we want it filled with stuff, any stuff, so the lorry can ferry something around. Channelling Hoffman, Trott thinks that is what content has become: just undifferentiated and irrelevant stuff. It's the shiny systems that count.

In a funny turn of events, Trott may also be just the person to show that maybe not all is lost. Following his diatribe, another blog post, from the US content production and creative studio Across The Pond, pointed to Dave Trott as the very example of creating great content! The studio does a lot of work with Google, among other clients.

Agreeing that a vast amount of content produced is wasted by people who didn't really understand the opportunity put in front of them, the blog explained that good content is thinking about what audiences find valuable in terms of attention. If we deliver on that we can make more substantial connections than an ad that is interrupting what people want to be doing. We are creating a product people want, rather than something advertising a product (Waddilove, 2015).

Then they proceeded to tell a really insightful and funny story from Trott's talk at a conference they visited. He was explaining about how he approached his Twitter account and that he had an expert to 'teach' him how to use the platform. Trott said he ignored all of the expert's advice and just started writing some jokes, posting quotes and some links to interesting articles relating to advertising. He would then intersperse this by promoting his blog posts and his books.

As the agency noted, by treating the content of his tweets as seriously as his books (like a cultural product created to interest and illuminate people),

Trott now has over 28,000 Twitter followers. He also mentioned the expert had around 400.

It seems the problem and the solution around Content is in the eye of the beholder. Trott was right about how a big part of the industry approaches Content; the agency was also right that that is the wrong way around…

Another reaction to Trott's article, in a similar vein, came from BBH's digital publishing director Richard Cable (2015). Point by point, he went with the fine comb through Trott's objections and tried to answer each. Echoing, but also qualifying Hoffman's point above, Cable states that 'content' may be a bad word, but that we are now in a situation of lacking another one:

> It's the stuff that used to be over the wall that we'd built between Church and State until the Digital Revolution came along, kicked down that wall and told us we could do whatever the hell we liked.

On the point of definition, Cable was simple: it's marketing communication that people choose to spend their time on. He also argues that it could be a much harder proposition to do right than advertising, as it has to think of the consumer as well as the brand, but it potentially could also be much more powerful.

On the delivery systems issues, Cable also calmly reminds us that this is the nature of the modern media space and that we are ignoring it at our own peril. Our audiences are there and we cannot do much about it. Each of those spaces has its own 'grammar' and rules of engagement and it is our job to understand them. Not to glorify them, we may add, just to understand them.

Finally, Cable proceeds to challenge the notion that ideas don't matter in Content. He was brutally direct here: content without ideas is not content. After all, people don't read magazines and other articles or spend time on social media because of the adverts. They are there for content, or, more precisely, ideas within content. They are after experiences – and those don't happen without ideas.

So, what Dave Trott was actually talking about was *bad* content. Like bad advertising, it is something we should all call out to and resist, as it diminishes the industry. Great, inspirational ideas are much desired not because of their aesthetic value, but because we know they work business-wise. Filling the lorry with junk – no matter whether it's a shiny digital, or the battered old direct one – is bad business. Sadly, it is the easiest thing to do, as we will see below.

Bob Hoffman was also very keen on this point in our interview:

Why is so much of everything else – books, movies, songs, TV shows – crappy? Because it is really, really hard to create good stuff and there are very few people who can do it well. Every copywriter has a blog, there's about 50 million blogs in the world and only about 130 of them get any attention from anyone. That's because it's really hard to write well. It's really hard to be interesting. To me, it's too easy now for anyone to claim they are content creators.

We are never more than 20 metres away... What we collectively should not forget, and why we need a more educated, strategic approach to Content, is that democratization of content creation has not, so far, brought up more Virginia Woolfs just by itself. Content is a strategic and creative business tool, first and foremost.

As one Trott-admiring blog sums it up (Latitude Group, 2015):

Creativity is the last legal unfair advantage we can take over our competitors.

Content doesn't work – brands don't understand how attention flows online

Probably the most meticulous and most devastating deconstruction of the Content hype, bad practices and the outright delusion within the industry has been provided by Mark Higginson, from Twenty Thousand Leagues. A prominent blogger, social media and analytics expert, his weapon of choice is the numbers, not opinions. Without too much bother, he follows various breathless claims about content successes in the trade press with publicly available analytics for those destinations – mostly via tools such as Arefs, Moz and similar – only to reveal the Potemkin-like nature for many of those claims. Mark Ritson, among others, is a fan.

Higginson throws not one, but several gauntlets into the industry's face. The first one is probably the biggest: it is very difficult to make Content work, statistically, as **very few people around seem to understand how attention flows on the web.** In the much-quoted blog post with the same title (2014), Higginson draws on the findings of scientist Albert-László Barabási about clustering-network effects of the internet – and what it means for all web content (Barabási, 2015; Barabási Lab, 2017).

Many networks exist like this in nature, however it was the evolution of the web that made the study of these 'network effects' easier. The key finding, explained by Higginson in our conversation, is that:

The number of links pointing to a page is the ultimate arbiter of attention, for it is this act of sharing that fixes a page in the topology of the wider web – affecting all subsequent activity. There are fundamental rules that govern how this attention flows from page to page that, while easy to understand, have huge ramifications for whether the things you create will be seen. The rule is that only a minority of pages receive a majority of people's attention over any given period of time. This is due to the structure of the web itself — formed of an ever-increasing number of pages and defined by their complex and shifting links to one another. In other words, in a given sample of pages that link to one another a few would be disproportionately popular. As users, because we rely on links to take us from page to page, it is inevitable that our attention becomes focused on these places. A handful of very heavily visited and linked-to pages forms the head, followed by an exceptionally steep drop-off that encompasses the rest, with very little in-between. If a page has a few links in, it isn't likely to have either been popular, or to become popular again, as it is not sufficiently embedded in the topology of the web. Ergo, the vast majority of pages that exist on the web have zero value for marketing purposes as they are never seen by large numbers of people.

The implications for the marketing people are quite stark if they want to use Content as advertising: either invest sufficiently in production of content strong enough to generate attention in its own right, which is extremely difficult to do today, or invest in promoting it. In reality, both are mandatory if content is to become a contender. All media today are both paid and earned.

When Higginson (2016) unleashed his analytical bombs onto some publicized examples, he found that, barring a few outliers, the majority of content published to these sites receives next to no links and goes nowhere, receiving few shares. He commented on it in our interview:

In this winner-takes-all environment where only a few hubs thrive it's most unlikely any business not solely focused on publishing and promotion could compete for attention. For a brand site to compete requires an unsustainable level of quantity and quality in terms of content production, followed by an equally unsustainable amount of promotion; however, this still wouldn't guarantee a return. For a brand there is simply no viable way to recover the investment required to set up and maintain a web-publishing operation if each page isn't directly generating a monetary return. Trying to defy this fundamental rule is akin to trying to launch yourself into space by jumping. I salute the aspiration but you look ridiculous in the execution.

The only thing regular and predictable about brand publishing for a client is that posts will get fewer shares than the number of people they hired to create them and be seen by fewer people than they employ.

The second gauntlet he throws at the industry is the one of delusion and vested interests to big up, as Higginson calls it, this 'content mirage':

The fact we're working in a space of almost infinite content means there is no cost to the reader to take their attention elsewhere, instantly. Not only that, we can apply a technical fix to remove the adverts – in the face of the unstoppable rise in adblocking the best the marketing sector can come up with is the often repeated idea that 'we must make better ads' or 'we need to disguise our message as something that looks like editorial'. Neither of those 'solutions' makes anyone more likely to desire or indeed see or hear our messages.

Years ago I looked at the analytics for a project that was providing content with an environmental slant for a consumer-facing insurance client. What was immediately apparent was that despite several hundred posts being published the majority of individual posts had less than 100 visits. In internet terms this is just noise from having a website that exists with a few external links pointing to it. It signifies nothing. Furthermore, greater than 9-in-10 visitors never came back. People not only didn't want this content, it was barely even visible compared to the numbers coming on-site elsewhere looking for insurance quotes. This didn't change in over a year, yet was being sold to the client as a type of 'content marketing' and 'search marketing'.

What amazed me at the time is that rather than figure out what might work instead, I ran into the issue of presenting hard facts to people whose salaries depended on me being wrong. Many were betting their careers on propagating this view. Many people I knew from that time are making exactly the same recommendations to clients today. No matter what the problem is, the solution is always 'produce more content' in some form, because that is what is billable. That sums up the whole predicament of content creators working on behalf of brands to produce content for the web face today. It's insanity.

Unflinchingly, Higginson challenges brands and agencies in the way we can only call 'The Higgs X-Prize': the invitation to compile a list of their top 100 posts from last year that individually received over 1,000 links from more than 100 domains that were shared more than 10,000 times on any combination of social platforms. So far, he didn't mention anyone taking him up on that challenge...

Higginson is not alone in the drive to quantify the bad effects of bad Content thinking. Beckon is a consultancy that aggregates marketing spend and performance data for many of the world's biggest brands, running analytics to help them understand what is working best across it all. With more than $16 billion in marketing spend across 203 brands and 120 countries in their system, and performance data across every channel imaginable, one would say they are well positioned to offer an objective, bird's eye view of various aspects of marketing performance industry-wide.

In Beckon's 2016 'Marketing Truth or Marketing Hype?' report they found that in the period August 2015–16 brands had pumped out *three times* more content than in the previous measurement year – with no increase in engagement! Some brands had created 29,000, or even 50,000 pieces of content in that period – way more than in the previous years. What is really striking is what happened with consumer engagement (views, clicks, likes, forwards) during that period: it had grown by exactly 0 per cent. We, as consumers, obviously don't want more content. In an almost mathematical proof of Higginson's findings above, Beckon noticed that just 5 per cent of the branded content generated 90 per cent of all engagement. The punchline, with a punch of Mike Tyson, is that 19 out of 20 content pieces get little to no engagement.

As Beckon warns, let's keep in mind that lack of engagement is the best-case scenario here. The worst case is that low-quality content is actually hurting the perception of the brand and, ultimately, sales. Brands ARE focusing more on content volume than on content performance, maybe because the new content publishing platforms have made it much easier to create and publish at scale, and, particularly, at speed – while at the same time, warns Beckon, often lack robust measurement tools.

One can only look at these figures and share the despair of the people we quoted above. Suddenly, none of them look like a laggard and a digital illiterate. It seems they have a big and critical point. We may protest that Higginson is focusing only on brand publishing as a replacement for advertising, or Dave Trott only on delivery systems (rightly, as it turns out), but Beckon's figures bring it uncomfortably close to Ritson's 'bollocks' metaphor above.

TV is still doing well – even with young people

At Brandcast 2015, a big YouTube advertising and media industry bash in London, Eileen Naughton, then the Google UK and Ireland managing director, dropped a bomb among the assorted luminaries (O'Reilly, 2015):

> Advertisers reach their target audiences far more efficiently by adding YouTube to their media plans... especially the hard-to-reach 16- to 34-year-olds where cost per reach point is optimized when 24 per cent of your TV budget is allocated to YouTube.

She then went on to quote Ipsos and GfK research, commissioned by Google, which found that ads seen on YouTube and TV are more effective than ads seen the same number of times on TV alone.

Much commotion had ensued in the trade press in the weeks to come, with the result of various sets of statistics being produced to show that the news about the death of TV are still a bit exaggerated. It echoed, again, IPA's seminal research, which demonstrated, on their set of data, that TV is still not just one of the most cost-efficient marketing media, but also the best for building emotional resonance in the long term.

Although TV is, of course, key popular content in its own right, in this debate it also often stands as a symbolic proxy for the 'old world' that digital is slowly (or rapidly, depending on who one talks to) dismantling. Content in the digital space is, on the contrary – in many conversations and particularly if taken as 'online video' – seen as the new TV of a sort: non-linear, authentic, personal and 'unofficial', a grass-roots sort of thing that is supposed to rewrite the rules. What a surprise, then, to learn that TV as we know it is far from giving up the ghost among the screen generations!

One of the responses to Naughton's challenge, as expected, was delivered by Thinkbox – the marketing body for commercial TV in the UK, in all its forms. Its shareholders are Channel 4, ITV, Sky Media and a few other partners who together represent over 99 per cent of commercial TV advertising revenue through their owned and partner TV channels.

Collating and integrating the data from half a dozen top research companies specializing in audience measurement, Thinkbox had a reminder for all advertisers (Clay, 2016):

> 0.6 per cent of video advertising is seen on YouTube; 94 per cent is seen on TV, in full and with sound. For 16–24s that rises to 1.4 per cent versus TV's 87.6 per cent. The fact that 80 per cent of YouTube's viewing is done by 20 per cent of viewers also hampers their reach potential for advertisers.

Then, a bit of a shock, when the next chart revealed that those much sought-after age 16–24s spend 10.3 per cent of their daily video time on YouTube (double the time of the general UK population), but a far cry from 73 per cent of time spent on combined live and playback TV! Even put together, YouTube, Facebook, 'other online video' and – brace yourself! – pornography, command only 29 per cent of their daily video time! To some, it was like a hammer blow to a Jeff Koons statue.

These findings reflected the key points from research of a year before (2015) on the role of video in the lives of young UK people and their overall media habits and motivations. What Thinkbox found, again with the help of a panel of big media research partners, was very similar stats on the online video/TV divide, but also some interesting dynamics (Thinkbox, 2015). For example, young people typically had limited control of the main household TV set, busting boredom is one of the key motivations for watching online video, and that identity formation and fear of missing out (FOMO) influences content sought and shared.

For someone who spent most of their professional life in the digital arena, like many readers of this book, it could be a world-view-changing moment. Here it is, if we are to believe the very credible sources, even in one of the most sophisticated digital (and digital media and marketing) markets in the world, a proof that our filter bubble was, indeed, real! Content does work for attracting attention in the digital world, true, but it tends to be on TV as well! What then to make of other countries and world regions where digital is just developing and TV is, by and large, still the queen of the media mix? Some painful realignment of the optics, the removal of the Content myopia, was maybe required...

Tom Goodwin has an explanation for this phenomenon, something he called in our interview 'the problem of generality' in our professional discourse:

I think we have this narrative that somehow everything is different and what we did before isn't working now. I don't think that is actually true. I think most of the things we have done for years still work really well. I think it's quite embarrassing that we have let this counter-narrative develop, because it suggests that everyone who is doing their job is doing it badly. The idea that TV no longer works is not supported by the data, and brands are continuing to commit to it because it does still work.

To say, generally speaking, 'advertising is still working' is fine, but that implies 'doing things the way you have done them before' is fine, when it's not true. It's just that on aggregate it is still working, but if you are trying to launch a chewing gum today then it's probably remarkably stupid to use TV because you'll discover that the people you are trying to talk to spend most of their time on phones. Similarly, if you are trying to launch a stair lift then there is probably been no better time to use TV. So just be careful that by the time you aggregate everything up to a general level you end up removing a lot of detail you are missing out on.

In general, there's a lot of crap out there and people like to appear to sound like they are modern. It's easy to be a 38-year-old saying that TV is a great media, but more difficult as a 48-year-old as it could look like being out of touch. It's a bit like Picasso saying you need to be able to paint before being able to unpaint, it's easier being a millennial saying something that others wouldn't feel comfortable saying.

That provides some context for me to say that what we know is that most of the things we have done for a long time still continue to work. There is a lot of change happening, including aspects of how we are behaving, so we always need to be looking out for how we can exploit the power of the new. We always need to be checking things that have worked before in order to check that they are still working. But generally speaking most of the tactics we have been using since the 1850s, up to the 1970s are still working fairly well. In some categories and in some market conditions they do not do as well as they used to, and in some they perform far worse than they used to, but in some they do better than they used to do.

Several times already in this book we have called for the sense of balance when Content is being thought through. On one hand, we have those successful cases of deployment across the customer journey that some of our contributors talked about. On the other, without a doubt too, we have this vast Content landfill that is the whole of the industry in aggregate. Again, both sides cannot be totally right. We believe that, looked at from that particular hill where the Content castle was meant to be standing, this changes the frame of the conversation from whether Content should exist at all, to how to do it better. If we are to use the cooking analogy, we are now in the 'fast-food phase' of content production and are learning – and some are already there – how to do 'slow cooking'. How to be more strategic, more creative, more relevant; how to create a better experience. Not just of the kind that people would go to publishers for, but also what brands with their particular expertise can do to charge the Moments that Matter with the maximum Empathic Utility. We hope this book provides at least part of the answer to this challenge.

Omaid Hiwaizi from Blippar has a timely reminder:

> Anyone who says that Content is insignificant needs to remember that advertising was invented to subvert Content and over time it made a real nuisance of itself!

Now, it seems, it is Content's turn to make a nuisance of *itself*. The sooner we understand that, the better.

References

Barabási, A-L (2015) [accessed 30 December 2017] Network Science Book [Online] networksciencebook.com

Barabási Lab (2017) [accessed 30 December 2017] Think networks [Online] barabasilab.com

Beckon (2016) [accessed 30 December 2017] Marketing Truth or Marketing Hype? [Online] pages.beckon.com/rs/976-IET-418/images/Marketing-Truth-or-Marketing-Hype-Beckon-Report.pdf

Cable, R (2015) [accessed 30 December 2017] How Long? 2–3 Minutes Content Without Ideas Isn't Content: A Retort to Dave Trott, *Campaign*, 3 November

[Online] campaignlive.co.uk/article/content-without-ideas-isnt-content-retort-dave-trott/1371060

Clay, L (2016) [accessed 30 December 2017] Reluctantly Responding to YouTube Research (Blog), *ThinkBox*, 20 June [Online] thinkbox.tv/News-and-opinion/Blogs/20160620-Reluctantly-responding-to-YouTube-research

Gossage, H L and Goodby, J (2006) *The Book of Gossage*, Copy Workshop, Chicago

Higginson, M (2014) [accessed 30 December 2017] How People's Attention Flows on the Web (Blog), *Mark Higginson*, 27 November [Online] markhigginson.co.uk/pages/attention_flow.html

Higginson, M (2016) [accessed 30 December 2017] Why the 'Brands as Publishers' Trend Is Utter Nonsense (Blog), *Econsultancy,* 20 January [Online] econsultancy.com/blog/67426-why-the-brands-as-publishers-trend-is-utter-nonsense/

Hoffman, B (2014a) [accessed 30 December 2017] Why I Hate Content (Blog), *The Ad Contrarian*, 22 September [Online] adcontrarian.blogspot.rs/2014/09/why-i-hate-content.html

Hoffman, B (2014b) [accessed 30 December 2017] Content: Hiding behind the C-Word (Blog), *The Ad Contrarian*, 6 October [Online] adcontrarian.blogspot.rs/2014/10/content-hiding-behind-c-word.html

Latitude Group (2015) [accessed 30 December 2017] *Six Tips on Content Marketing* from Dave Trott (Blog), *Latitude Group*, 28 September [Online] latitudegroup.com/blog/six-tips-on-content-marketing-from-dave-trott/

Mancini, J (2008) [accessed 30 December 2017] What's in Your Digital Landfill?, 12 June [Online] slideshare.net/jmancini77/whats-in-your-digital-landfill

O'Reilly, L (2015) [accessed 30 December 2017] Google Just Told Advertisers That If They Want To Reach Young People Youtube Will Need To Take 24% of Their TV Budgets, *Business Insider*, 14 October [Online] uk.businessinsider.com/at-brandcast-google-tells-advertisers-to-shift-tv-money-to-video-youtube-2015-10

Ritson, M (2016) [accessed 30 December 2017] Is Content Marketing a Load of Bollocks?, *Marketing Week,* 11 October [Online] marketingweek.com/2016/10/11/is-content-marketing-a-load-of-bullsht/

ThinkBox (2015) [accessed 30 December 2017] The Truth about Youth [Online] thinkbox.tv/Research/Thinkbox-research/The-truth-about-youth

Trott, D (2015) [accessed 30 December 2017] A View from Dave Trott: Content, Content, Content, *Campaign*, 29 October [Online] campaignlive.co.uk/article/view-dave-trott-content-content-content/1370207

Waddilove, R (2015) [accessed 11 March 2015] Dave Trott Loves Content Really (Blog), *Across The Pond*, 2 November [Online] blog.atp.tv/blog/2015/11/2/dave-trott-loves-content-really

Content marketing and ethics

11

Challenges, threats and balancing acts

If in Chapter 10 Content was at best an irrelevance, a folly and an illusion, in this it has a darker tonality. It's not about just missing quarterly agency targets or wastage in the communications spend. We are talking the demise of our liberal, democratic civilization, under attack from many forces.

Strong words, indeed. But, Content is here part of a more sinister media atmosphere. Paradoxically, it is predominantly the very benefits of Content for marketers that are deemed to be its biggest societal threat: the fact that it doesn't look like just any old advertising and that it could be wickedly engaging when done well. How marketing upsides and their societal down-sides will be reconciled, no one yet knows – at least within the current prevalent ideological and economic models.

Overall ethical challenges in which Content is playing a part could be clustered into four groups of considerations. They are very rarely, in our experience, discussed within the marketing communications industry, particularly in boardrooms. Survival (at all cost) and profit (if possible), still rule. That is what makes this chapter a mirror for all the players in the communications industry to look into – and check which hat they really wear: the black, the white or, as is often the case, the grey one.

The 'dark comms' challenge: manipulation by opacity

Ask good creative directors what they consider to be key elements of successful advertising and the word 'clarity' will come high up the list. How ironic, then, that opacity and confusion increasingly look like marketer's best friends. This repertoire of various technology-powered sleights-of-hand is not just expanding, but becoming sophisticated at a rate that leaves even the most nimble (self)regulators hopelessly behind.

Opacity here works in several well-documented ways. One of those, garnering a lot of press in 2017, is connected to how digital technology empowers various operators to exercise their influence under the radar of public scrutiny. We have entered the era of super-personalized propaganda powered by algorithms and ever-expanding data sets, where a person sees messages specifically tailored to their behaviour and preferences, often quite different from what someone next door – or even in the same room – will see. It's direct marketing on steroids. This was brought to global attention during the US presidential elections in which Donald Trump emerged as a surprise winner, as well as in the equally surprising Brexit vote in the United Kingdom.

Much ink has been spilt over how the data consultancy involved in both of the above, Cambridge Analytica, allegedly used Big Data sets and targeting based on some of the traits of the OCEAN personality framework. The focus was on undecided voters, nudging them to disfavour Hillary Clinton, in the United States, or favour Brexit, in the UK (Doward and Gibbs, 2017).

Although claims of the levels of sophistication and impact have been subsequently downplayed by various insiders, the staggering amount of analysis deployed by Cambridge Analytica still demonstrates the ever more granular levels of targeting, very near, or almost equal, to the 'ideal' one-to-one paradigm (Peppers and Rogers, 1998). It is 'mass customization' on a very deep level, hitherto preserved for the super-sophisticated data-driven commerical marketers such as Tesco or Target.

It is also a big challenge. Apart from the data privacy issues, in order to be able to react to any dubious practices the society and the regulators have to be *aware* of those in the first place. That is exactly what is lacking here, as the public media sphere of old has been replaced by millions of individual screens touched by proprietary 'black box' algorithms. In this space, public scrutiny as a concept is much diluted, poorly defined and poorly enforced. These *Weapons of Math Destruction* (2016), as the author and ex-Wall Street analyst Cathy O'Neil calls them, are darkening our social environment.

This has raised various concerns. In the case of the UK 'snap' elections in June 2017, it generated some citizen-activism initiatives around collecting evidence of and shedding some light on the super-targeting ad practices by the main political parties (Gallacher and Kaminska, 2017). What the examples demonstrated is a communications eco-system bent on exploiting the private nature of the digital media space to ramp up divisive, negative – even offensive – rhetoric that would cause much consternation, even outcry, if deployed in the traditional public media spaces such as TV or outdoor (Ellison, 2017).

The issue is recognized as enough of a credible threat to democratic values that it sparked inquiries and activities of various watchdogs into misuse of data in politics (Cadwalladr, 2017). Something everyone grapples with is the lack of credible regulation for the increasing cross-pollination between the, so far, much more sharply delineated commercial and political communications worlds. As Professor Andrew McStay, from Bangor University, pointed out in our interview:

> In the UK, the Committee of Ad Practice does not regulate in this area (political ads) and the Electoral Commission does not cover advertising. The ICO (Information Commissioner's Office) is going to have to walk a fine line on this one as it gets into the nuts and bolts of democratic functioning.

So, at the moment, non-transparent, commercially protected algorithmical super-personalization is a no-man's land...

Professor Mara Einstein, a prominent media scholar from Queens College in New York and author of a book on opacity in modern marketing communications, *Black Ops Advertising* (2017), believes there are clear dangers in riding the 'filter bubble' too much. In an important point in our interview she sees the coarsening of the US culture as partly the result of us communicating with each other more online rather than in person, so the context and meaning get lost, which diminishes the way we relate to each other as human beings.

> If someone had to speak with someone the way they tweet it would be a very different conversation. As the saying goes, 'no one is as angry as they are on Twitter or as happy as they appear on Facebook'. We just don't relate in the same way online as we do when we engage face to face. Underlying this is not only the interface, but the manipulation by the platforms. Facebook really needs to step up and start taking ownership of their culpability for a lot that has been going on; you can't tell me that they couldn't hold off on the fake news stuff or that they need to be digging into people's personal data the way they are. I think that's crazy.

Pope Francis has denounced the fake news as evil, comparing it to the snake in the Garden of Eden (Associated Press, 2018). It is the message echoed, in even stronger verbiage, by the writer John Lanchester in his review of three books on 'post-truth' for *The London Review of Books* (2017). He asks an intriguing question: whether lies peddled through advertising platforms such as Facebook are tolerated because they actually serve a useful purpose for the platform and its advertisers?

> The key to understanding this is to think about what advertisers want: they don't want to appear next to pictures of breasts because it might damage their brands, but they don't mind appearing alongside lies because the lies might be helping them find the consumers they are trying to target.

Lies could, in this political economy of attention, become hooks and data signals teasing out and flagging up passions and interests of individual users and like-minded others, subsequently connected to various vast online and offline data sources for hitherto unprecedented personal message targeting.

But, there is another, even more troubling, side of the 'dark comms'. If the stealth-messaging schemes look like direct marketing on steroids, the stealth *user experience* manipulations are marketing and sales on opium. Beyond messages, it is about a planned and structured, but concealed or downright deceptive, engineering of the interface itself. This group of approaches encompasses things such as 'dark user interface (UI)', 'brain hacking' and sometimes, directly or insidiously, the industry's beloved ideology (and a set of tools) known as 'behavioural economics' (BE).

Most of us are, even the professionals within the marketing industry, oblivious of the 'dark UI' (or 'dark UX') ethical challenges. As an official definition does not yet exist, it could be best described as tricks that user-interface designers deploy to fool us into doing something within that interface (or missing doing something) to produce result we have not quite intended. Think unwanted registrations, downloads or purchases – generating additional revenue. Even the biggest brands don't seem to be immune to its lure, as evidenced by examples on the Darkpatterns.org website, an activist initiative by some concerned members of the user experience (UX) design community (Darkpatterns.org, 2017a). Microsoft was using the 'bait and switch' tactics, where the user sets to do one thing, but another – undesirable – one happens instead, for example clicking the 'X' button at the top right of the box that previously meant 'close' and here was changed, without notice, into action to upgrade the OS to Windows 10 (Darkpatterns. org, 2017b).

The list of those 'dark patterns' is illuminating and sounds like the marketing jargon from hell: 'disguised ads', 'forced continuity', 'friend spam', 'hidden costs', 'misdirection', 'price comparison prevention', 'privacy Zuckering' (being tricked into publicly sharing more information about yourself than you really intended to, usually through the small print), 'roach motel', 'sneak into basket' or 'trick questions' (Darkpatterns.org, 2017c). It does feel, after a while, that there is a whole ideology rooted in deceiving the user at every turn.

There is something unnerving in realizing that the actual screen – the interface – our primary means of relating to the world and our lives (at least in the developed countries), is left so unprotected and open to manipulation. Because, for a lot of us, interface IS the reality. If the interface is fundamentally manipulated, our reality is fundamentally manipulated. It is hard to fathom that we try to regulate all other aspects of the media, but that we abandoned organized and informed protection of this critical space. There are no interface watchdogs yet.

One particular aspect of the 'dark UI' has exploded in the media at the end of 2017 – claims of deliberately in-built addictiveness of mobile phones and the apps on them. 'Brain hacking' is the label gaining notoriety. Is it possible that the situation has become ethically so serious that even senior former executives of Google and Facebook had to break silence and alert the public?

App alerts may seem an innocuous service for users, but the mechanism behind it was compared to a slot machine by the author Douglas Rushkoff in his prescient book (among many) *Present Shock* (2014): we are driven to check 'what did I get?' with each glance. It creates a habit (and distraction, even measurable anxiety from the fear of missing out on all those text messages), as well as *a little shot of serotonin* when we do check it – 'a pleasant ping from the world of chronos' (Cooper, 2017). Snapchat's 'streaks' are another example, so addictive that kids leave their passwords with friends to keep the streaks active while on holiday.

'They are programming people', said Tristan Harris, former Google product manager, who spilled the beans on CBS's '60 Minutes'. He was, again, channelling Rushkoff and his book *Program or Be Programmed* (2011). The phrase Harris used to describe the thinking behind this is as illuminating as it is chilling: 'the race to the bottom of the brainstem'. The more automatic, habitual and... *mindless*... an action becomes, the more hooked we are, the more attention the app gets, the more money that attention generates. No wonder that, in the United States, 50 per cent of all young people think they are addicted to their devices (PBS, 2016).

Paul Snoxell, a former creative lead in several well-known London agencies, who brought the 'dark UI' phenomenon to our attention in the interview for the book, believes the industry does have a choice here:

> 'Dark UI' is what happens when really smart people do things just because they can. They show less smart people what can be done and because they respect academic intelligence more than emotional intelligence these ideas become reality.

In other words, it is what happens when an organization and its helpers are so blinded by the actual possibility to manipulate the primal power of the interface, enabled by findings of various academic disciplines, that they forget about empathy and morals. For Snoxell, at the root of it all is marketers' fear that without some underhand 'nudging' they won't gain competitive advantage:

> The sleight of hand provided by 'Dark UI' allows lazy marketers and their corporate bosses to avoid holding up a mirror to themselves and fix what is fundamentally wrong and instead use what is ostensibly a suite of tools and tactics to do public good to prop up a broken business proposition...
>
> That's the other problem with 'dark UI'; the name itself sounds a bit sexy, a bit cool. Call it 'dirty UI' and no marketer will want to touch it. (Although I can imagine some individuals in agencies would find it even more appealing...)

The remark about the appeal of the 'secret' knowledge agencies sometimes peddle is more than a joke. Rare is an agency that does not promote a proprietary framework, a process, a thinking tool or a 'black box' that should give them a fighting chance in the cut-throat agency markets such as London or New York – then copied globally. Anything that may give an impression that an agency is plugged into some source of magic that can influence consumer thinking, feelings or behaviour is fair game.

One recent wave of such thinking that swept the industry was adoption of behavioural economics (BE). Based on ground-breaking work of luminary social scientists such as Daniel Kahneman, Cass Sunstein, Richard Thaler, Don Ariely and Robert Cialdini, BE has, for a while, become the new 'science' of advertising. It welcomed it in a desperate need of the new framework of effectiveness and quantification of creative efforts, so desired by the procurement gatekeepers. It was also helped, unexpectedly, by credibility conferred to BE by the UK government, as the vanguard in this regard, through setting up its colloquially known 'nudge unit' to help with making policies more effective.

Suddenly, pitch slides were replete with 'cognitive biases', 'choice architectures', 'social proofs', 'loss aversions' and 'post-purchase rationalizations'. Agencies were creating BE teams, departments and even institutes. Consumers were, according to that noise, incessantly 'nudged' towards brand-beneficial outcomes. Yet, no one had asked a simple question: did consumers know that they were nudged? If not, is that ethical? If the BE was so effective in tapping into the basic heuristics of our mind, should it be left completely unregulated? Should something so predatory be left unchecked and unleashed? For agencies, there was another question: if the BE is just one new tool in the arsenal, did it deserve such brouhaha? Was it oversold, a new toy for agencies to charge the clients for? It can't be both. It is a discussion that significantly surpasses the reach of this chapter, but is yet another example of the marketing industry's zeal for a competitive advantage and natural inability to put ethical questions even on a par with, let alone on top of, profit (Dzamic, 2017).

Many readers of this book will be familiar with the concept of the Net Promoter Score (NPS), one question and one number used widely for correlating attitudes towards a brand with its potential for growth. But what about the Net Civilizational Score (NCS)? An ethical measure that doesn't exist yet, but the authors of this book think it should be considered as a tool. It's a simple question, too: is what you, your company or your industry does, overall, beneficial or detrimental to the individual consumer, society and the world? It is also a question that plagues the next challenge directly related to Content.

The crumbling separation between advertising and editorial

There is another issue residing on the red-flag-list of many actors in the media, marketing and academic space: our increasing inability to differentiate between ads and 'proper' editorial content. This is not about super-targeted ads or interface deceptions, where Content may have a secondary role. Content is here at the centre of the storm. It is a debate often attached to considerations and effects of 'native advertising' and similar approaches.

In the old media order, it was easier to make that distinction. Advertising had a much more distinct 'signature' expressed in standardized formats and, largely, tonality. It 'looked' and 'felt' like advertising. Not any more, or not that easily. The richness of the digital eco-system, the duopoly of Google and Facebook in the online advertising game and the subsequent redrafting of this 'political economy of communications' (a phrase used by digital media critic Evgeny Morozov (2017) and several others) are blasting out this wall too.

Professor Mara Einstein, who covered 'native advertising' in her book mentioned above, is a passionate defender of the existing separation of the two 'estates', pointing to an interesting inversion: publishers have started behaving like advertisers, who in turn are behaving ever more like publishers, broadening the definition of content marketing, and the audience confusion, by the minute.

In her interview with us, Professor Einstein highlighted several issues with this trend:

The biggest one is that readers are not able to discern what is sponsored content and what is editorial. There are three major recent studies showing that only 17 per cent of readers in the United States, including middle-school readers (so-called digital natives), are able to distinguish between the two. The ability of people to understand when something is being pitched to them, versus balanced objective journalism, is being undermined.

We engage with ads differently from editorial content and even when the message is coming from a well-known brand psychologically we know that, ultimately, they are trying to sell us something – that the info is coming to us with a very slanted bias.

Second, more 'native content' is being written by the producer's editorial team, not a dedicated marketing team, which is confusing people even more as these in-house writers and artists know the tone of voice of a specific publication; advertising truly becomes indistinguishable from editorial. There has to be a better and more uniform way to label this content across various touchpoints, so people can tell the difference.

Finally, the use of influencers and the lack of labelling on social media sites is very misleading: #ad is simply not enough to let consumers know they are engaging with advertising. Marketers may start pulling back, or at least use these people more judiciously, either because of regulatory pressure or more likely because of the bad press associated with scandals such as the ill-fated Fyre festival in the Bahamas in 2017, and the Kendall Jenner 'Jump In' Pepsi ad, which formed part of their 'Live for Now' campaign (Schultz, 2017).

Although the issue of 'fake news' is overall outside the scope of this book, Professor Einstein has an interesting angle on the point of overlap between this phenomenon and 'native advertising':

I would put native advertising under fake news, frankly, because people are looking at it as if it is 'news' and it is not. On the other hand, the clickbait nature of the headlines is also an important factor: it is not a reporter who is writing the headlines, it is headline writers; this is also something that needs to be rethought. Headlines have become more important in the world of digital media because a lot of people read the headlines and never get to the story. The 'real' fake news, and we have seen some examples of that, have been driven by the imperative to drive ad revenue. Facebook and Google are private pipelines, not like traditional, regulated media. However, we tend to think of these sites as protected and working for our best interest, but it is not the same; the internet was – and still is – overwhelmingly controlled by young, white, male, privileged people without the foresight to think 20–30 years down the line.

If it all sounds a bit grim, it's because it is. The stakes cannot be higher. The opacity of those 'private pipelines'? 'It scares me to think about experiments going on Facebook every day', says Professor Einstein.

So, is the ethical cause doomed then? If brands and agencies are actually relishing all of this as an opportunity to survive or thrive, and if regulators are still shuffling their feet, are we just sleepwalking into a civilizational nightmare, of the kind Douglas Rushkoff and Tristan Harris were warning about above?

We need to find ways to fight addictive issues surrounding technology, particularly around social media, which is not going to be easy as it is all about hyper-generating emotions in us, so we keep on buying products. You and I are old enough to remember a time when you saw a commercial when it was on TV and you turned off the TV and you walked away and went on with your life and you weren't surrounded by that stuff all the time. So the problem is that every time we open up our phone, or go to Facebook or Google or whatever it is, we are constantly being bombarded with someone trying to sell us something, someone trying to get us excited about something, so I don't think it's about reducing the amount of those messages, as that is not going to happen, I think it's about getting *us* to reduce the amount of time spent engaging with technology and then we end up being able to manage our emotions. Otherwise, ad people are too smart for us.

Or, as Douglas Rushkoff put it in *Present Shock*: 'We must retrain ourselves instead to see the reward in the amount of time we get to spend in the reverie of solo contemplation or live engagement with another human being. Whatever is vibrating on the iPhone just isn't as valuable as the eye contact you are making right now.'

One of the strongest opponents of native advertising, since its inception as a 'new' marketing concept, has been the prominent US journalist Bob Garfield. As the host of one of the most regarded US radio shows, *On The Media*, he is deeply immersed in the everyday struggle of keeping objectivity alive in the world of 'fake news' and 'fake fake news'. A vigorous fighter for sanity and rationality, he is a unique species among like-minded journalists for also being an insider in the world of advertising: he was the chief ad critic for the industry's leading publication *Advertising Age*. As such, he is quite familiar with the thinking, approaches and the elastic ethical standards of the industry he used to cover. He gets both sides of the story, and he doesn't like what he sees.

For Garfield, the collapsing separation between editorial and advertising is not just a *perceived* ethical risk, but – in his own punchy answers in our interview – 'a widespread contemporary reality' with huge consequences, both for the media world and society:

They call it 'native advertising', which means content produced not by the editorial department based on normal editorial values, but by third parties – brands or their agencies or separate 'studios' created by publishers – in order to blend organically with the surrounding editorial matter. By blend, they mean, to the casual consumer, 'be mistaken for'. It is outright deception, advertising disguised as content. Some of it is fairly good, but that is irrelevant. What is relevant is that audiences are being deceived about the nature, provenance and independence of the content. Some publishers include an ambiguous disclose ('sponsored content'), for instance, in varying degrees of visibility, but the key fact is this: when people think it is an ad, they don't click on it. When they think it is organic editorial they will click. It's not just deception, but a conspiracy of deception, but desperate publishers – whose business models are circling the drain – find themselves bartering away their only true asset: trust.

In some corridors of the global media world this is just a codified form of corruption. Publishers have been trading ad revenue for favourable coverage, even naked PR, since time immemorial. That is, of course, grossly unethical, but remains pervasive throughout the world. They are brothels with printing presses, and some countries are already the red-light district. But it follows the law of diminishing returns. What does a publication or channel offer its audiences but trustworthiness, whether about politics or Rhianna's baby? Native advertising and similar practices over time erode the trust, which is the goose that lays the Golden Egg.

Garfield believes that we cannot be in the dark about the motives of reporting, and we chafe when even the goofiest Hollywood movie has made itself a 35mm catalogue of product placements. 'We want our crap uncontaminated by other crap. And when we discover that we are being conned, we get angry.' Or, as John Oliver put it in his inimitable way (LastWeekTonight, 2014): 'ads are baked into content like chocolate chips into a cookie; except, it's actually more like raisins into a cookie because no one ****ing wants them there!'

Garfield is also adamant that journalists should never write paid-for content for brands:

This is like the chief of police asking his cops to go undercover to rob liquor stores. Ugh. But, no problem. The aforementioned digital disruption has put many talented journalists out of work. And a lot of them have gone native.

Digital Revolution blew up the business model that had rewarded publishers (and, later, broadcasters), almost obscenely for 300 years. Fragmentation, an infinite glut of supply, instant ad-avoidance and fraud have destroyed profitability. At my Media Future Summit in November 2016, I asked a room of publishers which was more important: the mission, or survival? One cable exec said: 'The mission IS survival.' That was heartbreaking.

It was also echoed in the much-commented-on exclamation by Leslie Moonves, the CEO of CBS, on Donald Trump's presidential campaign in February 2016: 'It may not be good for America, but it's damn good for CBS' (Hunt, 2017). In times like this, all is fair:

The media and their trade organizations have consistently misrepresented their culpability in this, offering lip service about full disclosure while simultaneously doing everything in their power to bury that disclosure where it is least likely to be seen, in language that is least likely to be understood.

Garfield's last point is reiterated by Ken Auletta, a contributor to the venerable *New Yorker*, who explained on John Oliver's *Last Week Tonight* what this new approach is and what message publishers now send to advertisers: 'we will camouflage your ads to make them look like news stories' (LastWeekTonight, 2014).

There are differing voices, though. Paul Snoxell begs to disagree here, pointing out that brands have and will always enjoy presenting themselves in a journalistic style.

It's an easy and effective way to tell longer, multi-layered stories, as exemplified by the work of Howard Gossage and David Ogilvy in the first half of the 1960s. There is no need to pretend to be 'real' or unbiased as all journalists write with a point of view, or are pushing a certain agenda, which makes it perfectly acceptable for brands to do the same – as long as they make it clear that they have presented that argument. Just like a journalist has a byline, brands could have a byline too.

What this implies, though, is two things. First, that brands want to have a 'byline' – which is now increasingly under suspicion, unless forced by the regulators – and that users are able to discern it, which research mentioned by Professor Einstein shows not to be the case for the majority of us. Some figures are quite striking: analysis of the 50 most-followed celebrities on Instagram, by the US marketing firm Mediakix in May 2017, found that 93 per cent of posts promoting a brand were not compliant with the US's Federal Trade Commission (FTC) guidelines (Hunt, 2017). So, a huge amount of #sponcon remained unidentified. This is what Professor Jonathan Hardy from the University of East London calls 'corporate ventriloquism'. In our interview, he mentions one important additional point that goes beyond the issue of just identification:

> One fundamental problem is that the FTC, restricted by remit but also predilection, is only concerned with consumer deception, not with the impact of sponsored content on the quality of communication services. Once we are past the hurdle of consumer recognition there is little regulatory counterweight against advancing ad integration.

This visibility, or the absence, of the brand 'byline' is also what bothers Tim Lindsay, CEO of the legendary D&AD association:

> The piece I don't understand but I'm concerned about is when branded content does not declare itself. That's why I hate the phrase 'native advertising', and hate this notion of promoting content because I think it damages the integrity of everyone involved. For example, *Behold: Reveries of the Connected World*, the 90-minute documentary produced by Pereira & O'Dell and directed by Werner Herzog for Netscout. It is an absolutely amazing documentary about the perils of the internet; it's only when it is about 80 minutes in that you realize it has been brought to you by a cyber security company – and that changes your whole attitude to what you have just seen: you have been absolutely absorbed by this thing and think it is brilliant and then suddenly you think they are just trying to scare you into buying their stupid product. That's a very crass example, I know, but I think branded content needs to declare itself.

Back in the day when advertising was good, people openly accepted the quick-exchange deal, so you make me laugh in 30 seconds, or the more optimal 45 seconds, and in return I will give you the gift of my attention and might take some of what you say on board. That's how the agencies back then did business, but the deal was obvious and one you didn't have to enter into because you could do something else such as make a cup of tea, yet people usually did enter in because they were happy to interact with the good stuff and you knew what was going on. Not knowing what is going on makes people more wary and more mistrustful. That's why I think branded content carries the seeds of its own destruction. Advertising, or at least the way we now understand it, will be gone soon, but if the quality hadn't declined I think we would still be in a position where it is effective. Technology may have made it easier to avoid advertising, but I think we have connived in its demise being more rapid than it could have been. Therefore, the idea of branded content being a substitute is a complicated thing.

Professor Hardy believes that despite some recent moves by the regulators FTC in the United States and Ofcom in the UK – that caused some sharp intake of breath from the industry because of what amounted to the first crackdown on what one may call 'dark influencer marketing' (Hunt, 2017) – there is still a lot of work to be done:

Consumers are confused. We have to come up with a much more consistent industry-wide labelling, not the situation where the publishers may come up with their own rules, for example using the label 'branded content' where the brand has influenced the editorial and 'sponsored content' when it hasn't, but still paid the money to be associated with the topic.

So labelling and consumer awareness are vital, but there is a real danger that a narrow regulatory focus on these issues tends to displace two other concerns. The first is the effect of native advertising on the **quality** and **integrity** of channels of communication. I take that quaint phrase from public relations codes. For instance, the International Public Relations Association says its members should 'not engage in practice that tends to corrupt the integrity of any channel of communication'. The second concern is the power and extent of marketers' voice in communications. Societies have sought to allow marketers to communicate, but set limits to serve a variety of public-interest purposes – from rules on where outdoor posters can appear, to regulations on product placement.

The key concerns are not just consumer identification, but also what happens to the media channel and what happens if the voice of marketers extends into spaces governed by other values, such as editorial independence. Historically, societies have set limits to marketers' power to promote, and I think we haven't worked out what those should be in the 21st century. We also haven't yet worked out the best label for all the sophisticated ways a brand can influence content in the digital space. The labelling game is still in its early phases as new media formats evolve, but I don't think we should shy away from calling all these approaches just 'advertisements'. That would certainly be clear to consumers! Another proposal is to borrow from the product placement regulations in the television industry and introduce a universal logo. In UK television production, the paid presence of brands has to be identified by a universal logo – a 'P' sign. There is no such equivalent across publishing. Publications that contain branded editorial content might be required by law, or incentivized by industry self-regulation, to display a universal logo – perhaps a 'B' sign for brand content – at both masthead level and content level. As publications search out viable economic and ethical models that might serve as a marker for reader awareness, a point of difference among publications, and bring greater public attention to important media literacy issues. Such a measure may at least stimulate a debate that is, deep down, about securing trust. While there is plenty of conflict over proposals to strengthen regulation, there are also points of commonality between brands, media and societies at large, and trust seems to be just such a point from which to kick-start the debate.

The 'empathic media and datafication of emotional lives' challenge

For Professor Andrew McStay from Bangor University, the real challenge and the danger for all of us lies less in the opacity of messaging or the confusion between Content and editorial, but in too much uncontrolled knowledge that brands and their data systems could accumulate about us over time, allowing them more perfect manipulations of our behaviours and emotional states. Think Cambridge Analytica, writ large. It is another door into 'us', and the key to our defences is to be able to control who has what information about us for what purposes. We will lose if we lose the afore-mentioned 'agency' to control the extent to which the marketing process can impose on our lives – and that in the digital world largely means controlling the flow of data.

The main thrust of his thinking could be glimpsed from the title of the 18-month project that Professor McStay is currently leading: 'Empathic Media: Theory-Building and Knowledge-Exchange with Industry, Regulators and NGOs' (Research Councils UK, 2017).

'Empathic media' here refers to the capacity of new media technologies to sense, interpret and act on the emotional states of people, and to make use of people's intentions and expressions in generating textual and person-alized media experiences. McStay is on a mission to investigate how our emotional lives – via incessant data gathering that digital space allows – increasingly get 'datafied' and how, in return, various players create more sophisticated ways to mediate emotions back to us.

Empathy here could mean two things, the good and the bad one. In its more benign expression, empathic media could be compared to a friend who listens intently to what we need and tries to help. In its more sinister form, it is a psychopath who picks up on our emotional states in order to manipu-late us more easily. In a memorable analogy used in one of *The Economist's* reports on data, the good digital media empathy is like having many little helpful brothers; the bad empathy is the Big Brother (Suich, 2014).

How do digital media become more 'empathic'? First, by reading users' sentiment as they go about using digital channels: posts, images, emojis and any other material that could be harnessed to indicate our emotional states, in the moment and over time. Second, by a rising tide of 'biometrics', either initiated by us through, for example, a wearable, or by systems such as face or voice recognition. The internet, and organizations and brands that use it for marketing and sales, is learning how to, in McStay's words, 'mediate intimacy'.

While clearly there are causes for concern, some have been oversold and I'm really not sure though that native signals 'the end of days', nor that it indicates constant erosion between editorial and ads. It's also worth noting that even high-minded media have always bent for commercial reasons, for example, moving a story elsewhere to avoid offending an advertiser and similar. What is more troubling for me is the overall low level of trust in media due to fake news and other factors, where native does play a role, but not a critical one. It's a question of transparency, how obvious it is to the user that they are moving into a 'creative branding affective space'.

For example, Red Bull offers excellent content of mountain bike footage unavailable elsewhere. In this sense branded content plays a highly useful role and both interests are served (the brand and the viewer). I have less truck with branded content in newspapers though, where it is unclear what is journalism and what is not.

The real ambush for consumers, though, for Professor McStay, is the data collection and the control over its use. He believes that there has to be the element of 'agency' here, in other words, customer understanding about what data is being collected and what for, so that they can make informed choices about how much they are prepared to give away. There is nothing wrong with using data about emotions for work that is genuinely of value to people, but it is the *consumer* who has to make that decision.

Given what we now know about how our minds work online, are we too negligent about those decisions, too eager to share even our embarrassing moments, stretching the definition of privacy to a breaking point? Can we make a good call on it?

There is a fallacy of the younger audiences being more careless with their data or privacy, but what I've seen is that everyone wants control over their data; there may be age difference in how we are willing to share: younger audiences are certainly more willing – even older ones are now posting things publicly that we wouldn't 10 or 20 years ago. So, the notion of privacy may change, like we may share more emotional stuff, but privacy is about **maintenance** and **boundaries**, modulating the amount of information we share with others, so notions of being able to have **control** over our information is the same. Gaming is an interesting example: the commitment to privacy is strong and users are willing to share a lot of emotional and bio stuff because of that upfront commitment, plus creativity is the answer here: give people something they are willing to engage with.

Where Professor McStay *is* concerned is that some data practices are quite shoddy and that we are witnessing an appropriation of that data without proper consent and control. He also worries about the mass surveillance of both online and offline life – exemplified, for example, by Amazon buying Whole Foods, which will allow them to do much deeper profiling of consumers. If done with integrity and opportunity for consumers to exercise control, it doesn't have to be detrimental, it could be creative... data and content connect via personalization, better emotionality ('if I understand you better, I can better help'), time, location and meaningful choices.

All the key players would have to find a way to fight their predatory impulses by adopting some new approaches. One is a proper and thorough embrace of the new value proposition of 'empathic understanding' that the IPA report was espousing in previous chapters – which our 'Empathic Utility' expression is connected to. We will know the agencies mean empathy business when they create a role of the Chief Ethical Officer, with the power to override managing, planning and creative directors!

The other approach is the prevention of the abuse of empathy, the descent into the 'dark UI' or other questionable ethical practices. It should be guided by what Rushkoff, in yet another of his far-sighted books, *Throwing Rocks at the Google Bus* (2016), calls the need to 'retrieve the human purpose of technology rather than the technological (and market) exploitation of humans'. A glimpse of that potentially more exploitative side of machines' 'empathic' abilities, growing by the day, is the news from August 2017 about Stanford University's algorithm capable of deducing whether someone is gay, based just on a photograph of the person, with an accuracy of up to 81 per cent (Levin, 2017).

If the science behind it is robust, and the name and the reputation of the university indicate it, the implications for various aspects of our lives are quite staggering. From dating and recruitment, to political debates, human rights and religion, a lot could be affected. One algorithm, out of millions currently being developed, can significantly complicate our daily lives. To go back to some of Professor McStay's worries highlighted above, who decides when to use such an algorithm? Should it be regulated and even licensed, or will we just move into a more rigorous enforcement of existing rules? Will it be used for targeting ads and Content, by brands and agencies keen to tap into the vast purchasing power of the 'pink pound'? Is the notion of libel going to change, now that there is a more robust scientific proof for a public claim? These are all huge, transformative questions.

The concept of 'control' becomes even more interesting in the fast-developing new digital spaces of VR and AR. Given the immersiveness of these technologies and their current, yet still nascent, ability to 'override' our brains and make us feel things more strongly, does Professor McStay see them as potent machines for making us lose control not just over our data, but time, attention and money?

VR offers a more visceral, more corporeal experience and there is truth in how the sense of presence is manufactured to be incredibly affective, which puts a lot of responsibility on creators. However, I do not have a sense of danger or a threat to the public, I'm not all doom and gloom and think it could be compared to the rise of the early mass media, when there were cries that TV is going to be the death of literacy. However, it IS a thing for concern that industry bodies don't seem to be up to speed with developments, based on my recent talks to them, which is strange given that one can now buy a VR set at a petrol garage.

There are some good ideas, though. I have recently been at a conference in Brussels concerning a potential watchdog for AI decisions concerning the public sphere. Underpinning the idea is a good simple proposition: it's not just about the construction of algorithms and potential decision-making biases therein, but a human check on important decisions. In other words, the algorithm could stay proprietary as long as its decisions are scrutinized, validated and, if needed, corrected by a human being before being deployed. This is a shift from transparency of machine decision-making to specialist human analysis of inputs and outputs, rather than the bit in the middle, which is more sensible.

The 'Huxleyan' challenge: Content as the tool for amusing ourselves to death

Empathy and immersion fuel each other. That is exactly where brilliant content could become the most lethal.

In Neil Postman's seminal book *Amusing Ourselves to Death* (1985), which should be read by everyone working in media and advertising, the US media theorist and critic compares two competing media-related paradigms, incredibly prescient in this digitally powered world: the 'Orwellian' and the 'Huxleyan'. Most of the time we talk about the former, while it could be the latter that may be our undoing – and that one cannot work without engaging content.

The Orwellian one, in our collective consciousness, represents the main 'threat paradigm': how we imagine the media in a repressive society. Its roots reside in the familiar tropes: total erosion of privacy in a total-surveillance state; deprivation of knowledge by controlling the flow of information; incessant state propaganda based on emotions, lies and the threat of an external enemy. We are collectively and instinctively drawn to this narrative, as it reflects our past experiences, the pre-internet legacy media eco-system and the ideological focus on totalitarianism as the archetypal anti-democracy. Many of the 'opacity' challenges described above tap into this thinking.

However, the other Postman scenario – the Huxleyan one – is seldom discussed. It is the world where we numb ourselves to the reality through the sheer power of numerous media sources of pleasure. The infinite abundance of trivialities – a fair depiction of the modern internet – is our 'soma'. There is no need for the Big Brother, as we *ourselves* are removing our democratic agency in the world around us by getting terminally distracted with entertainment and trivial aspects of ours and other people's lives. So far, at least in the developed world and given some recent developments, this attention- and cognitive-depletion scenario has an alarmingly shriller ring of truth (Postman, 2017).

It is marvelously expressed by Postman himself in the foreword to his book (1985):

We were keeping our eye on 1984. When the year came and the prophecy didn't, thoughtful Americans sang softly in praise of themselves. The roots of liberal democracy had held. Wherever else the terror had happened, we, at least, had not been visited by Orwellian nightmares.

But we had forgotten that alongside Orwell's dark vision, there was another – slightly older, slightly less well known, equally chilling: Aldous Huxley's *Brave New World*. Contrary to common belief even among the educated, Huxley and Orwell did not prophesy the same thing. Orwell warns that we will be overcome by an externally imposed oppression. But in Huxley's vision, no Big Brother is required to deprive people of their autonomy, maturity and history. As he saw it, people will come to love their oppression, to adore the technologies that undo their capacities to think.

What Orwell feared were those who would ban books. What Huxley feared was that there would be no reason to ban a book, for there would be no one who wanted to read one. Orwell feared those who would deprive us of information. Huxley feared those who would give us so much that we would be reduced to passivity and egoism. Orwell feared that the truth would be concealed from us. Huxley feared the truth would be drowned in a sea of irrelevance. Orwell feared we would become a captive culture. Huxley feared we would become a trivial culture, preoccupied with some equivalent of the feelies, the orgy porgy, and the centrifugal bumblepuppy. As Huxley remarked in *Brave New World Revisited*, the civil libertarians and rationalists who are ever on the alert to oppose tyranny 'failed to take into account man's almost infinite appetite for distractions'. In *1984*, Huxley added, people are controlled by inflicting pain. In *Brave New World*, they are controlled by inflicting pleasure. In short, Orwell feared that what we hate will ruin us. Huxley feared that what we love will ruin us.

This book is about the possibility that Huxley, not Orwell, was right.

These words should be on the wall of every agency planner and creative director, not to mention brand and marketing clients. We are becoming not just addicted to technology, but also 'digitally obese', to use Gerd Leonhard's phrase, and that largely means 'content obese' as well, strikingly shown in the fact that Netflix now competes with sleep: 'supersizing' its offer, so that viewers can binge for hours on whole seasons of content (Kemp, 2017). This digital obesity is driven by our manifested 'attention illiteracy', as one of our professional friends calls it. Here's another important concept to put in our school curriculums...

At the moment, the Huxleyan threat is the most difficult for the marketing people to grasp, as it goes against every single grain of adopted wisdom and reflex about what constitutes great work: the more attention-arresting, the better. However, it also puts into focus the very moral ground of advertising as such, on its perennial journey from persuasion to seduction to, finally, affectiveness. As McStay framed it:

Persuasion (rational arguments based on facts) used to be the moral ground of advertising, as well as the whole of economics: that consumers can exercise free will to make up their mind. That moral ground has been undermined with our realization that advertising also works with influence, where the industry is using any means, including not very visible ones – targeting our emotional states, maybe catching us off-guard, deploying neuroscience and similar – to achieve its objectives. What really staggers me about the advertising industry is its ethical blindness, not discussing things that are even discussed on the high street!

No industry, particularly one that is so tightly woven into the fabric of the modern world in so many of its crucial aspects – politics, media, commerce, diet, lifestyle, aspirations and anxieties – can distance itself from genuine ethical self-examination.

The biggest battle in our consumer-based civilization is the one between two neurotransmitter chemicals: dopamine and serotonin. The former is the 'addiction' chemical telling us 'this feels good, want more of it', which drives our obsession with more, new, improved and the latest of everything. The other chemical, serotonin, is the 'contentment' chemical. 'Aahh, I've had enough, this feels good.' The problem is that dopamine reduces serotonin and, with that, also drives depression. Personally and, it seems, collectively: a big point made by the US doctor Robert Lustig (2017). Branding and advertising are an industrial-strength dopamine stimulator machine. Content, with its myriad ways of expressing itself, and when done well, may just exacerbate it.

So, are we ending in a world that paraphrases CBS's Leslie Moonves: 'It may not be good for the world, but it's damn good for brands!' (Bond, 2016)? Only time will tell, but we can't say we haven't been warned.

References

Associated Press (2018) [accessed 27 January 2018] Pope Francis Compares Fake News to Snake in Garden of Eden, *The Guardian*, January, https://www.theguardian.com/world/2018/jan/24/pope-francis-fake-news-snake-garden-of-eden

Bond, P (2016) [accessed 30 December 2017] Leslie Moonves on Donald Trump: 'It May Not Be Good for America, but It's Damn Good for CBS', *Hollywood Reporter,* 29 February [Online] hollywoodreporter.com/news/leslie-moonves-donald-trump-may-871464

Cadwalladr, C (2017) [accessed 30 December 2017] Revealed: Tory 'Dark' Ads Targeted Voters' Facebook Feeds in Welsh Marginal Seat, *The Observer*, 27 May [Online] theguardian.com/politics/2017/may/27/conservatives-facebook-dark-ads-data-protection-election

Cooper, A (2017) [accessed 30 December 2017] What is 'Brain Hacking'? Tech Insiders On Why You Should Care, *CBS News | 60 Minutes*, 9 April [Online] cbsnews.com/news/brain-hacking-tech-insiders-60-minutes/

Darkpatterns.org (2017a) [accessed 30 December 2017] Dark Patterns [Online] darkpatterns.org

Darkpatterns.org (2017b) [accessed 30 December 2017] Bait and Switch [Online] darkpatterns.org/types-of-dark-pattern/bait-and-switch

Darkpatterns.org (2017c) [accessed 30 December 2017] Types of Dark Pattern [Online] darkpatterns.org/types-of-dark-pattern

Doward, J and Gibbs, A (2017) [accessed 30 December 2017] Did Cambridge Analytica Influence the Brexit Vote and the US Election?, *The Guardian*, 4 March [Online] theguardian.com/ politics/2017/mar/04/ nigel-oakes-cambridge-analytica-what-role-brexit-trump

Dzamic, L (2017) [accessed 30 December 2017] Should Behavioural Economics in Marketing Be Regulated – Or Hyped-Down? (Blog) *BOBCM*, 21 January [Online] bobcm.net/2017/01/21/should-behavioural-economics-in-marketing-be-regulated-or-hyped-down/

Einstein, M (2017) *Black Ops Advertising: Native ads, content marketing and the covert world of the digital sell*, OR Books, New York

Ellison, M (2017) [accessed 30 December 2017] Election 2017: Scottish Voters Targeted by 'Dark Ads' on Facebook, *BBC*, 7 June [Online] bbc.com/news/ uk-scotland-scotland-politics-40170166

Gallacher, J and Kaminska, M (2017) [accessed 30 December 2017] Facebook Needs To Be More Open About Its Effect On Democracy, *The Guardian*, 12 June [Online] theguardian.com/commentisfree/2017/jun/12/ general-election-social-media-facebook-twitter

Hunt, E (2017) [accessed 30 December 2017] Social media Stars Face Crackdown Over Money From Brands, *The Guardian*, 16 September [Online] theguardian.com/technology/2017/sep/16/social-media-stars-face-crackdown-over-money-from-brands

Kemp, N (2017) [accessed 30 December 2017] Compulsive Content: When Netflix Is Competing With Sleep Are We Entertaining Ourselves To Death?, *Campaign*, 28 April [Online] campaignlive.co.uk/article/compulsive-content-when-netflix-competing-sleep-entertaining-ourselves-death/1431200

Lanchester, J (2017) [accessed 30 December 2017] You Are the Product, *London Review of Books*, **39** (6), pp 3–10 (August) [Online] lrb.co.uk/v39/n16/ john-lanchester/you-are-the-product

LastWeekTonight (2014) [accessed 30 December 2017] Native Advertising: Last Week Tonight with John Oliver (HBO) [Online] youtu.be/E_F5GxCwizc

Levin, S (2017) [accessed 30 December 2017] New AI Can Guess Whether You're Gay or Straight from a Photograph, *The Guardian*, 8 September [Online] theguardian.com/technology/2017/sep/07/new-artificial-intelligence-can-tell-whether-youre-gay-or-straight-from-a-photograph

Lustig, R (2017) [accessed 30 December 2017] The Pursuit of Pleasure is a Modern-Day Addiction, *The Guardian*, 10 September [Online] theguardian. com/commentisfree/2017/sep/09/pursuit-of-pleasure-modern-day-addiction

Morozov, E (2017) [accessed 30 December 2017] Moral Panic Over Fake News Hides the Real Enemy – the Digital Giants, *The Guardian*, 8 January [Online] theguardian.com/commentisfree/2017/jan/08/blaming-fake-news-not-the-answer-democracy-crisis

O'Neil, C (2016) *Weapons of Math Destruction: How big data increases inequality and threatens democracy*, Crown Publishing Group, New York

PBS (2016) [accessed 30 December 2017] The Drug-Like Effect of Screen Time on the Teenage Brain, *PBS News Hour*, 4 May [Online] pbs.org/newshour/show/the-drug-like-effect-of-screen-time-on-the-teenage-brain

Peppers, D and Rogers, M (1998) *The One to One Future*, Bantam Doubleday Dell Publishing Group, New York

Postman, A (2017) [accessed 30 December 2017] My Dad Predicted Trump in 1985 – It's Not Orwell, He Warned, It's Brave New World, *The Guardian*, 2 February [Online] theguardian.com/media/2017/feb/02/amusing-ourselves-to-death-neil-postman-trump-orwell-huxley

Postman, N (1985) *Amusing Ourselves to Death: Public discourse in the age of show business*, Penguin Books, New York

Research Councils UK (2017) [accessed 30 December 2017] Empathic Media: Theory-Building and Knowledge-Exchange with Industry, Regulators and NGOs [Online] gtr.rcuk.ac.uk/projects?ref=AH%2FM006654%2F1

Rushkoff, D (2011) *Program or Be Programmed: Ten commands for a digital age*, Shoemaker & Hoard, New York

Rushkoff, D (2014) *Present Shock: When everything happens now*, Penguin, New York

Rushkoff, D (2016) *Throwing Rocks at the Google Bus: How growth became the enemy of prosperity*, Penguin, New York

Schultz, E J (2017) [accessed 12 December 2017] See Kendall Jenner in Her New Pepsi Ad, *AdAge*, 4 April [Online] http://adage.com/article/cmo-strategy/kendall-jenner-pepsi-ad/308551/

Suich, A (2014) [accessed 30 December 2017] Little Brother, *The Economist*, 11 September [Online] economist.com/news/special-report/21615869-technology-radically-changing-advertising-business-profound-consequences

Conclusions

This book is our contribution to building the answer to the much-debated question of 'Why Content?' The more we discovered various points of view, the more we realized that the picture is more complex than we anticipated. Hopefully, that complexity has been somewhat reduced by reading the book. What do *we* make of it? Here are the key conclusions for us.

The 'why?' is becoming more important than the 'how?'

To quote Simon Sinek, and Dave Packard before him, starting with the above question of 'why?' much of the 'how?' of Content could be answered too. The confusion, the divisions, the controversy, were all reduced. We firmly believe now that Content should be an ethos and a way of thinking, a broader view of the ways to earn consumer attention in the attention-scarce world. It doesn't seem to us an isolated discipline any more, something that should be placed in its own department. It should not be a tactic, maybe not even a strategy, but a *philosophy* that should fuel everything an organization does at all points where it touches the consumer. It particularly should not be a set of quick and dirty tactics, a 'solution', as it is often the case today. It is not yet a replacement for advertising, but it could make it better. Content is a key lens for keeping the customer in the centre of the picture and for allowing brands to meet them at the 'intersection of permission and desire'.

Content is a symptom *of the evolution of marketing*

It reflects deep and wide evolutionary trends in modern marketing and, as such, it is quite difficult, if not impossible, to define beyond glibness. Any attempt, bar one, we have seen so far, reduces its scope and is detrimental to its potential. That is why we adopted the capital 'C' to denote the principle, as opposed to delivery. The exception is the above-mentioned 'philosophical' one, focused on customer experience: most of those we talked to agree that good Content has to *earn* the attention of the audience. It's pull, not push. It provides a good value exchange, it's empathic. It makes efforts to define it beyond that obsolete. It's old and it's new, but what we see today is a transitional, 'liminal' phase, an evolutionary stepping stone and a 'place-holder' towards a more widely adopted approach – whatever the name – to base more of the brand-building efforts on deserved 'opt-in impressions'. Money follows attention, which is increasingly more difficult to merely buy.

Experience and purpose could be answers to the attention deficit

The set of forces driving the media, marketing and agency landscape transformation is too fundamental to be easily dismissed. Digital, as an almighty commodification force of everything, has reiterated the need for *relevance* and *experience* to fight the attention scarcity and the explosion of 'skippability'. Brands should think 'less about how to avoid being tuned out, but how to get chosen'. Focus on experience and purpose may be the answers. The mindset of 'designing for time and place' moves things away from just communication – just 'messaging' – and into product and service delivery too. It is the essence of the human-centred design thinking and a place where communication meets experience. It has *empathy* – a much used and needed, but also much abused word – at its heart; the word that is increasingly becoming a transformational focus for both clients and agencies.

Many of the experts we spoke to, on all sides of the industry, believe that organizations don't have a choice but to start better defining their purpose of existence beyond just making profit. That is difficult to do without empathy. Once they do that, though, many of the traditional rules of doing business and marketing start getting eroded too. It becomes a free pass to go into any direction and expression – messaging, product, service – that provides an emotional, meaningful and useful experience to consumers. The shackles of formats and product categories, even business categories, start to break too. Creating an enterprise experience business, still a formidable challenge for many, turns things upside down: marketing becomes a profit centre, Content becomes a business model. It is an opportunity for the more enlightened CMOs to start gaining a wider remit in their companies again, beyond just marketing communications and the current role of the 'colouring-in department'.

Content could be the bedrock of 'cultural branding'

Purpose, experience, values and authenticity are nothing more than cultural constructs. Brands should never forget that 'connecting with people is a social exercise that is conducted through the messy, murky construct called culture'. In the world where attention and trust have to be earned, cultural resonance matters. This applies both internally, and externally. Content, looked through the cultural lens, becomes a potentially powerful expression of the organizational purpose and culture. It helps both consumers and employees to align their values with the organization's. For consumers, instead of just shoving sales messages down their throats, it provides a meaningful platform for making the brand part of their personal cultural repertoire and a means of self-expression: *I like that, I AM like that.* A similar, but slightly amended, mantra works for employees too: *I value that, I AM like that.* Given a broader emotional and utilitarian space that Content provides for not just telling but demonstrating companies' cultures to their audiences, it has a role that is way beyond the current marketing communications. Modern business and marketing theory and practice have recognized this, offering a raft of approaches for building a brand's cultural resonance. This is also acknowledged in many interviews with clients and agencies in the book.

Customer journey is now everyone's game

There is not a part of it that Content can't play a role in. It is now, or it should be, Content journey. Content is the only real candidate, based on what we have seen, for the overall digital 'archetypal' approach, above and beyond the atomized delivery formats and discipline boxes. The good, old funnel is far from dead, but is now also much more detailed and real-time: consisting of a myriad of everyday touchpoints where consumers – prospects and current customers of brands – look for things related to the category they need something from. These Moments that Matter (MTMs), in Google parlance, are small units of *context* where great content could be delivered. It encompasses everything from SEO and shopper marketing to all the steps that are currently owned by CRM. But now, that's everyone's game, as TOFU (top of the funnel – advertising) merges with BOFU (bottom of the funnel – CRM). Focus on delivering meaningful and emotional relevance, largely via Content, could be a unifying factor that heals the current rift between the parts of the funnel. Legacy business models and established 'muscle memories' of various agencies are the biggest barriers for adopting this mindset for business development.

New theory of 'agency product' is needed to heal the current binary divide

There is a rift in the agency industry, a binary equation of a sort driven by the existing business models and cultures of specialization. This rift has various descriptions, but all are relating to the intellectual divide between the so-called 'deep branding' and the 'touchpoint optimization' paradigms. The former is often referred to as 'brand', 'emotional', 'creative', 'big idea' or 'right brain', as opposed to the latter of 'promotional', 'programmatic', 'platform', 'performance' and 'left brain'. We think this is deeply wrong and reflects the industry in its initial stages of confusion while trying to answer to the digital challenge.

But, a new kind of consolidation is already taking place, largely driven by media and PR agencies on one side, and more nimble consultancies on the other. They realized there is a new place of 'insertion' between the clients and the traditional creative agencies, powered by the combined understanding of data, technology and consumers' consumption of media. Various new recipes are being tried out, from merging 'stories and systems' and borrowing skills from publishers and Hollywood, to enhancing the traditional 'two-atom' creative team with creative technologists and data scientists.

However, we believe that there may be another way to think about it, a set of optics more than a predetermined set of formatted deliverables. It is within every agency's grasp, irrespective of expertise. We call it Empathic Utility (EU), as it contains two of the most powerful ingredients of every experience: Emotional Resonance and Intent Utility. They are not either/or; EU should be the charge of every MTM. What is useful does not have to be boring; what is emotional does not have to be expensive. 'YouTubers' have shown that convincingly. It is a way for agencies to heal the rift, even within the current business models. What is needed is more open-mindedness.

Finally, another space for agencies to grow to is to do for their clients, collectively and individually, what they now do for their products: to sell them better *internally*. Organizations, as well as the key people in them, are a cultural product that employees have to *buy into* in order to maintain or increase their growth. It is founded in their purpose – which creative agencies are the best positioned to articulate, and then to emotionally narrate. The future of advertising (and agencies) may as well be internal, too.

Data is still an unfulfilled promise

It is the hype of the promise that smears the postcard landscape of the delta where data flows into empathic and meaningful Content. Data was supposed to help inform and inspire great content ideas, support optimization pre- and post-deployment and pinpoint targeting contextually. However, the promise is still unfulfilled. Large data sets are difficult to process, despite yet another promise of Big Data, as they are mostly private, anonymized or just not very useful; legal challenges abound; cheaper and easier alternatives are often equally, or more, effective. Programmatic has so far been marred in controversies depicting it as a gargantuan waste-generating machine. To add insult to injury, the broader perspectives that the Big Data should have provided have turned out to have their own sort of narrow-mindedness. In the rush to get the newest shiny promise of the 'big' automatic efficiency, the industry has forgotten to maintain the 'rich' and the 'thick' data insight sources – the qualitative ethnographic insights that often provide the answer to the 'why?' of consumer behaviour, not just the 'what?' It eventually led to the creation of the ever more efficient 'robots for picking fruit', while forgetting to water the brand tree via emotions and empathy to keep it growing.

The syndrome of 'Content myopia' is real – and dangerous!

Content is not just a symptom, but a *syndrome* as well, in itself a feeble, yet unfulfilled, promise of a more experiential and purposeful way to do business. Warnings and criticisms about the current state of Content thought and practice are, we believe, largely justified. After all, the fact that only one in 20 pieces of content produces any engagement, and that 5 per cent of it produces 90 per cent of all engagement is sobering. Theodore Sturgeon's dictum that 90 per cent of everything is crud applies here too, not helped by the fact that in but one year the industry had pumped out three times more stuff than in the previous one! Content, overall, doesn't work – falling into the same silo trap as the very thing it was supposed to be a better alternative to: bad advertising.

Part of the problem is hype. Theoretically positioned as the new answer to everything in marketing, the super-strategy of the new thinking, it lost the perspective of currently being only a tiny fraction of a small slice of marketing communications, in itself a small slice of marketing. The other problem is infatuation with 'shiny new delivery systems', 'martech' that made it possible to create and publish *something* with increased speed and efficiency, without stopping to ask *what* that is and *why*. Those 'lorries' for carrying content are vastly contributing to the media clutter they were supposed to be the solution for. They also contributed to larger parts of communications budgets being allocated to Content, helping in the process to generate the perception of the arriving future – and to increasingly turning Content into a 'C-word'. Strategic refocusing is now desperately needed, but the industry dynamics are currently not conducive to it.

Ethical challenges with Content and modern media are growing

Looking at the daily developments, sometimes it feels there is a whole industrial complex bent on deceiving the public. Opacity of algorithmical 'weapons of math destruction', dodgy data practices, 'dark UI' manipulations and in-built addictiveness of modern consumer tech platforms, the erosion of walls between the editorial and advertising – all of this is contributing to the perception that ever more marketing practices are going 'black ops' in a relentless 'race to the bottom of the brainstem'. In other words, to try to bypass, in more nefarious ways, the psychological and functional barriers contributing to the demise of online advertising.

There is a bit of a paradox in it: it is predominantly the very benefits of Content for marketers that are deemed to be its danger to us as well: the fact that it doesn't look like just any old advertising and that it could be wickedly engaging when done well. On top of this, there is the issue of technology getting increasingly clever and more 'empathic', fed with ever more data about us, some of it willingly given. Despite the potential huge benefits to society, the breakdown happens when we as consumers and, even more important, citizens, lose control over that. We are already seeing that happening and in this light initiatives such as GDPR look quite different than from just the point of view of the marketing industry. One of the most serious accusations of the data-based marketing of today is that it is becoming a surveillance business.

The most serious ethical challenge for brands, agencies and the modern media (platforms) is, however, the most insidious. It is the accusation of trivialization of our lives. In the West, at least for now, Orwell is largely placed aside; the system of checks and balances is keeping the repression at bay. We don't have to fear information starvation and state-imposed isolation. On the contrary, we need to fear the Huxleyan 'Brave New World' threat – the information glut and pandering to our basic impulses and opinions; the premise that no one has to ban any books as very few are actually read; no one has to hide the truth from us, as we are drowning in a sea of irrelevance; we are not controlled by inflicting pain on us, but by inflicting pleasure. Brands have always understood 'man's almost infinite appetite for distractions'.

How the industry is going to respond to these challenges will define the way we are going to live in the near future.

New immersive spaces could be 'Content-only' paradigm changers

What may help answer the above collective challenges is the arrival of the new immersive environments such as AR and VR (mixed together into MR) and intelligent virtual assistants powered by machine learning and AI. Highly emotionally charged, empathetic and visceral, they are not kind to the crass advertising interruptions of old. Some of them, such as virtual assistants, are not even created to be interrupted by brands, or at least we don't have plausible models for that yet without incurring brand damage. It is permission marketing on nuclear power. In this world 'without edges' that will fully immerse us, Content could mean something completely different from the largely textual- and film-based deliverables of the moment. Content can, and will, become part of our environment, embedded into our visual field and inseparable from 'R' (reality). It is a game-changer, a huge opportunity, but also a huge responsibility for brands. Storytelling will not be enough any more; 'storydoing' and 'storyliving' will become the norm. It may turn out that the new reality will provide the key ingredients for the final victory of *invitation* versus *interruption*. Given the adaptability and creativity of the best brands in their collective history so far, though, that victory may still be the promise of a more distant future. One thing is for sure, Content thinking will be at the heart of it.

Epilogue – the Quaker story

The Quakers offer examples of business leaders who founded banks and other major businesses still around today such as Barclays and Cadburys, whose business success helped fund their philanthropy and bring about social change. They had a purpose.

For those readers inclined to try how it feels thinking about Content as a better promise for doing marketing in the digital world via the ways touched upon above, here is a simple Quaker visualization exercise for gauging purposeful actions.

Sit comfortably and close your eyes. Picture the world in which you, your family and your friends would like to live; for 5–10 minutes think of the relationships you have, what you do and why.

Then build on to it: think of the part you play in it professionally (or personally) to make that world happen; your actions, the way you conduct your role and business, the way people work, behave and interact with each other; how business is done generally in such a world and the impact it has on the society, culture, planet...

Then, after that, every time before you are about to make a professional decision or do something, ask yourself just two simple questions: 1) Does it increase the chances of making that better world happen? 2) Does it decrease the chances of making that better world happen?

Strip away the Quakerism, and it still works for everyone, for everything. Including building more successful brands and better Content. Unless you have insurmountable moral challenges – and modern global businesses are often in the vicinity of such positions – this creative visualization helps us frame where we are trying to get to, rather than let any road simply take us somewhere.

INDEX

Note: Page numbers in *italics* indicate Figures.